Summer Institute of Linguistics and
The University of Texas at Arlington
Publications in Linguistics

Publication 99

Editors

Virgil Poulter
University of Texas
at Arlington

William R. Merrifield
Summer Institute of
Linguistics

Assistant Editors

Rhonda L. Hartell

Marilyn A. Mayers

Consulting Editors

Tense and Aspect in Eight Languages of Cameroon

Stephen C. Anderson and Bernard Comrie

Editors

A Publication of
The Summer Institute of Linguistics
and
The University of Texas at Arlington
1991

Cover sketch and design by Hazel Shorey

Copies of this and other publications of the Summer Institute of Linguistics may be obtained from

International Academic Bookstore
7500 W. Camp Wisdom Road
Dallas, TX 75236

Table of Contents

Section Three: Chadic Languages

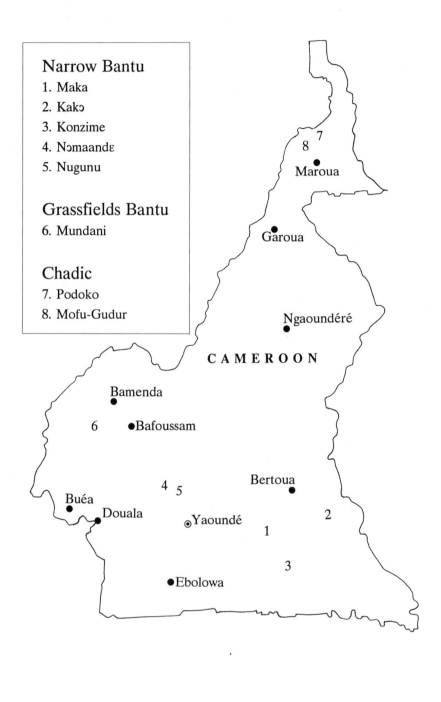

Narrow Bantu
1. Maka
2. Kakɔ
3. Konzime
4. Nɔmaandɛ
5. Nugunu

Grassfields Bantu
6. Mundani

Chadic
7. Podoko
8. Mofu-Gudur

C A M E R O O N

Maroua

Garoua

Ngaoundéré

Bamenda

●Bafoussam

Bertoua

Buéa

Douala

Yaoundé

Ebolowa

Preface

Bernard Comrie

When a potential reader approaches a linguistic work entitled "Phenomenon X in Language(s) Y", a reasonable question to ask is: "Why this particular phenomenon in this particular language?" Of course, if the reader is directly interested in both phenomenon X and language(s) Y, then no further encouragement is needed. But the reader directly interested in X but not in Y might well ask: "What new insights will this language/these languages give me into X?" While the reader directly interested in Y but not in X might equally ask: "Is X a sufficiently important phenomenon in Y for me to take the effort to read this work?"

The linguistic diversity and richness of Cameroon is well documented, with over 250 languages representing two of the major phyla of Africa: Niger-Congo and Afroasiatic, the latter essentially restricted to the Chadic family, but the former including not only Bantu languages in the narrower and broader senses but also languages of the Adamawa-Ubangian group.

One of the areas in which many languages of Cameroon are particularly rich is precisely their tense-aspect systems. It is not unusual to find languages like Nomaande with four past tenses, differentiated according to the degree of remoteness from the present moment, or like Nugunu, with three past tenses and three future tenses differentiated essentially in this way. For those interested in the general theory of tense-aspect, material from the languages of Cameroon, and more specifically from those discussed in this volume, can throw important light on general theoretical problems. For instance, while most languages with different past tenses distinguished according to degrees of remoteness have as one cutoff point the division between today and before-today, Makaa presents an alterna-

façon explicite, alors que cette expression explicite est indispensable au futur.

Bien que les systèmes aspecto-temporels des langues tchadiques soient généralement moins complexes que ceux des langues bantu, on y relève toutefois des phénomènes intéressants, tels que la possibilité d'un aspecto-temporel non-marqué en mofu-gudur, et le fait qu'il n'y a pas de corrélation directe entre les oppositions parfait/imparfait et informations de premier-plan/informations d'arrière-plan en podoko, les informations d'arrière-plan étant soit au parfait, soit à l'imparfait selon les relations temporelles apparaissant dans le fil du discours.

L'étude des systèmes aspecto-temporels est un élément très important pour notre compréhension de la structure générale des langues du Cameroun, l'une des raisons en étant que le système aspecto-temporel est étroitement lié à d'autres phénomènes, et qu'ils s'influencent réciproquement. Par exemple, le système aspecto-temporel du kɔɔzime, qui est très riche, entretient d'étroites relations avec le système tonal complexe de cette langue, avec la structure morphologique (en particulier à cause de la structure morphologique discontinue d'une grande partie des catégories aspecto-temporelles) et avec l'expression de la focalisation. Bien que la plupart des études portant sur les systèmes aspecto-temporels des langues camerounaises, ceci étant vrai aussi pour la plupart de celles de cet ouvrage, se concentrent soit sur la structure et le sens de base des catégories aspecto-temporelles ou sur leur fonction au niveau du discours, on ne peut négliger l'interdépendance entre système aspecto-temporel et syntaxe. A ce sujet, le lecteur pourra se référer à l'étude faite sur le système aspecto-temporel et la subordination en mundani.

Les articles rassemblés dans cet ouvrage ont été développés en partie durant l'atelier sur le système aspecto-temporel des langues camerounaises que nous avons dirigé à Yaoundé durant l'été 1987, à l'invitation de la filiale de la Société Internationale de Linguistique au Cameroun. Nous tenons à remercier tous ceux qui ont participé à cet atelier d'une façon ou d'une autre.

Que ce volume sera d'un intérêt réel pour ceux qui s'intéressent au système aspecto-temporel des langues camerounaises va sans dire. Mais nous souhaitons que la variété des travaux et le niveau des contributions s'avérera intéresser à la fois tous ceux qui étudient les langues du Cameroun et tous ceux qui ont un intérêt pour la théorie générale des systèmes aspecto-temporel.

Section One

Narrow Bantu Languages

Tense and Aspect in Makaa

Daniel Heath

Abstract

The Makaa verbal system has five tenses and three aspects. The tenses are marked by morphemes at the beginning of the verb phrase: remote past by toneless *a*, near past by ` *ámɔ̀*, present by a replacive high tone, near future by toneless *e*, and remote future by *bá*. As for the aspects, habitual is marked by the morpheme *dù* and progressive by the morpheme *ŋgɔ̀*, but perfective is marked only with tone. Of particular interest are the tonal morphemes and rules. A replacive high tone located after the tense marker, which is found in all constructions but present progressive, is only manifested when occurring between two low tones, in which case the preceding low becomes high. A second replacive high tone occurs at the end of the verb phrase in most nonprogressive constructions. This tone replaces right, and is manifested on the following morpheme when that morpheme is a segment. When the morpheme that follows is nonsegmental, an epenthetical vowel is created to carry the tone.

Résumé

Le système verbal mɔkaa comprend cinq temps et trois aspects. Les temps sont signalés par des morphèmes au début du syntagme. Le passé lointain est signalé par le morphème atonal *a*, le passé récent par ` *ámɔ̀*, le présent uniquement par un ton haut, le futur proche par le morphème atonal *e*, et le futur lointain par le morphème *bá*. En ce qui concerne l'aspect, l'habituel est marqué par *dù*, et le progressif par *ŋgɔ̀*. Intéressant à signaler est la manière dont agissent les tons. Dans le syntagme, le morphème temporel est suivi d'un ton haut dans toutes les constructions verbales, sauf celles du présent progressif. Cependant, ce ton ne manifeste que lorsqu'il se trouve entre deux morphèmes qui chacun porte un ton bas. Dans ce cas, ce ton haut change en ton haut le ton bas précédent. Un deuxième ton haut situé à la fin du syntagme est aussi présent dans la plupart des constructions non-progressives. Ce ton remplace le ton suivant.

> Quand le morphème suivant est 'segmental', le ton se manifeste sur celui-ci. Par contre, lorsque le morphème est 'nonsegmental', une voyelle épenthétique est créée, et porte le ton.

This paper[1] describes how tense and aspect are marked in Makaa indicative and affirmative constructions with dynamic (nonstative) verbs. Only absolute tenses are treated. Makaa[2] is a Narrow Bantu language of the northwest zone, identified by Guthrie (1971:33) as A.83; it is spoken in the southeastern part of the Republic of Cameroon.

Before the individual tense and aspect markers are discussed, the basic ordering within the verb phrase is shown in (1).

(1)   (SUPR) (TENSE) (H1) (P1) (HAB) (PROG) STEM (H2) (OBJECT)

The verb phrase usually begins with a subject pronoun (SUPR). This pronoun is often followed by one of several tense markers (TENSE) followed in turn by a replacive high tone tense-aspect marker (H1). Next is the position of the near past tense marker (P1) when it is present, followed by optional habitual (HAB) and progressive (PROG) aspect markers. The verb stem (STEM) follows, and then the verb phrase may be closed by another replacive high tone tense-aspect marker (H2) preceding an optional object. All constructions must be marked for tense and aspect. There are other verbal auxiliaries which occur within the verb phrase, but they are outside the scope of this paper.

1. Tonal morphemes

Within the verb phrase, there are two separate replacive high tone nonsegment morphemes which spread to adjacent syllables and delete tones already associated with those syllables. Each of these unusual tonal morphemes is triggered by tense-aspect features.

---

[1]The paper was produced during a linguistic workshop in Yaoundé, Cameroon, under the leadership of Bernard Comrie. The author has been influenced by the lectures given by Comrie and has received personal input from him in the writing of the paper. The terminology used is from Comrie 1976 and 1985. Thanks also go to Stephen C. Anderson who gave valuable suggestions, especially in the analysis of the tone and in the general presentation of the findings. Errors are my own.

[2]Makaa has twenty-two consonant phonemes: b c d f g h j k l m n n ny ŋ p s sh t v w y z and zh, and nine vowel phonemes: a e ɛ ə i ɨ o ʉ, and u. There are two tone levels, high and low, which are indicated in this paper by acute (´) and grave (`) accents respectively.

The first of these tonal morphemes (H1) is a replacive high tone which occurs immediately after the tense marker position and is present in all constructions except the present progressive (i.e., constructions marked for both present tense and progressive aspect). The direction in which this first replacive tone docks is dictated by the tonal environment. This rule is formalized in (2).

(2)   H1 Docking Rule

$$/\text{H1}/ \quad \rightarrow| \quad \text{H} \rightarrow \quad \backslash\_\text{H}$$
$$\leftarrow \text{H} \quad \backslash\_\text{L}$$

The rule says that H1 is realized by high tone (H) which docks to the right if the next tone is H, but to the left if the next tone is a low tone (L). Since it is a replacive tone, it always deletes the tone which is already associated with the syllable to which it docks. The result of this rule is that the presence of this replacive tone is apparent on the surface only when it is trapped between two L tones, and then it manifests itself on the syllable to the left.

In examples that follow, H1 is either preceded by '←' or followed by '→' to indicate the direction in which this tone is posited to dock; and the symbol →| indicates 'is realized phonetically as'.

Example (3) shows that the H on the verb *wííŋg* 'chase away' causes the H1 to dock to the right and to be absorbed into the H already there. This means that the presence of the H1 marker is invisible in this environment.

(3)   *Mə̀ a   ´   wííŋg   ò-mpyâ.*   →| *Mə̀ à wííŋg òmpyâ.*
       1s   P2   H1 → chase^away   c2-dog[3]
       I chased the dogs away (before yesterday).

Example (4), on the other hand, shows that the L on the verb *càl* 'cut down' causes the same H1 to dock to the left. Since the H1 marker is now preceded by the toneless P2 marker, which normally takes its tone from the preceding syllable, we can actually see the H1 in this environment.[4]

(4)   *Mə̀ a   ´   càl   mə̀-lə́ndú.*   →| *Mə̀ á càl mə̀lə́ndú.*
       1s   P2 ←   H1 cut^down   c6-palm^tree
       I cut down the palm trees (before yesterday).

---

[3]Throughout the paper, 1s indicates first person singular, P2 indicates remote past tense, and C, followed by a number of 1–10, indicates a class noun prefix.

[4]The P2 marker, as well as the F1 tense marker, is a toneless morpheme, as discussed in §§2.1 and 2.4. These toneless tense markers take the tone of the subject pronoun they follow before the replacive tone H1 can act upon it.

In (5), the L of the following progressive marker *ŋgɔ̀* also causes the preceding H1 to dock to the left, and again it is visible on the P2 marker.

(5) *Mɔ̀ a   ´   ŋgɔ̀   wííŋg   ò-mpyɔ̂. →| Mɔ̀ á ŋgɔ̀ wííŋg òmpyɔ̂.*
    1s   P2 ← H1   PROG chase^away C2-dog
    I used to chase away the dogs (before yesterday).

The second replacive high tone (H2) occurs following the verb stem and before the object. In P2, it occurs only in nonprogressive constructions marked for polar focus.[5] In the other tenses, it occurs in all nonprogressive constructions, whether marked for perfective or habitual aspect and whether or not it occurs with polar focus. This tone immediately follows the verb and replaces whatever tone occurs on its right, usually the first tone of the object, whether prefix or root.

In (6), H2 replaces L of the class 2 prefix *ò* of the noun *mpyɔ̂*.

(6) *Mɔ̀   ´   ` ámɔ̀   wííŋg   ´   ò-mpyɔ̂.→| Mɔ́ ámɔ̀ wííŋg ómpyɔ̂.*
    1s ← H1 P1   chase^away H2 →C2-dog
    I chased away the dogs (earlier today or yesterday).

However, this same H2 often occurs immediately preceding a pronoun, a preposition, another verb, or an object without a prefix with a L root. In all these environments, the H2 creates its own epenthetic *u* vowel. We know that the epenthetic vowel is *u* because of its realization between a consonant-final verb and a consonant-initial object, as in example (7).

(7) *Mɔ̀   ´   ` ámɔ̀   wííŋg   ´   ø-ncwòmbè.*
    1s ← H1 P1   chase^away H2→ C7-sheep
    I chased them away.

    →| *Mɔ́ ámɔ̀ wííŋg ú ncwòmbè.*

If the verb ends in a vowel, however, the epenthetic vowel which is created assimilates to the quality of the final vowel of the preceding verb. In (8), the zero object prefix (ø-) of noun class 7 results in the emergence

---

[5]The polar focus marker *shí* is limited to past tense. Like *sì* in the neighboring language Kɔɔzime (Beavon 1991:61), it is most likely derived from the verb *shîn* 'to be done, to be finished'. However, unlike Kɔɔzime, where it indicates perfective aspect, in Makaa it is used to counter-assert the truth value of a statement.

of an epenthetic vowel to which the H2 can dock, the underlying *u* harmonizing to the final *u* of the preceding verb.[6]

(8) *Mə̀ a*   ´   *gù*   ´   *ø-gwòó.*   →| *Mə̀ á gù ú gwòó.*
    1s   P2 ← H1   pick   H2 →   c7-mushroom
    I picked the mushroom.

Now that we have examined the rather complicated nature of the two floating tones, we turn to a discussion of the various tense and aspect markers.

2. Tense markers

Makaa has a five-way temporal distinction with two past tenses (remote and near), a present tense, and two future tenses (also remote and near).[7]

Morning marks the beginning of a new day for the Makaa people; night belongs to the preceding day. A day starts, therefore, when a person gets up in the morning.

In order to focus on the grammatical markers of tense, the examples in this section are given with perfective aspect which is unmarked. The H1 morpheme is always present, however, and one might posit the H1 to be the mark of perfective aspect if it did not also occur in many nonperfective constructions.

2.1. Remote past (P2). Remote past is used for situations which existed or took place earlier than yesterday (i.e., before yesterday morning). It is marked by the toneless morpheme *a*, as seen in (9) and (10). Toneless tense markers (which include both the P2 and F1 markers) usually take their tone from the immediately preceding subject pronoun. In (9), the L of the first-person-singular pronoun *mə̀* spreads onto the toneless *a* (P2). In (10), it is the H of the third-person-plural pronoun (3p) *bwó* which spreads onto the P2 marker.

(9) *Mə̀ a*   ´   *wííŋ*   *ò-mpyɔ̂.*   →| *Mə̀ à wííŋ òmpyɔ̂.*
    1s   P2   H1 →   chase^away   c2-dog
    I chased the dogs away (before yesterday).

---

[6]A similar phenomenon occurs in the associative construction as described in another paper by Heath (1989:12).

[7]A poorly understood perfect (PERF) construction is mentioned briefly in §4.

(10) *Bwó a   ´   wíiŋg   ò-mpyɔ̂. →| Bwó á wíiŋg òmpyɔ̂.*
      3p   P2 H1 → chase^away c2-dog
      They chased the dogs away (before yesterday).

It is therefore concluded from examples like these, where H1 is posited to dock to its right, that the P2 marker is indeed toneless, adopting the tone of the preceding pronoun. If L were posited on P2, the verb in (10) would be downstepped; but it is not.

2.2. Near past (P1). Near past is used to refer to situations which existed or took place before the present moment, either earlier today or yesterday. This tense is marked by ` *ámɔ̀*, which includes a preceding floating L. This floating L is never realized on the surface, but its presence accounts for the preceding H1 always docking to the left in P1 constructions, a process which occurs elsewhere only when H1 is followed by L.

In (11), the floating L of P1 causes the H1 to replace left, in turn causing the L of *mɔ* (1s) to be replaced by this H. In (12), the H1 is also posited to dock to the left, but its presence is not seen on the surface because *bwó* (3p) normally carries H.

(11) *Mɔ̀   ´   ` ámɔ̀ wíiŋg   ´   ò-mpyɔ̂.*
      1s ← H1 P1   chase^away H2 → c2-dog
      I chased the dogs away (earlier today or yesterday).

      →| *Mɔ́ ámɔ̀ wíiŋg ómpyɔ̂.*

(12) *Bwó   ´   ` ámɔ̀ dɔ̀ ´   ì-kwódò nɔ̀kùgú.*
      3p ← H1 P1   eat H2 → c8-yams yesterday
      They ate yams yesterday.

      →| *Bwó ámɔ̀ dɔ̀ íkwódò nɔ̀kùgú.*

2.3. Present (PRES). Present tense is used in conversation to describe situations which are presently taking place or which will be taking place in the immediate future. The present tense construction is not marked for tense, but it does occur with H1 except in progressive aspect.

In (13) and (14), which are both perfective, the only marking is H1.

(13) *Mɔ̀   ´   càl   ´   mɔ̀-lɔ́ndú. →| Mɔ́ càl mɔ́lɔ́ndú.*
      1s ← H1 cut^down H2 → c6-palm^tree
      I am about to cut down the palm trees.

(14) *Mà* ˊ *wíìŋ* ˊ *ò-mpyô.* →| *Mà wíìŋ ómpyô.*
    1s H1 → chase^away H2 → C2-dog
    I am about to chase the dogs away.

The present perfective construction has two different uses. In the middle of a narrative discourse, it has a consecutive meaning which carries along the main storyline. In normal conversational dialogue, it has an inceptive meaning, indicating an action that is about to happen. In this section, constructions are glossed with inceptive meaning.

In (15), which is marked for progressive aspect, the meaning is the normal one of an action currently in the process of taking place.

(15) *Mà ŋgà wíìŋ* *ò-mpyô.* →| *Mà ŋgà wíìŋ òmpyô.*
    1s PROG chase^away C2-dog
    I am chasing away the dogs.

2.4. Near future (F1). Near future is used to refer to situations which will occur subsequent to the present moment but during the same day. It is marked by a toneless *e*. In (16), the pronoun *mà* (1s) spreads its low tone onto *e*.

(16) *Mà e* ˊ *wíìŋ* ˊ *ò-mpyô.* →| *Mà è wíìŋ ómpyô.*
    1s F1 H1 → chase^away H2 → C2-dog
    I will chase away the dogs (later today).

When the preceding pronoun has H, as in (17), it is the H that spreads onto the toneless tense marker.

(17) *Bwó e* ˊ *wáámbùlà* ˊ *ø-mbààdô* *mpwó kùgú.*
    3p F1 H1 → sweep   H2 → C3-courtyard toward evening
    They will sweep the courtyard this evening.

    →| *Bwó é wáámbùlôô mbààdô mpwó kùgú.*

Finally, in (18), while *e* is expected to take the L of *mà*, it is realized instead with H because the L verb following H1 causes H1 to dock to the left.

(18) *Mà e* ˊ *càl* ˊ *mà-lôndú.* →| *Mà é càl môlôndú.*
    1s F1 ← H1 cut^down H2 → C6-palm^tree
    I will cut down the palm trees (later today).

2.5. Remote future (F2). Remote future refers to situations which will occur after today (i.e., beginning tomorrow morning). This construction is marked by *bá* (F2), as seen in (19).

(19) *Mə̀ bá ´   wííŋ   ´   ò-mpyɔ̂.* →| *Mə̀ bá wííŋ ómpyɔ̂.*
      1s   F2 H1 → chase^away H2 → C2-dog
      I will chase away the dogs (tomorrow or later).

3. Aspect markers

A three-way aspectual distinction exists in Makaa—perfective, habitual, and progressive. Makaa makes a morphological distinction between constructions which are progressive and those which are not, thereby grouping perfective and habitual actions together. H1 is present in all constructions except present progressive. H2 is present in all constructions except those which have the progressive aspect and P2. (It does occur in a nonprogressive P2 construction that also has polar focus.). Therefore both H1 and H2 occur in all perfective and habitual constructions, with H1 also occurring in progressive constructions, except for present.

3.1. Perfective (PRFV). Perfective aspect "involves lack of explicit reference to the internal temporal constituency of a situation" (Comrie 1976:21). A construction with perfective aspect thus looks at a situation as a whole, as has been seen in our examples up to this point. Perfective aspect is unmarked in that the absence of habitual or progressive marking is the best indication of perfectivity in Makaa. We now examine nonperfective constructions in like detail.

3.2. Habitual (HAB). Habitual aspect describes "a situation which is characteristic of an extended period of time, so extended in fact that the situation referred to is viewed not as an incidental property of the moment but, precisely, as a characteristic feature of a whole period" (Comrie 1976:27–28). Habitual aspect in Makaa can be used with all five tenses and is marked by *dʉ*, as illustrated in (20).

(20) Mə̀ a   ´   dù   ŋgùl mə̀-lwòg mə̀ `-lə́ndú.
     1s P2 ← H1 HAB drink c6-drink of c5-palm
     I used to drink palm wine (before yesterday).

→| Mə̀ á dù ŋgùl mə̀lwòg mə̀ lə́ndú.

Since the habitual marker immediately follows H1, the L of the habitual
marker always forces the H of H1 to dock to the left.

3.3. Progressive (PROG). Progressive aspect indicates continuous action
and is marked by ŋgə̀. Like habitual aspect, progressive can be used with
all five tenses. A typical progressive sentence is illustrated in (21).

(21) Mə̀ a   ´   ŋgè wííŋg   ò-mpyə̂. →| Mə̀ á ŋgə̀ wííŋg òmpyə̂.
     1s P2 ← H1 PROG chase^away c2-dog
     I was chasing the dogs away.

It might seem that this aspect should be glossed as continuous rather
than progressive because it can be used with verbs that are generally
classified as stative. When it is used with a stative verb such as bwàs 'to be
sick,' however, the verb takes on a nonstative meaning and indicates a
process. In (22), for example, the perfective form of gwág keeps the stative
meaning of 'to understand' or 'to hear'. In (23), on the other hand, the
same verb is given a nonstative meaning of either 'to be listening' or 'to
be in the process of understanding' when it occurs with the progressive.

(22) Mə̀   ´   ` ámə̀ gwág ´   mə̀-kûl. →| Mə́ ámə̀ gwág mə̀kûl.
     1s ← H1   P2   hear H2 → c6-news
     I heard (or understood) the news.

(23) Mə̀ ŋgə̀ gwág   `-yígùlì. →| Mə̀ ŋgə̀ gwág yígùlì.
     1s PROG listen^to c1-teacher
     I am listening to (or am understanding) the teacher.

3.4. Habitual and progressive. Sentences marked for both habitual and
progressive aspects also occur. Such sentences take on a special habitual
meaning which is different from that when only dù (HAB) is present. When
dù and ŋgə̀ are both used, it means that the situation, though occurring
often, is less frequent than when the habitual morpheme is used alone.
This is illustrated by the following two pairs of examples, contrasting HAB
with HAB + PROG.

(24) *Mə̀ a   ′ dù   də̀ i-dûw kú   nə̀   `-bààgè.*
      1s P2 ← H1 HAB eat C8-food NEG with C1-hot^pepper
      I used to eat food without hot pepper.

      →| *Mə̀ á dù də̀ idûw kú nə̀ bààgè.*

(25) *Mə̀ a   ′ dù   ŋgə̀ də̀ i-dûw kú   nə̀   `-bààgè.*
      1s P2 ← H1 HAB PROG eat C8-food NEG with C1-hot^pepper
      I often ate food without hot pepper (but not always).

      →| *Mə̀ á dù ŋgə̀ də̀ idûw kú nə̀ bààgè.*

(26) *Mə̀ a   ′ dù   bwàs   ø-kwésh.* →| *Mə̀ á dù bwàs kwésh.*
      1s P2 H1 HAB be^sick C7-cough
      I used to be (frequently) sick with a cough.

(27) *Mə̀ a ′ dù   ŋgə̀ bwàs   ø-kwésh.*→| *Mə̀ á dù ŋgə̀ bwàs kwésh.*
      1s P2 H1 HAB PROG be^sick C7-cough
      I often was sick with a cough (but not all the time).

This habitual-progressive has been found to occur with P2, P1, PRES, and F2. Further research is needed to discover if this combination of aspects may also occur with F1.

4. Perfect (PERF)

Although it is not, strictly speaking, a pure tense, Makaa also has a present perfect construction which indicates, as Comrie states, "the continuing present relevance of a past situation" (1976:52). It can refer to a situation which occurred any time in the past whose present result is of importance to the speaker. More research needs to be done on this construction in order to fully understand how the tones work.

Perfect is marked by *mə́* plus a floating L which causes a following H to be downstepped (!). This is shown in (28) and (29).

(28) *Mə̀ mə́ ` wííŋg   ′ ò-mpyə̂.* →| *Mə̀ mə́ !wííŋg ómpyə̂.*
      1s PERF   chase^away   H2 → C2-dog
      I have chased the dogs away (and they haven't returned).

(29) *Mə̀ mə́* ` *wóós.* →| *Mə̀ mə́ !wóós.*
      1s   PERF   arrive
      I have arrived (and am still here).

5. Summary

Makaa makes a three-way aspectual distinction—perfective, habitual, and progressive—and a five-way temporal distinction—remote past, near past, present, near future, and remote future. A summary of how tenses and aspects are marked is presented in (30). Two examples of the perfective are given in each tense to indicate how H1 docks before a H stem versus a L stem.

The interaction of five grammatical tenses with three grammatical aspects has been examined in detail, with special care given to tonal changes which result from certain grammatical markers. The most complicated tonal changes result from the replacive high tone morphemes H1 and H2. These morphemes are not only unusual in their tonal behavior; they also mark the absence of present progressive and progressive notions. Perhaps most unusual is the way they mark perfective and habitual as opposed to progressive constructions. The H2 marker, especially, seems to mark nonprogressiveness, a rather unusual semantic distinction.

Finally, Makaa is also unusual in allowing progressive and habitual markers to occur together in the same construction. The special meaning resulting from this is that the action is seen to be habitual in nature though not quite so frequent as if the habitual marker had been used by itself. The reason the progressive marker is used in this way (instead of a specific adverb, for example) seems to be just another manifestation of the particularity of the Makaa language.

(30) Tense and aspect constructions

	1s	TNS	H1	P1	HAB	PROG	STEM	H2	OBJ
P2:									
PFV	mɔ̀	a	′→				wííŋ		ò-mpyɔ̂
	mɔ̀	a	←′				càl		mɔ̀-lándú
PROG	mɔ̀	a	←′			ŋgɔ̀	wííŋ		ò-mpyɔ̂
HAB	mɔ̀	a	←′		dù		wííŋ		ò-mpyɔ̂
HAB/PROG	mɔ̀	a	←′		dù	ŋgɔ̀	wííŋ		ò-mpyɔ̂
P1:									
PFV	mɔ̀		←′ `	ámɔ̀			wííŋ	′→	ò-mpyɔ̂
	mɔ̀		←′ `	ámɔ̀			càl	′→	mɔ̀-lándú
PROG	mɔ̀		←′ `	ámɔ̀		ŋgɔ̀	wííŋ		ò-mpyɔ̂
HAB	mɔ̀		←′ `	ámɔ̀	dù		wííŋ	′→	ò-mpyɔ̂
HAB/PROG	mɔ̀		←′ `	ámɔ̀	dù	ŋgɔ̀	wííŋ		ò-mpyɔ̂
PRES:									
PFV	mɔ̀		′→				wííŋ	′→	ò-mpyɔ̂
	mɔ̀		←′				càl	′→	mɔ̀-lándú
PROG	mɔ̀					ŋgɔ̀	wííŋ		ò-mpyɔ̂
HAB	mɔ̀		←′		dù		wííŋ	′→	ò-mpyɔ̂
HAB/PROG	mɔ̀		←′		dù	ŋgɔ̀	wííŋ	′→	ò-mpyɔ̂
F1:									
PFV	mɔ̀	e	′→				wííŋ	′→	ò-mpyɔ̂
	mɔ̀	e	←′				càl	′→	mɔ̀-lándú
PROG	mɔ̀	e	←′			ŋgɔ̀	wííŋ		ò-mpyɔ̂
HAB	mɔ̀	e	←′		dù		wííŋ	′→	ò-mpyɔ̂
F2:									
PFV	mɔ̀	bá	′→				wííŋ	′→	ò-mpyɔ̂
	mɔ̀	bá	←′				càl	′→	ò-mpyɔ̂
PROG	mɔ̀	bá	←′			ŋgɔ̀	wííŋ		ò-mpyɔ̂
HAB	mɔ̀	bá	←′		dù		wííŋ	′→	ò-mpyɔ̂
HAB/PROG	mɔ̀	bá	←′		dù	ŋgɔ̀	wííŋ		ò-mpyɔ̂

References

Beavon, Keith. 1991. Kɔɔzime verbal system. (In this volume).

Comrie, Bernard. 1976. Aspect. Cambridge: Cambridge University Press.

———. 1985. Tense. Cambridge: Cambridge University Press.

Guthrie, Malcolm. 1971. Comparative Bantu 2. Farnborough, England: Gregg International Publishers.

Heath, Daniel. 1989. Tone in the Makaa associative construction. ms.

Temps et aspect en kakɔ

Urs Ernst

Résumé

Cette étude étant essentiellement inspirée par le modèle de pensée de Bernard Comrie, est consacrée au kakɔ, une langue parlée dans l'est du Cameroun et appartenant au groupe des langues bantu. Elle cherche à démontrer les moyens grammaticaux, au niveau de l'énoncé verbal dont dispose la langue pour exprimer les trois références temporelles par rapport au moment d'énonciation, à savoir: le temps présent (identique au moment de l'énonciation), le temps passé et le temps futur. La temporalité est envisagée sous un double angle: absolu et relatif. L'étude traite ensuite de la notion d'aspect, mettant l'accent sur l'aspect imperfectif et la construction du parfait. Enfin, des modifications aspectuelles telles que le duratif, l'ingressif, le cessatif ainsi que le prioritaire sont traitées. Bien que les deux concepts de la temporalité et de l'aspectualité soient discutés séparément, nous avons remarqué les cas où il y a chevauchement des deux.

Abstract

This study of a Bantu language from eastern Cameroon uses Bernard Comrie's theoretical model to examine the grammaticalization of time concepts. The Kakɔ language grammaticalizes past, present and future time, each of which can be used to mark absolute or relative tense. This study goes beyond a discussion of the obligatory marking of perfective and imperfective aspects to examine the optional aspectual marking of perfect, durative, ingressive and terminative constructions as well as a construction expressing an action having priority over another action. Also included is a discussion of which tense and aspect markers can occur in the same construction.

17

La langue kakɔ parlée au Cameroun dans le département de la Kadey (Province de l'Est), ainsi que dans la région voisine de la République Centrafricaine (autour de Gamboula), est classée par Guthrie (1971:34) sous A.93 dans les langues bantu, et sous Nº 237 dans ALCAM (Dieu et Renaud, 1985:25).

Le but de cette étude[1] est de présenter les éléments principaux du système aspecto-temporel en kakɔ. Etant donné que nous sommes au début de l'analyse grammaticale du kakɔ, la présente étude ne constitue qu'un premier essai d'une description systématique de la grammaire de cette langue. Une future étude plus approfondie cherchera à analyser et à décrire le système des tons.

La terminologie adopté dans cette étude est essentiellement celle de Houis (1977). Les deux termes PERFECTIF et IMPERFECTIF sont employés par Comrie (1976, 1985).

Il convient ici de dire un mot quant à la catégorie grammaticale qui est au centre de la présente étude, à savoir le verbe. Selon Houis, la description du verbe doit inclure celle de la base verbale (BV) ainsi que du (ou des) paradigme(s) de prédicatifs (p). Quand on parle de VERBE, on parle d'une base verbale actualisée par des prédicatifs. Le terme VERBE est toujours employé pour parler du verbe conjugué, qui, lui seul, peut assumer la fonction de prédicat dans l'énoncé. Nous ne tenterons pas de présenter une description exhaustive du système des prédicatifs, mais nous nous contenterons de donner un aperçu des éléments de base du système. Des aspects spécifiques relatifs au système des prédicatifs sont traités dans d'autres études mentionnées ci-dessous.

---

[1] La présente étude est le fruit de recherches menées entre 1987 et 1988. La partie principale de cette recherche a été faite pendant un séminaire de la Société Internationale de Linguistique (SIL). Ce cours avait lieu à Yaoundé au Cameroun en mai-juin 1987. L'étude se situe dans le cadre des programmes de recherche entrepris par le Centre de Recherches et d'Etudes Anthropologiques (CREA) et a été effectuée sous l'autorisation de recherche Nº 22/1987 accordée par le Ministère de l'Enseignement Supérieur, de l'Informatique et de la Recherche Scientifique.

Notre reconnaissance va en premier lieu à la Direction du Ministère de l'Education Supérieure, de l'Informatique et de la Recherche Scientifique ainsi qu'au Gouvernement Camerounais qui ont permis que cette étude soit entreprise. Nos remerciements s'adressent ensuite au Professeur Bernard Comrie à l'enseignement duquel nous devons beaucoup. Nous remercions aussi nos collègues de la SIL, notamment les Drs Steve Anderson, Robert Hedinger et Carol Stanley qui ont lu et annoté le manuscrit ainsi qu'à Mme Carol Holmes qui a vérifié le français. Enfin, nous tenons à dire que rien de ce qui va suivre n'aurait été possible sans la collaboration amicale de notre assistant de langue, M. David-Didérot Kombo Dee. Qu'il en soit remercié.

Contrairement au système des nominants, celui des prédicats est très peu homogène. Dans ces paradigmes on peut trouver des formes très variées:

(1) La forme du prédicatif:[2]
    -ton (marqué sur l'unité BV-p)
    -suffixes de BV
    -morphèmes indépendants

L'infinitif, toujours d'après Houis, n'est pas un verbe parce qu'il n'est pas actualisé par des prédicatifs et ne peut pas assumer la fonction de prédicat.

Nous appelons INFINITIF la forme du verbe qui a la diffusion la plus large parmi les formes verbales attestées dans la langue. La forme infinitive est notamment utilisée dans les séries verbales (2). Elle apparaît ensuite dans les constructions imperfectives (3–5), dans le futur (6) et dans le parfait (7). Enfin, c'est cette forme qu'un informateur autochtone fournira lorsqu'on lui demande l'infinitif d'un verbe quelconque en français. Dans les exemples de cette étude, toute forme non spécifiée représente la forme infinitive (cf. (8) *kὲ* 'aller').

(2)   *Bὲmbìyὲ kwàŋ-má tìlɔ̀ ndàmbà nyέ*
    Bembiye partir-PAS extraire caoutchouc mettre

    kɛ yótú né hénὲ njὲ yɔ̀kwὲ.
    à corps son tout venir rentrer
    Bembiye parta extraire du caoutchouc; il s'en enduit, puis revint.

(3)   *Mi kέ kwàdyé sùmɔ̀ tụ̀.*
    je IPF aimer construire maison
    Je veux construire une maison.

(4)   *Bo kέ tuyɔ́ ŋgwáŋ.*
    ils IPF défricher champ
    Ils sont en train de défricher le champ.

(5)   *Wùsὲ ndi kέ bétὲ gɛy.*
    nous DUR IPF jeter hameçon
    Nous sommes toujours en train de faire la pêche à la ligne.

---

[2]L'aspect tonal du système des prédicatifs est traité dans Ernst 1989a. Un aperçu des formes morphologiques des prédicatifs liés fait part de Ernst 1989b.

(6)   *À tǎ kèlɔ̀ mèsay.*
       il FUT faire travail
       Il fera le travail.

(7)   *Ɓó mǎ ɓìyè mɔ́ gubɔ̀.*
       ils PAR saisir personne voler
       Ils ont saisi le voleur.

(8)   *À kwàŋ-má kɛ̀ ɓèŋɛ̀ sɔ wénɛ.*
       il partir-PAS aller voir ami son
       Il partait voir son ami.

Formellement, l'infinitif en kakɔ est constitué, au niveau segmental, par un radical verbal qui peut ou non être suivi par une extension. La base verbale, c'est-à-dire, respectivement le radical, et le radical plus l'extension, est suivie par une voyelle finale (VF). Les formes infinitives peuvent être résumées comme dans l'exemple (9). Les paradigmes des voyelles finales sont présentés en (10).

(9)   **Base**   -VF

       monosyllabiques: CV   -∅   *wó*   'tuer'
                            CVC   -VF   *ɓèŋɛ̀*   'voir'
       polysyllabiques: CVC-EXT   -VF   *lép-ìn-à*   'bavarder'

(10)   c-(*i̧ e ɛ ɛ̧ a a̧ ɔ ɔ̧ o u̧*)
           cvc-(*e ɛ a ɔ*)
           cvcvc-(*e ɛ a*)

On notera les particularités phonologiques (11).

(11) Particularités phonologiques:

l'absence des voyelles de première aperture (*i u*), à l'exception des variantes nasalisées dans le cas des bases monosyllabiques du type CV.

les voyelles nasalisées sont limitées aux bases monosyllabiques du type CV.

l'absence des voyelles postérieures dans le cas des bases dissyllabiques dont une majorité peut être considérée comme des bases dérivées.

Au niveau tonal, l'infinitif est caractérisé par des structures tonales bien définies. Ces tons ne semblent pas subir des changements provoqués par le contexte phonologique. Nous distinguons les schémas ci-dessous. Il est à noter que ces schémas sont considérés dans le contexte de l'énoncé d'au moins trois termes—Sujet-Prédicat-Expansion (S-P-X). Par expansion (X) nous entendons tout constituant post-prédicatif. Selon une règle tonale générale affectant l'infinitif ainsi que quelques autres formes verbales, tout ton non-bas en position finale devient bas devant pause. L'absence de l'expansion n'aurait donc pas permis d'établir deux catégories de verbes à base monosyllabique, à savoir les verbes à ton bas d'une part et les verbes à ton haut d'autre part. Il en est de même quant aux bases dissyllabiques où l'identité du deuxième ton du schéma 'HH n'est révélée que dans le contexte S-P-X. Nous distinguons donc les schémas tonals des bases verbales (12). En sommaire, la forme infinitive en kakɔ peut être définie en fonction de deux traits caractéristiques, à savoir la tonalité et le paradigme de la voyelle finale.

(12) Bases monosyllabiques
du type cv

| | B | ɓà | 'dépecer' |
| | H | ɓṹ | 'prendre' |

Bases dissyllabiques
du type cvc-

	BB	ɓèŋè	'regarder'
	'HH	ɓɔmɔ́	'acheter'
	HB	tédyè	'montrer'

Bases dissyllabiques

| | BBB | kòmbìlè | 'arranger' |
| | HBB | wúmbìdyè | 'balayer' |

Dans (13–14), on peut analyser les éléments comme faisant partie des prédicatifs (p). Pour ce qui en est des morphèmes suivant BV, on remarquera la distinction entre morphèmes liés à valeur prédicative (14) et le morphème /-ɔ/ lié à valeur non prédicative (13). Les premiers servent à actualiser la base verbale kèl- 'faire' lui permettant ainsi d'assumer la fonction de prédicat dans l'énoncé. Le second, par contre, ne fonctionne pas comme actualisateur de la base verbale. Il s'agit plutôt de la voyelle finale (VF) caractérisant l'infinitif.

(13) Morphèmes libres

prédicatifs	infinitif	
ké	kèl-ɔ̀	'est en train de faire/fait (IMPF)'
tǎ	kèl-ɔ̀	'fera (FUT)'
mǎ (sì)	kèl-ɔ̀	'a fini faire (PRF-CESS)'
sì ké pà	kèl-ɔ̀	'finit d'abord faire (IMPF-CESS-PRI)'

(14) Morphèmes liés

    kèl-má   'a fait/faisait (PAS)'
    kel-ɛ   'a fait/faisait (NAR)'
    kél-∅   'fait/faisait (AR)'

La présentation ci-dessus, sans être complète, nous permet toutefois de dire que les prédicatifs en kakɔ forment un système de deux paradigmes qui se complètent. On pourrait proposer comme hypothèse le schéma de système des prédicatifs en (15) ci-dessous. On notera deux catégories de prédicatifs, à savoir (a) les prédicatifs précédant la base verbale (p_w, p_x, p_y) et (b) les prédicatifs suivant la base verbale (p_z). Les deux catégories de prédicatifs diffèrent non seulement quant à leur position par rapport à BV, mais aussi quant à leur nature morphologique.

(15)

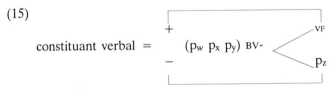

constituant verbal = (p_w p_x p_y) BV-

Les prédicatifs précédant la base verbale (BV) sont des morphèmes libres caractérisés par leur capacité d'être combinés entre eux. Il y a néanmoins réstriction quant au nombre et au genre des prédicatifs qui peuvent se combiner pour actualiser la base verbale (cf. §2.3). Il est à noter que ces prédicatifs sont suivis par la forme infinitive du verbe (BV-VF). On remarquera aussi que les prédicatifs libres ne provoquent pas de changements tonals au niveau de la forme infinitive du verbe qu'ils précèdent.

Les prédicatifs suivant la base verbale par contre, sont des morphèmes liés (suffixes) phonologiquement conditionnés dont la description exacte fait objet de notre étude "Description morphologique de quelques formes verbales en kakɔ" (Ernst 1991b). Nous n'avons relevé qu'un seul cas, relatif au mode impératif, où les deux catégories de prédicatifs, qui normalement ne coexistent pas dans un même énoncé, se combinent dans l'actualisation de la base verbale (Ernst 1991a).

Les valeurs liées au système des prédicatifs concernent (a) les modalités du procès, (b) la situation du procès dans le temps et (c) la position du locuteur vis-à-vis du procès.

Quant aux modalités du procès, nous ne traiterons ici que du mode indicatif affirmatif. Quant à la situation du procès dans le temps, nous étudierons brièvement l'expression des valeurs temporelles en faisant référence au passé, d'une part et, au futur, d'autre part. Pour ces deux références de temps, c'est la temporalité qui est marquée par un morphème respectivement lié et libre tandis que l'aspectualité est marquée par l'absence de tout marqueur soit segmental soit tonal. Enfin, quant à la position du locuteur vis-à-vis du procès, en cas du temps dit PRESENT, c'est plutôt l'aspectualité qui est marquée au niveau segmental tandis que la temporalité est caractérisée par un morphème zéro (∅). Nous en parlerons sous §2.2.

1. Temps

Le temps, selon Comrie (1976:9), peut être défini comme la localisation grammaticalisée dans le temps. Le temps indique le moment du procès. Pour le situer, il faut avoir un temps de référence fixé, à savoir le moment de l'énonciation ou n'importe quel autre point de référence situé sur la ligne du temps. Comrie distingue ainsi deux systèmes temporels, à savoir (a) le temps absolu, et (b) le temps relatif. Selon le premier système, le temps de référence est le moment de l'énonciation. Selon le deuxième par contre, le temps de référence est n'importe quel autre moment qui reste à être précisé, mais toujours par rapport au moment de l'énonciation.

En nous basant sur une vingtaine de textes de genres littéraires différents, tels que contes, descriptions, dialogues, exhortations, nous constatons que, dans la grande majorité des cas, lorsque référence est faite soit au temps passé soit au temps futur, la temporalité de la forme verbale est marquée au niveau segmental. Quant à l'aspectualité, elle est marquée par l'absence de tout marqueur tant segmental que tonal. Nous appelons ces formes respectivement PASSE et FUTUR.

Pour résumer, nous constatons que la langue kakɔ, lorsqu'elle exprime le temps présent, met en évidence l'attitude du locuteur vis-à-vis du procès, donc l'aspectualité, tandis que, lorsqu'elle exprime un temps non présent, elle souligne la situation du procès dans le temps, donc la temporalité.

1.1. Référence au passé. Le kakɔ atteste les formes verbales de (16) pour faire référence au temps passé.

(16)   le passé
        le passé narratif
        le parfait
        l'imperfectif passé
        l'aoriste
        la forme verbale caractérisant la mise en emphase du constituant
            préverbal

L'imperfectif passé sera traité sous le système d'aspect (§2), le parfait sous §3, et l'aoriste sous §4. La forme verbale caractérisant la mise en emphase du constituant préverbal sera étudiée en relation avec le narratif (§1.2).

Le passé (-má (PAS)). Le passé envisage le procès dans sa totalité. Bien qu'il soit caractérisé par l'absence de toute modalité aspectuelle, on peut, du point de vue du contenu sémantique de l'événement qu'il désigne, le considérer comme perfectif qui lui, est marqué par /∅/ (§2.2).

Le passé a comme valeur la plus fréquente la référence à un fait passé relatif au moment de l'énonciation. Il est à noter aussi que les degrés d'éloignement temporel en kakɔ ne sont pas exprimés, en général, par des modalités verbales, mais plutôt par des adverbes.[3]

(17)   *À   wò-má   nyámɔ   ɓèmɛŋménè   múkà.*
        il   tuer-PAS animal   matin   aujourd'hui
        Il a tué un animal ce matin.

(18)   *Ɓó kwàŋ-má   kwéy.*
        ils partir-PAS hier
        Ils sont partis hier.

(19)   *Mí ɓèŋ-má   nyɛ njómbú   nyáŋà.*
        je voir-PAS lui vieux   chose
        Je l'ai vu il y a longtemps.

Le kakɔ, ne disposant pas de forme verbale distincte pour exprimer l'antériorité d'un événement par rapport à un point de référence situé, soit dans le passé, soit dans le futur (temps relatif), peut se servir du passé à cet effet. L'antériorité peut aussi être exprimée par le parfait.

---

[3]Une exception à cette règle est discutée sous §2.3.

(20)   *Bó lèpì-má   ndé à kwàŋ-mà.*
       ils parler-PAS que il partir-PAS
       Ils ont dit qu'il était parti.

(21)   *Jean dyàŋ-má   yítè Màríyà kwàŋ-mà.*
       Jean arriver-PAS cela Marie   partir-PAS
       Jean arriva lorsque Marie était partie.

(22)   *À   tă   lɛpɔ́ nyé wɛ ndé à kwàŋ-mà.*
       il FUT dire à   toi que il partir-PAS
       Il te dira qu'il était parti.

(23)   *Kómè   wé tă   njè   nèmɛnɔ ké,*
       lorsque tu FUT venir demain SUB

       ɔ́ tă   dolɔ́   ndé à kwàŋ-mà.
       tu FUT trouver que il partir-PAS
       Lorsque tu viendras demain, tu verras qu'il sera parti.

Enfin, un emploi particulier du passé concerne l'expression dans le discours direct de faits imminents quasi-simultanés par rapport au moment de l'énonciation. Dans ce contexte, le passé a pour but d'atténuer l'énoncé; il s'agit ici d'une forme de politesse.

(24)   *Mí kwàŋ-má mbè!*
       je partir-PAS moi^EMPH
       Je voudrais partir!

(25)   *Ndá   wùnè ké lìnjà   ké, wùsè kàndì-má   sú*
       comme vous IPF tarder SUB je   commencer-PAS nous^EMPH

       kèndì.
       voyage
       Comme vous tardez, nous commençons à partir!

(26)   *Ndá   wùnè séŋ-má   ké, mí tìkì-má   mbé   yo.*
       comme vous refuser-PAS SUB je laisser-PAS moi^EMPH ça
       Comme vous avez refusé, je veux le laisser!

Le passé dénotant un fait imminent est caractérisé par certaines restrictions lexicales. La fonction de nominal est assumée exclusivement par les pronoms *mí* et *wùsè* de la 1ère personne respectivement du singulier et du pluriel. La fonction de prédicat, obligatoirement suivie par le pronom emphatique *mbè* et *sú* respectivement, ne peut être assumée que par une classe restreinte de verbes. Ceux-ci semblent avoir comme particularité commune le trait INCHOATIF indiquant le début d'une action qui va progresser. Nous ne l'avons trouvé qu'avec les verbes sous (27).

(27) Verbes inchoatifs

dùwè	'rentrer'
kwą́	'partir'
témè	'se lever'
jìsè	'quitter'
pundɔ́	'sortir'
tikɔ́	'laisser'
kàndè	'commencer'

   Suivant Comrie (1985:2–6, 36, 82), les divers emplois du passé peuvent être résumés en sommaire sous forme de schémas représentant sur la ligne temporelle les événements (E) situés par rapport au moment de l'énonciation (En), d'une part, et par rapport à un point de référence (R) fixé par le contexte, d'autre part. On notera que les exemples (20–21) constituent un cas particulier de la relation E avant En.

(28) Les divers emplois du passé

Ligne temporelle	Situation des événements sur la ligne temporelle	Exemple
E En	E avant En	17, 18, 19
E R En	E avant R-passé	20, 21
En R (E- - -)	E avant R-futur	22, 23
En/E	En = E	24, 25, 26

Le passé narratif ('Hⁿ, -ɛ (NAR)). Le passé narratif, lui aussi, envisage le procès dans sa totalité. C'est la forme verbale par excellence dans les récits et surtout dans les contes. Le narratif se combine, dans le discours narratif, avec le passé (cf. lignes 1 et 2 de l'exemple (29)). Ce dernier a pour fonction de marquer le début d'un narratif ainsi que le début d'un nouveau paragraphe. Ce sujet sera traité plus à fond lors d'une étude future sur le discours. Quant à la traduction en français, le passé narratif sera normalement traduit par le passé. Bien qu'il raconte des événements qui sont effectivement situés dans le passé par rapport au moment de l'énonciation, il pourrait toutefois, pour des fins stylistiques, être traduit en français par le présent. Les paragraphes suivants tirés des textes serviront à illustrer le passé narratif.

Au niveau de l'énoncé, le passé narratif est caractérisé, tout d'abord, par un morphème libre /à/ ou /è/, selon les locuteurs, apparaissant en début de l'énoncé. Ensuite, le verbe en fonction de prédicat est caractérisé par un paradigme de prédicatifs ayant la forme /-ɛ/. Les réalisations de ce prédicatif sont (a) -v́, désignant une voyelle soit orale soit nasalisée identique à la voyelle finale de la forme infinitive, et (b) -ɛ dans le cas des verbes dont la voyelle finale est -ɔ. Le passé narratif est enfin caractérisé, au niveau tonal, par un schéma tonal qui, ne comprenant que des tons hauts rabaissés ('H^n), qualifie l'unité actualisée BV-ɛ.

(29) *Ŋgurú ɓé-nɛ́   ŋgò   ɓiy-má   sɔ.*
       tortue c2-avec sanglier tenir-PAS ami

     À   ŋgó   tɛm-ɛ   ɓémɛŋménɛ̀ kɛ̀
     NAR sanglier se^lever-NAR matin   aller

     pɛ mbósè pɛ yi   ŋgurú   kɛ̀   dyénà   njè   dùwɛ̀.
     à visite à chez tortue aller manger venir rentrer

     À   ŋgurú nj-é   témɛ̀, sèndí kɛ̀ pɛ̀lɛ̀ yi   ŋgó.
     NAR tortue venir-NAR se^lever aussi aller à   chez sanglier
La tortue se lia d'amitié avec le sanglier. Le sanglier se leva le matin et alla rendre visite à la tortue. Il mangea, puis rentra. Ensuite, la tortue se leva aussi et alla chez le sanglier.

(30) *Tòmbá ɓé-né ndèmbi dǐy-má   kɛ wété dyàri. À   ɓó*
      aîné   c2-avec cadet rester-PAS à un village NAR ils

      tɛm-ɛ   wété yesɔ́ kwá̧ kɛ̀ pɛ sákɔ pɔ́ndɔ̀. À   ɓó
      se^lever-NAR un jour partir aller à lieu piège NAR ils

      kɛy-ɛ   sàɓìdyè duku yínî. À   tómbá k-a
      marcher-NAR traverser ruisseau quatre NAR aîné   dire-NAR

      ndé: "Hɛ kêl-∅   gurú wakà." À   ndémbí té k-a
      que nous faire-INJ cabane ici   NAR cadet ce dire-NAR

      ndé: "Bɛ̀, tǎ kɛ̀ mbé   mbɔ́mbu."
      que non FUT aller moi^EMPH devant
      Un frère aîné et son cadet vivaient dans un village. Un jour ils se
      levèrent et partirent pour un séjour de piégeage. Ils marchèrent,
      puis traversèrent quatre ruisseaux. Puis l'aîné dit: "Construisons la
      cabane ici!" Le cadet dit: "Non, moi j'irai plus loin!"

La forme verbale du narratif sert aussi à exprimer la mise en emphase
du constituant préverbal. Elle concerne tout premièrement le sujet, constituant préverbal par excellence (31–32, 34) mais peut aussi, de façon
générale, concerner tout constituant en position préverbale (33). Cette
forme verbale peut, selon le cas, faire référence aussi bien au passé qu'au
présent. On notera le statut facultatif du morphème emphatique *yé*
(EMPH).

(31) *(Yé) nda kel -ɛ   yò?*
      EMPH qui faire-NAR cela
      C'est qui qui a fait cela?

(32) *(Yé) Kombo kel-ɛ.*
      EMPH Kombo faire-NAR
      C'est Kombo qui l'a fait.

(33) *(Yé) ŋge wé dyaŋgw-ɛ kɛ̀?*
      EMPH quoi tu vendre-NAR REL
      Qu'est-ce que tu vends?

(34) *(Yé) mɔnɔ wénɛ lel-ɛ.*
      EMPH enfant son pleurer-NAR
      C'est son enfant qui pleure.

1.2. Référence au futur. Comme pour le temps passé, le kakɔ dispose de plus d'une forme verbale pour faire référence au temps futur. Nous distinguons entre (a) le futur, et (b) l'imperfectif futur. Le dernier sera traité sous le système aspectuel (§2.2).

Le futur (tǎ (FUT)). Le futur, comme le passé, envisage le procès dans sa totalité, mais ayant lieu dans l'avenir immédiat ou un temps futur plus ou moins lointain. Les degrés d'éloignement temporel sont exprimés, en général, par des adverbes. Un futur proche peut, cependant, aussi être exprimé par l'imperfectif futur. Le futur est, lui aussi, caractérisé par l'absence de toute modalité aspectuelle. La forme verbale exprimant le temps présent, à savoir l'imperfectif, ne peut pas être utilisée pour faire référence au temps futur.

La forme du futur est caractérisée par le prédicatif libre *tǎ* préposé à la forme infinitive du verbe.

(35) *À tǎ   njè   ndánà.*
      il FUT venir tout de suite
      Il viendra tout de suite.

(36) *Bè-jeŋgwé tǎ kwá̧ nèmɛnɔ.*
      c2-étranger FUT partir demain
      Les étrangers partiront demain.

(37) *Mí tǎ dîyɔ̀ mè-sèw kamɔ kɛ Bertoua.*
      je FUT rester c6-année dix   à Bertoua
      Je resterai dix ans à Bertoua.

Le futur sert également à exprimer la postériorité d'un événement par rapport à un point de référence fixé par le contexte. Ce point de référence peut être situé soit dans le passé soit dans le futur.[4]

(38) *À lèpì-má ndé à tǎ   njè   nèmɛnɔ.*
      il dire-PAS que il FUT venir demain
      Il a dit qu'il viendra demain.

(39) *À lèpì-má ndé à tǎ   njè.*
      il dire-PAS que il FUT venir
      Il a dit qu'il viendra.

---

[4]Un cas particulier où référence à un temps futur est faite par une forme verbale autre que celle sous discussion ici sera traité sous §2.2.

(40) *À lèpì-má ndé à tǎ njè   kwèy.*
il   dire-PAS que il FUT venir hier
Il a dit qu'il viendrait hier.

(41) *Nèmɛnɔ́ à tǎ   lɛpɔ́ nyé mí   ŋgìmɔ̀ té yi   nyé tǎ   njè   kè.*
demain il FUT dire à   moi temps ce REL il   FUT venir REL
Il me dira demain quand il viendra.

(42) *À dyènà-má   kɛ ŋgímɔ yítân,*
il   manger-PAS à   temps cinq

   kɛtó   à tǎ kwą́ kè ŋgímɔ̀ yítân jɔ yiɓá.
   parce^que il FUT partir à temps cinq   et deux
   Il a mangé à cinq heures parce qu'il partira à sept heures.

Les divers emplois du futur peuvent être schématisés comme en exemple (43). On notera que les exemples (38) et (41) constituent des cas particuliers de la relation 'E après En'.

(43) Ligne temporelle   Situation de l'événement   Exemple
                                sur la ligne temporelle

Ligne temporelle	Situation de l'événement sur la ligne temporelle	Exemple
En E	E après En	35, 36, 37
R En E	E après R-passé et En	38
R En	E après R-passé	39
R E En	E après R-passé avant En	40
En R E	E après R-futur	41

2. Aspect

Il y a un chevauchement entre l'aspectualité et la temporalité en kakɔ. Nous pouvons distinguer deux catégories aspectuelles principales, à savoir: PERFECTIF et IMPERFECTIF. Suivant Comrie (1976:16–24, 52–65), nous leur attribuons les définitions en (44).

(44) PERFECTIF: On envisage le procès dans sa totalité sans tenir compte de sa structure interne.

     IMPERFECTIF: On envisage le procès quant à sa structure interne (son déroulement).

2.1. Le perfectif (∅). Le perfectif constitue un cas particulier dans le système aspectuel du kakɔ. Contrairement aux autres catégories aspectuelles mentionnées ci-dessus, le perfectif n'est pas marqué formellement. Autrement dit, il est marqué par l'absence de la marque de l'imperfectif. Un événement quelconque rendu par la forme du perfectif sera toujours envisagé par le locuteur kakɔ sous l'angle de sa totalité. Le contenu sémantique de tous les exemples présentés respectivement sous PASSE, PASSE NARRATIF, et FUTUR est donc PERFECTIF.

La notion du PERFECTIF est considérée comme valable du simple fait qu'il y a opposition entre deux formes aspectuelles, l'une marquée et clairement identifiée comme IMPERFECTIF et l'autre non marquée. Nous donnons les exemples (45–48) à titre illustratif.

(45) *À   sànà-mà.*
    il   travailler-PAS
    Il a travaillé.

(46) *À ɓ-ǎ̰   ké sánà.*
    il   être-PAS IPF travailler
    Il était en train de travailler.
    Il travaillait.

(47) *À tǎ   sánà.*
    il   FUT travailler
    Il travaillera.

(48) *À tǎ ɓé ké sánà.*
    il   FUT être IPF travailler
    Il sera (tout de suite) en train de travailler.
    Il travaillera.

2.2. L'imperfectif (ké IPF). L'imperfectif envisage le procès sous l'angle de son déroulement plutôt que dans sa totalité, et constitue, en kakɔ, la forme non marquée pour exprimer le temps présent (51–52). Référence au présent peut aussi être faite par l'aoriste (§4) et par la forme narrative

(§1.1) lorsqu'elle sert à exprimer une mise en emphase du constituant préverbal.

Lorsque l'imperfectif apparaît dans une construction périphrastique, il y exprime, avec le verbe *ɓé* 'être', respectivement un temps passé (53–54) et un temps futur (56–57). L'imperfectif par lui-même n'implique donc pas de valeur temporelle déterminée.

L'imperfectif a comme valeurs aspectuelles les plus fréquentes la progression et l'habitualité. La dernière peut aussi être exprimée par l'aoriste.

L'imperfectif est caractérisé, formellement, par le prédicatif *ké* suivi par la forme infinitive du verbe. On notera que le prédicatif *ké* a la même forme que la préposition *ké* dont la signification principale est 'à' dans le sens locatif. L'exemple (49) démontre l'emploi des deux homonymes dans le même énoncé.

(49)   *Mbam ké dyàŋgwè táɓɔ̀   ké lùmɔ̀.*
       homme IPF vendre   chèvre   à   marché
       L'homme vend la chèvre au marché.

(50)   *Ɓo ké lùmɔ̀.*
       ils à   marché
       Ils sont au marché.

(51)   *À ké dyé   kámɔ̀.*
       il IPF manger couscous
       Il est en train de manger du couscous.
       Il mange du couscous.

(52)   *À ké sá   ŋgwáŋ kɔ̀fì.*
       il IPF travailler champ café
       Il est en train de travailler le champ de café.
       Il travaille le champ de café.

Les deux énoncés (51–52) trouveront deux interprétations différentes selon le contexte. Comme nous l'avons déjà dit ci-dessus, on peut leur attribuer (a) une interprétation progressive qui recevra la traduction française 'Il est en train de manger/travailler' ou (b) une interprétation habituelle: 'Il mange/travaille habituellement.'

Les exemples (53) et (54) font référence au temps passé.

(53) *À ɓ-ǎ̰   ké kèlɔ́ mésay.*
il être-PAS IPF faire travail
Il était en train de faire le travail.
Il faisait le travail.

(54) *Mí ɓ-ǎ̰   ké sùmɔ̀   tṵ.*
je être-PAS IPF construire maison
J'étais en train de construire la maison.
Je construisais la maison.

L'imperfectif passé s'exprime à l'aide du verbe 'être' dans sa forme passée *ɓǎ̰* précédant le prédicatif *ké*. Il est à noter que *ɓǎ̰* constitue un verbe de plein exercice compatible avec toutes les modalités verbales conformes à sa nature spécifique de verbe statique. La forme *ɓǎ̰* a probablement évolué à partir de la forme *ɓɛ̀-má* (être-PAS), forme qui est toujours attestée, côte à côte avec la forme raccourcie *ɓǎ̰*, par exemple dans le dialecte béra. Nous proposons l'analyse schématisée sous (55).

(55) Analyse du passé à l'imperfectif:

          R1   R2
ɓɛ̀-má → *ɓà-má* → *ɓǎ̰*

Selon une règle d'assimilation (R1), la voyelle *ɛ* devient *a*. Ce phénomène est attesté ailleurs dans la langue. On distingue par exemple entre deux formes impératives/injonctives du verbe 'voir', à savoir *ɓèŋá* et *ɓàŋá*.
Selon une deuxième règle (R2), la forme *ɓàmá* a ensuite subi une réduction par perte de l'un des deux noyaux syllabiques. On remarque que les deux traits caractéristiques de celle-ci, à savoir la nasalisation et la tonalité du prédicatif, ont été conservés.
Enfin, l'imperfectif peut coexister avec la forme du futur où il fait référence au futur proche.

(56) *À tǎ ɓé ké kwǎ̰.*
il FUT être IPF partir
Il est sur le point de partir.

(57) *Wùsè tǎ ɓé ké ɗyénà.*
nous FUT être IPF manger
Nous sommes sur le point de manger.

L'imperfectif futur s'exprime, comme l'imperfectif passé, à l'aide d'une construction périphrastique, selon laquelle le verbe 'être' dans sa forme future *tǎ ɓé* précède la construction de l'imperfectif présent.

Il est à noter, que contrairement à l'imperfectif passé où aucune notion de degré d'éloignement sur le plan temporel n'est exprimée, l'imperfectif futur sert à exprimer qu'un procès se déroulera dans un avenir immédiat.

Enfin, remarquons que l'imperfectif est utilisé dans les textes où il est rencontré côte à côte avec le passé narratif. Dans ce contexte, il sert à fournir des informations supplémentaires portant sur l'arrière-plan plutôt qu'à la ligne principale des événements.

Nous avons relevé quatre prédicatifs servant à modifier l'imperfectif dont trois précèdent le prédicatif *ké* et un le suit. Ils sont présentés en (58).

(58)	*ndì*	*ké*		duratif
	mè	*ké*		ingressif
	sì	*ké*		cessatif
	(sì)	*ké*	*pǎ*	prioritaire

On notera que *sì* peut se combiner avec *pǎ*. C'est ici le seul cas, selon notre connaissance, où la base verbale est actualisée par trois prédicatifs.

2.3. D'autres aspects. Les valeurs aspectuelles traitées dans cette section servent à modifier des catégories aspectuelles et temporelles principales telles que l'imperfectif, le futur, et le parfait.

Le duratif (ndi (DUR)). Le duratif exprime la durée d'une action. Il peut être rendu en français par les expressions 'toujours' ou 'encore.'

Le duratif est exprimé formellement à l'aide du prédicatif *ndi* qui est antéposé au prédicatif *ké* de l'imperfectif. En dehors du système aspectuel, *ndi* signifie 'seulement'. L'exemple (59) démontre l'emploi des deux homonymes dans un même énoncé.

(59)   *À ndi ké ɗyé ndi kámɔ.*
       il DUR IPF manger seulement couscous de manioc
       Il ne mange toujours rien que du couscous de manioc.

Le duratif n'est jamais attesté comme seul prédicatif actualisant BV. Nous ne l'avons trouvé qu'en coexistence avec *ké*, prédicatif de l'imperfectif comme illustré dans les exemples (60–62).

(60) *Bo ndi   ké tuyɔ́   ŋgwáŋ.*
      ils DUR IPF défricher champ
      Ils sont encore en train de défricher le champ.
      Ils défrichent encore le champ.

(61) *À   ɓ-ă̆   ndi ké wó   ɓé-nɔ̀n.*
      il   être-PAS DUR IPF tuer c2-oiseau
      Il était encore en train de tuer les oiseaux.
      Il tuait encore les oiseaux.

(62) *À   tă   ɓέ ndi ké pεsɔ́   mé-jèti.*
      il FUT être DUR IPF couper c6-arbre
      Il devrait toujours être en train de couper du bois.
      Il devrait toujours couper du bois.

On remarquera qu'à l'imperfectif futur, le prédicatif *ndi* apporte une modification supplémentaire à valeur dubitative. Ainsi, l'exemple (62) implique qu'on présume qu'au moment de l'énonciation l'agent est toujours en train de couper du bois et le sera encore pour un temps futur non précisé. L'exemple (62) pourrait être une réponse naturelle à la question suivante.

(63) *À   ti   yá   yɔkwέ   na? Ɓὲ,...*
      il NEG^PAS encore rentrer NEG non
      N'est-il pas encore rentré ? Non,...

L'ingressif (mὲ (ING)). L'ingressif exprime une action en mettant l'accent sur son stade initial. Il correspond ainsi au français 'commencer à'.
    L'ingressif s'exprime à l'aide d'un prédicatif *mὲ* antéposé à la forme de l'imperfectif (61, 65). Nous ne l'avons relevé que dans cette construction spécifique. Il semble que le prédicatif *ké* peut être supprimé sans changer le sens, lorsque le prédicatif *mὲ* est présent.

(64) *Mi mε ké dyénà.*
      je ING IPF manger
      Je suis en train de commencer à manger.
      Je commence à manger.
      Je mange déjà.

(65)   *Bo mɛ ké dùmɔ̀ yombò.*
        ils   ING IPF piler   manioc
        Ils sont en train de commencer à piler le manioc.
        Ils commencent à piler le manioc.
        Ils pilent déjà le manioc.

Le cessatif (sì (CES)). Contrairement à l'ingressif qui exprime une action
en mettant l'accent sur son stade initial, le cessatif le met sur son stade
final. En ce faisant, il exprime parfois aussi une valeur d'intensif que le
français rendrait par les expressions telles que 'bien' dans l'énoncé 'Je l'ai
bien vu' et 'totalement' dans 'Il a totalement oublié'. La valeur de l'intensif
est particulièrement évidente dans le parfait (72–74).
    Le cessatif s'exprime à l'aide du prédicatif *sì* dont la ressemblance
formelle et sémantique avec le verbe *sìdyè* 'finir, terminer' est évidente. Il
est attesté en combinaison avec d'autres valeurs aspectuelles. Nous relevons notamment les cas suivants qui seront illustrés par les exemples
(67–75).

(66)   Le cessatif en combinaison avec d'autres aspects.

sì ké	imperfectif-cessatif
sì ké pǎ	imperfectif-cessatif-aspect à valeur prioritaire
tǎ sì	futur-cessatif
tǎ pǎ sì	futur-cessatif-aspect à valeur prioritaire
mǎ sì	parfait-cessatif
mǎ pǎ sì	parfait-cessatif-aspect à valeur prioritaire

On notera que le prédicatif *sì* se combine avec le prédicatif *pǎ* avec
lequel il partage une ressemblance sémantique. On comparera par exemple
(67) avec (76) ou (70) avec (79).
    Les énoncés entre parenthèses dans les exemples ci-dessous constituent
des contextes logiques et naturels permettant de mieux saisir la signification parfois cachée de l'aspect en question.

(67)   *À sì ké dyé kámɔ̀.*
        il CES IPF manger couscous
        Il est en train de finir de manger le couscous.
        Il mange (d'abord) le couscous.

(À tǎ   nje   njìmè.)
il FUT venir derrière
(Il viendra après.)

(68) *(Kombo tí   yɔkwé na).*
Kombo FUT^NEG revenir NEG
(Kombo ne reviendra pas.)

À   sì   ké   lèɓìdyè póndɔ.
il CES IPF tendre piège
Il est en train de finir de tendre des pièges.
Il tend (d'abord) des pièges.

(69) *Apou sì   kɛ lɔnjè mɔnɔsíkè.*
Apou CES IPF bercer enfant
Apou est en train de finir de bercer l'enfant.
Apou berce (d'abord) l'enfant.

(Kɛ kɔŋté à   nyàkà-má kè   jámbìnà.)
LOC dos il suffire-PAS aller réparer
(Ensuite, elle peut aller préparer.)

(70) *Wùsè tǎ   sì   wɔmbìlè tʉ̀.*
nous FUT CES balayer maison
Nous finirons de balayer la maison.
Nous balayerons d'abord la maison.

(Wùsè manjé kwą̀.)
nous puis partir
(Nous partirons après.)

(71) *Mí tǎ   pà   sì   sàkɔ   ŋgwàŋ.*
je FUT PRI CES sarcler champ
Je finirai d'abord de sarcler le champ.

(Manjé lòdyè.)
puis   brêler
(Je viendrai le brêler après.)

(72) *Mí mǎ   sì   wó   nyàmɔ.*
je PAR CES tuer animal
J'ai fini de tuer l'animal.

(Ndáná,   mí nyàkà-má ɓɔ̀lɔ̀   jèsɔ̀).
maintenant je suffire-PAS danser fête
(Maintenant je peux danser.)

(73) Mí mǎ sì ɓèŋè tʉ́   nè.
je PAR CES voir maison sa
J'ai bien vu sa maison.

(74) À mǎ sì lèŋsà lámbò.
il PAR CES oublier lampe
J'ai complètement oublié la lampe.

(75) Wùsè mǎ pà sì ɓétè gɛy,
nous PAR PRI CES jeter hameçon

       è wúsɛ nj-e   nɔ̀kɔ̀ ɓiya.
       NAR nous venir-NAR cueillir (fruit sauvage)
Nous avons d'abord fini de faire la pêche, puis nous avons cueilli
des fruits sauvages.

L'aspect à valeur prioritaire (pǎ (PRI)). L'aspect à valeur prioritaire sert
à exprimer que, dans un cadre temporel donné, un premier procès se
déroule pendant qu'un deuxième procès, qui le suivra, est déjà envisagé.
Ce deuxième procès peut ou ne peut pas être explicitement exprimé. Dans
la traduction française, l'aspect à valeur prioritaire peut être rendu par
l'expression 'd'abord'. A cette valeur est souvent lié celle de l'immédiat.
Dans ce cas-là, le français utiliserait l'expression 'tout de suite'. Il nous
paraît parfois difficile de déterminer, dans un exemple donné, laquelle des
deux valeurs est mise en évidence.
   L'aspect à valeur prioritaire s'exprime à l'aide du prédicatif *pǎ*. En se
combinant avec certaines formes modales, temporelles et aspectuelles, il les
modifie. Nous étudierons brièvement (a) la modification de l'imperfectif
présent, (b) la modification du futur et (c) la modification du parfait.
   L'aspect à valeur prioritaire peut aussi modifier la forme impérative du
verbe (Ernst 1991a). C'est le seul cas où l'aspect à valeur prioritaire se
combine avec une forme verbale caractérisée par un prédicatif lié.
   L'imperfectif du présent peut subir une modification aspectuelle à valeur
prioritaire. Dans sa forme modifiée il exprime qu'un procès se déroule
dans un temps présent avant qu'un autre procès puisse être envisagé.
   La modification aspectuelle à valeur prioritaire s'exprime à l'aide du
prédicatif *pǎ* qui s'insère entre le prédicatif principal *ké* de l'imperfectif et
la forme infinitive du verbe vue, en (76) et (77).

(76) *Mi ké pà ɓèŋè túmbɔ̀, manjé dyénà.*
je   IPF PRI voir lutte puis   manger
Je regarde d'abord la lutte, puis je mange.

(77) *Wùsè ké pà tɔ́kè   ɓé-koŋ,*
nous IPF PRI ramasser c2-chenille

wùsè manjé sùmɔ̀   balà.
nous puis construire cabane
Nous ramassons d'abord les chenilles, puis nous construisons la cabane.

Comme l'imperfectif du présent, le futur, lui aussi, peut subir une modification aspectuelle. A la différence de l'imperfectif, où plusieurs aspects de différentes valeurs sont combinés, la modification du futur constitue une combinaison d'une valeur temporelle avec une valeur aspectuelle. Dans sa forme modifiée, le futur exprime qu'un procès se déroulera dans un avenir plus ou moins éloigné et l'envisage dans la perspective d'un autre procès postérieur qui peut ou ne peut pas se réaliser.

La modification aspectuelle à valeur prioritaire du futur s'exprime à l'aide du prédicatif *pǎ* qui s'insère entre le prédicatif *tǎ* du futur et la forme infinitive du verbe.

(78) *À tǎ pà kɔ̀tɔ̀   ŋgwàŋ.*
il   FUT PRI labourer champ
Il labourera d'abord le champ.

(79) *Mí tǎ pà sùmɔ̀   tṹ,   manjé ɓṹ   nyári*
je   FUT PRI construire maison puis   prendre femme
Je construirai d'abord une maison, puis je me marierai.

La modification du parfait est analogue à celle de l'imperfectif du présent où l'aspect à valeur prioritaire modifie la valeur d'un aspect principal.

Dans sa forme modifiée, le parfait exprime qu'un procès, dont les conséquences subsistent dans le présent, s'est déroulé dans le passé. Ce procès est envisagé dans la perspective d'un autre procès postérieur par rapport au premier, mais passé par rapport au temps de l'énonciation.

Comme dans le cas de l'imperfectif du présent et du futur, la modification du parfait s'exprime à l'aide du prédicatif *pǎ*. Ici, contrairement à l'imperfectif du présent et du futur, où l'ordre des prédicatifs aspectuels est fixe, *mǎ* et *pǎ* peuvent changer d'ordre sans que le sens change. La modification du parfait diffère aussi des deux autres parce que le deuxième procès postérieur doit être explicitement exprimé. L'énoncé comportant la modification aspectuelle, bien qu'il soit complet du point de vue syntaxique, doit donc être obligatoirement suivi d'un deuxième énoncé coordonné par le marqueur *è* du narratif fonctionnant ici comme conjonction de coordination.

(80) *Mí pà mǎ sùmɔ̀   tú,   è   mí njé bǘ   nyari.*
      je PRI PAR construire maison NAR je   puis prendre femme
      J'ai d'abord construit une maison, puis je me suis marié.

(81) *À mǎ pà pɛsɔ́   yóta, è   nyɛ nj-e   dùwè.*
      il PAR PRI casser bois NAR lui venir-NAR rentrer
      Il a d'abord coupé du bois, puis il est rentré.

3. Le parfait (*mǎ* (PAR))

Le parfait, comme le dit Comrie (1976:52), combine l'idée d'un événement ou d'une situation passée et l'idée d'un état ou d'une situation présente. En kakɔ, il indique à la fois qu'un procès est parvenu à son terme, soit une action achevée et donc passée, et qu'une action est passée mais dure dans ces conséquences. En ce dernier cas, deux traductions sont possibles en français, l'une par un passé, l'autre par un présent. Les parenthèses dans les exemples (82) et (83) comportent l'information implicite, trait caractéristique du parfait.

(82) *À mǎ ɗyénà.*
      il PAR manger
      Il a mangé.
      (et est rassasié)

(83) *À mǎ wɔ́mbìlè tú.*
      il PAR balayer   maison
      Il a balayé la maison.
      (et elle est propre)

Les exemples (84) et (85) montreront aussi que le sens du parfait ressort nettement de l'emploi de certains verbes démontrant un changement d'état (par exemple *ɓɔ̀* 'pourrir', *ɗɔ̀kɔ̀* 'grandir'). Dans ce cas le parfait exprime, comme l'illustrent les exemples ci-après, l'état qui est l'aboutissement du processus.

(84) *Mè-mbùmɔ̀ mǎ ɓɔ̀.*
c6-fruit PAR pourrir
Les fruits ont pourri.
Les fruits sont pourris.

(85) *ɔ́ mǎ dɔ̀kɔ̀.*
tu PAR grandir
Tu as grandi.
Tu es devenu grand.

L'énoncé (85) est sémantiquement très proche à l'énoncé caractérisé par le morphème *nè* (87). Ce marqueur qui fonctionne ici comme marque grammaticale d'identité (ID) constitue un homonyme de la préposition *nè* signifiant 'avec'. L'exemple (86) illustre l'emploi des deux homonymes dans le même énoncé.

(86) *À nè mbùsà nè bíŋgɔ́.*
il ID maïs avec arachides
Il a du maïs et des arachides.

(87) *ɔ́ nè dɔ̀kɔ̀.*
tu ID grandeur
Tu es grand.

De faire ressortir ces nuances dans une traduction en français sera souvent tâche difficile. Stanley (1986:118), en décrivant un cas similaire en langue tikar, suggère que le choix pourrait porter sur une différence du point de vue du locuteur. Selon Stanley, l'énoncé copulatif en tikar qui correspond à notre énoncé caractérisé par le marqueur d'identité (ID) (87), servira à exprimer un fait en le constatant simplement comme tel tandis que le parfait (PAR) ferait plutôt valoir l'état actuel en tant que résultat d'un processus passé. Les deux exemples en question (85, 87) pourraient donc être interprétés comme en (88) et (89).

contexte sémantique possible

(88) Tu es *devenu* grand!   le locuteur s'adressant à son fils qu'il ren-
(voir (85))   contre après une longue séparation.

(89) Tu *es* grand.   le locuteur, en constatant que son fils est
(voir (87))   grand, peut lui accorder des privilèges.

Le parfait est caractérisé formellement par le prédicatif *mǎ* précédant la forme infinitive du verbe. Comme l'imperfectif, le parfait, lui aussi, peut être modifié par d'autres prédicatifs aspectuels, notamment *sì* (CES) et *pà* (PRI).

Comme l'illustrent les exemples (90–92), il n'existe en kakɔ qu'une seule forme distincte du parfait. Lorsque référence est faite, soit au passé soit au futur, le parfait exprime un passé relatif.

(90)   *À   mǎ   kwɑ̰̀.*
       il   PAR   partir
       Il est parti.

(91)   *Kɛ ŋgímɔ̀ té yi   mí tǎ   dyɑ̰̀   ké,*
       à   temps ce REL je FUT arriver SUB

       mi tǎ   dolɔ́   à   mǎ   dyénà.
       je FUT trouver il PAR   manger
       Lorsque je viendrai, il aura (déjà) mangé.

(92)   *Kɛ ŋgímɔ̀ té yi   mí dyàŋ-má   ké, à mǎ dyénà.*
       à   temps ce REL je arriver-PAS SUB il PAR manger
       Lorsque je venais, il avait déjà mangé.

Nous avons relevé deux modifications du parfait: (a) celle marquée par l'aspect à valeur prioritaire *pǎ* (76–81) et celle marquée par le cessatif *si* (72–75).

4. L'aoriste (*H^n*, -*Kv́* (AR))

L'aoriste en kakɔ exprime soit une action arrivée à son terme, faisant ainsi référence au temps passé, soit une action à son début ou au cours de son déroulement, faisant ainsi référence au temps présent. Il exprime en outre une action de caractère général ou universel. L'aoriste, n'impliquant pas de localisation dans le temps, sert aussi à mettre en emphase les constituants postverbaux, notamment l'objet direct et l'objet indirect ainsi que les expansions circonstancielles de temps, de lieu, de cause, de but et d'instrument.

La forme de l'aoriste est caractérisée par un morphème lié /-*Kv́*/ ayant les réalisations -*kí*, -*kú*, -*(í)kwé*, -*(ú)kwé*, -*ŋgwé*, -*é*, -*á* et -*∅*. Au niveau tonal, l'aoriste est marqué par le schéma tonal *H^n* qualifiant l'unité actualisée BV-*Kv́*. C'est par ce schéma tonal, qui ne comprend que des tons hauts, que la forme de l'aoriste ayant la réalisation -*∅* peut être identifiée sans équivoque. Les exemples (93–96) ci-dessous font référence au temps passé. Les exemples (95–96) font référence au temps présent tandis que les exemples (97–98) illustrent une action ou une situation de caractère atemporel exprimant une vérité générale ou universelle.

(93) *Bo dyá-ŋ   dyen?*
     ils arriver-AOR quand
     Quand sont-ils arrivés?

(94) *À wó-kú   nyàmɔ̀ nὲ   ŋge?*
     il tuer-AOR animal avec quoi
     Avec quoi a-t-il tué l'animal?

(95) *Ɔ kél-∅   nge?*
     tu faire-AOR quoi
     Que fais-tu?
     Qu'as-tu fait?

(96) *Mì dúm-∅   yòmbò.*
     je piler-AOR manioc
     Je pile du manioc.
     J'ai pilé du manioc.

(97) *Bè-kàkɔ dyá-kí   kàmɔ̀.*
     c2-Kakɔ manger-AOR couscous de manioc
     Les Kakɔ mangent du couscous de manioc.

(98) *Ndorú sídy-íkwέ mὲ-kàŋ.*
     (herbe) finir-AOR c6-gale
     L'herbe ndoru guérit la gale.

Les exemples ci-dessus illustrent le fait que l'aoriste est surtout attesté dans des énoncés du type QUESTION-REPONSE, ce qui n'est pas étonnant vu le fait que le mode interrogatif sert naturellement à mettre une certaine emphase sur le constituant postverbal. Il en est de même des énoncés affirmatifs lorsqu'ils constituent des réponses à de telles questions.

5. Conclusion

Nous avons essayé de décrire comment la notion du temps est réalisée grammaticalement en kakɔ. Nous avons constaté qu'on ne peut pas décrire le système temporel sans tenir compte en même temps de l'aspectualité. La grammaticalisation des deux concepts est réalisée essentiellement par des prédicatifs dont nous avons trouvé deux sortes: (a) marqueurs libres et (b) marqueurs liés (suffixes). Le système aspecto-temporel du kakɔ est clairement caractérisé par des marqueurs libres qui abondent en nombre et se distinguent par leur disposition combinatoire.

(99)   Le système aspecto-temporel en kakɔ

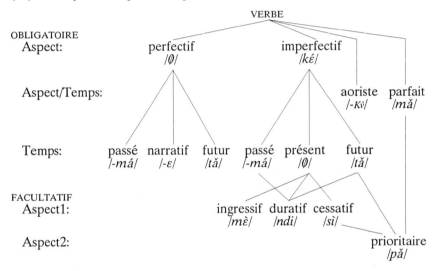

Le diagramme (99) présente, sous forme résumée, les éléments obligatoires du système aspecto-temporel d'une part et les éléments facultatifs d'autre part. On notera la position intermédiaire des deux concepts parfait et aoriste. Ils réunissent les traits de l'aspectualité avec ceux de la temporalité. Nous avons montré qu'ils servent à exprimer, selon le cas, une situation ou une action dans un temps présent ainsi que dans un temps passé.

Nous avons vu que les éléments facultatifs du système aspecto-temporel en kakɔ sont surtout au service de l'imperfectif. En dehors des constructions imperfectives, quelques-uns en peuvent modifier le futur perfectif ainsi que le parfait.

En plus de la dichotomie temporalité-aspectualité, nous avons étudié en quelque détail la dichotomie temps absolu-temps relatif. Ici nous avons constaté que le kakɔ, en se référant à un événement situé par rapport au moment de l'énonciation, utilise les formes verbales dont il dispose à cet effet de façon assez rigoureuse. Ainsi, nous n'avons trouvé qu'un seul cas exceptionnel, celui du passé. Cette forme peut être employée, dans le discours direct, pour atténuer un énoncé (24–26). Quant au temps relatif, en revanche, nous avons noté que, faute de forme grammaticalisée distincte, le kakɔ se sert des formes du temps absolu pour l'exprimer.

References

Bole-Richard, Rémy. 1983. Systématique phonologique et grammaticale d'un parler éwé: le gen-mina du Sud-Togo et Sud-Bénin. Paris: L'Harmattan.

Bouquiaux, Luc et Jacqueline M. C. Thomas, éds. 1976. Enquête et description des langues à tradition orale, tome I, II. Paris: Société d'Etudes Linguistiques et Anthropologiques de France.

Comrie, Bernard. 1976. Aspect. Cambridge: Cambridge University Press.

———. 1985. Tense. Cambridge: Cambridge University Press.

Creissels, Denis et N. Kouadio. 1977. Description phonologique et grammaticale d'un parler baoulé. LXV Université Nationale de Côte d'Ivoire, Institut de Linguistique Appliquée, Linguistique Africaine.

Dieu, Michel et Patrick Renaud. 1983. Situation linguistique en Afrique Centrale, Inventaire préliminaire: le Cameroun. Paris/Yaoundé: ACCT CERDOTOLA DGRST (Atlas linguistique de l'Afrique Centrale: Atlas linguistique du Cameroun). cartes.

Ernst, Urs. 1985. Phonologie du kakɔ. ms.

———. 1989a. Description tonologique de l'énoncé nominal associatif en kakɔ. ms.

———. 1989b. Lexique kakɔ-français/français-kakɔ avec tableaux de conjugaisons. ms.

———. 1991a. Impératif et injonctif en kakɔ. ms.

———. 1991b. Description morphologique des formes verbales en kakɔ. ms.

Guthrie, Malcolm. 1971. Comparative Bantu 2. Farnborough, England: Gregg International Publishers.

Houis, Maurice. 1977. Plan de description systématique des langues négro-africaines. Afrique et Language 7:5–65. Paris.

Hopper, Paul, ed. 1982. Tense-aspect: Between semantics and pragmatics. Amsterdam: John Benjamins.

Martinet, André. 1967. Eléments de linguistique générale. Paris: Armand Colin.

Stanley, Carol. 1986. Description phonologique et morpho-syntaxique de la langue tikar (parlée au Cameroun). Thèse présentée en vue du doctorat d'état. Université de la Sorbonne Nouvelle, Paris III.

Welmers, William, E. 1973. African language structures. Berkeley: University of California Press.

Kɔɔzime Verbal System

Keith H. Beavon

Abstract

This paper describes most of the verbal constructions found in Kɔɔzime, a Narrow Bantu language identified by Guthrie as A.84. It employs an autosegmental model for explaining various tone, intonation, and vowel changes present in these verbal constructions. An extensive inventory of tense and aspect markers exists, enabling Kɔɔzime speakers to refer contrastively and with precision to events that are distinct with regard to time and internal consistency. There is, alongside the absolute tense-marking system, a parallel system of relative tenses. Finally, the paper examines numerous possibilities for indicating mood, negation, and focus.

The many tonal markers which play an important role in distinguishing the various verbal constructions from each other are also noted. In addition to the many floating tones which are common in autosegmental descriptions of African languages, Kɔɔzime has need of a separate convention for indicating replacive tones. The author suggests one means of symbolizing these replacive tones, namely, an arrow on the tonal tier with no change to existing association lines.

Résumé

Le but principal de cet article est de décrire la majorité des constructions verbales en kɔɔzime, langue bantu identifiée par Guthrie comme A.84. L'auteur se sert d'une théorie autosegmentale qui lui facilite l'explication des phénomènes de ton, d'intonation, et des changements vocaliques qui sont impliqués dans ses constructions verbales. Le système verbal est basé sur un inventaire extensif des indices temporels et aspectuels, ces derniers permettant aux locuteurs du kɔɔzime de différencier avec précision entre des événements distinctifs par raison de leurs temps et leurs complexités internes. Il y a, en dehors de ce système des temps absolus, un système parallèle des temps relatifs. En plus, il existe maintes possibilités pour préciser des modes, la négation, la focalisation, chaque partie grammaticale étant examinée en détail.

L'auteur examine en détail les indices tonals multiples, ceux jouant un rôle important à la différentiation mutuelle des constructions verbales. Nombreux sont les tons remplacifs en kɔɔzime. Ils se distinguent des tons flottants qu'on connait déjà bien à travers plusieurs langues analysées selon la théorie autosegmentale. Ce phénomène de tons remplacifs nécessite la création d'une représentation conventionelle appropriée. L'auteur en propose une qui répond au besoin de la simplicité: il s'agit d'une flèche sur la rangée des tons entre le ton remplaçant et le ton remplacé. Cette notation conventionelle exige aucun changement des liens d'association déjà établis entre les tons et les voyelles.

Kɔɔzime is a Bantu language of the northwest zone, identified by Guthrie (1971) as A-84. It is spoken in southeastern Cameroon and represents a cluster of dialects (called Bajwe'e, Nzime, Njem, and Njeme) differing from each other with respect to the number of noun classes, the number of phonemes, and the character of certain tonal rules (Beavon 1978). Subdialectal differences also exist. The language variant described in this paper is a subdialect of Bajwe'e spoken to the northeast of the Bajwe'e region, known by the speakers as Upriver Bajwe'e. Any Bajwe'e subdialect is more progressive than any variant of the Nzime, Njem, or Njeme dialects. The Upriver Bajwe'e subdialect chosen is, however, relatively more conservative than other Bajwe'e subdialects.

This paper[1] is a description of the morphology and syntax of Kɔɔzime verb phrase constituents, including aspect, tense, mood, and negation markers. It also deals with focus markers—grammatical words usually associated with the noun phrase rather than the verb phrase. This section is included because of the influence of focus markers on the syntax of the verb phrase.

The parts of speech used in this paper have been defined in Barreteau and Beavon (1989). They have also been used in the context of other aspects of the phonology (Beavon 1983a, and Beavon 1984b) and of the grammar (Beavon 1986). The special uses of tense markers to indicate discourse units have been treated elsewhere (Beavon 1984a), as have the peculiar problems posed by the locative verb (Beavon 1990).

Before proceeding with the details of the Kɔɔzime verbal systems, a broad overview is here presented.

The fundamental distinction in the Kɔɔzime verbal system is that between the tense-marking and nontense-marking moods. The marking of

---

[1]This analysis of aspect and tense, as well as the final form of the article, reflects many suggestions and comments from Bernard Comrie and Stephen C. Anderson. Ursula Wiesemann contributed significantly to the analysis of toneless verbs which we follow in this paper.

tense (TNS) (and of focus (FOC) in the case of complements to the verb) is excluded in imperative (IMP) and hortative (HORT) moods. Tense markers, together with focus indicators on verb complements, are allowed only in the indicative (IND) mood. The interrogative (INT) mood may also be marked for tense but without complement focus. We can therefore draw (1).

(1) Mood restrictions

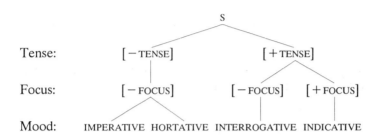

Within indicative constructions, the fundamental distinction is that between absolute and relative tenses (REL). The use of an absolute tense relates a situation in a direct and invariable way to a fixed point of reference, the present moment. Relative tenses, on the other hand, do not tie an event to this point of reference. They relate it rather to events in the preceding linguistic context. For example, the relative recent past tense may be employed to characterize a past, a present habitual, or a future situation. There is also the present perfect tense (PRES PRF) that can be thought of as a hybrid, or an absolute relative, tense. This marks a situation as having a direct relationship to the present moment, since the effects of a past event are felt in the present. However, when the present condition arose in the past is relative to the context. It could be due to an event in either the recent past (P1) or the remote past (P2). In this way it resembles the purely relative tenses. An event which occurs subsequent to a relative time reference may be expressed by either a consecutive (CONS) or future purpose (FUT PURP) construction. See (2).

Absolute tenses may be marked for perfective (PFV) or imperfective (IMPV), or be unmarked with respect to aspect. Imperfective constructions can be further marked to indicate only habitual (HAB) meaning in contrast with the unmarked imperfective construction which may take either a habitual or a continuous/progressive reading according to context. Absolute tenses marked as perfective must also be marked as past tense.

(2) Indicative tenses

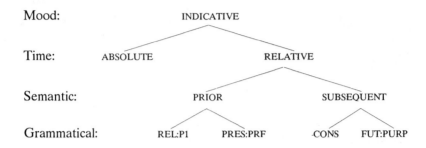

Imperfective constructions may be in any of the tenses—past (remote or recent), present, or future. These distinctions are captured in (3).

(3) Absolute indicative tense-aspect restrictions

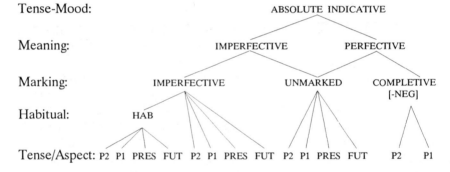

The distinction between indicative and interrogative is based not only on semantic criteria, but also on syntactic evidence. For example, focus marking is excluded in interrogative constructions. Furthermore, in the indicative mood, the negation marker (NEG) and the completive aspect marker may not occur together but both elements may be present in the interrogative and indicate that a question is rhetorical (see §§7, 9.2). Most importantly, a number of morphemes distinguish interrogatives from each other and from indicative sentences.

With this brief overview of the Kɔɔzime verbal system, we must now give a brief introduction to tone representation (§1) before proceeding to a detailed discussion of the specifics of the verbal categories of tense, aspect, and mood (§§2–7).

(4) Interrogative mood

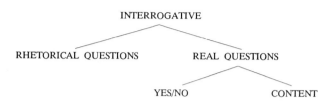

1. Autosegmental representation of tone

An autosegmental approach is used in this paper, since it is well suited to the data presented.

There is a simple two-tone distinction in Kɔɔzime, and there is also a small set of morphemes with toneless vowels. Toneless vowels are found only in the following: the marker of perfective aspect, six monosyllabic verbs, the serial verb meaning 'direction away from speaker', and the second vowel of disyllabic verbs. Surface tones assigned to these toneless syllables vary according to the tonal melody, which may include tonal morphemes (a morpheme with tone but no segments) indicating tense and aspect. The surface tones which result, therefore, always carry grammatical information.

In most verbal constructions, tense is marked discontinuously. For example, recent past tense is marked by three tonal morphemes: a low tone (L) following the subject noun phrase, a high tone (H) following either the verb or the perfective marker, and a high replacive tone (←H or H→) following the verb. This last tone associates with the first word after the verb, replacing an initial L which is thereby deleted. All of these tense markers are glossed P1 for 'recent past tense' rather than being distinguished one from the other. Where these tense markers need to be distinguished from each other, however, the first is identified as the 'main tense marker', the second, as the 'stem' tone, and the third, as the 'suffixal' tone, following Goldsmith (1976:71), whose model of autosegmental phonology is followed as closely as possible throughout this paper.

In the case of Kɔɔzime, however, there seems to be no possibility of adopting the first part of Goldsmith's Well-formedness Condition, which states: "All tones must be associated with some syllable" (1976:155). In Kɔɔzime, floating L noun class prefixes (C#) are left unassociated, but other floating Ls are associated to the left as predicted. For an example of the nonassociation of a floating L noun class prefix, see (5), where the class

seven prefix is not associated with the preceding syllable. (For an explanation of the line markings in the examples, see §1.1 below.)

(5) *Be   bee   o   Ø-lí.*
     |\ |\ | /\
     H L   L L   H→| H   L H H
     3p P1 see P1 P1   FOC C7-tree
     It was they who saw a tree (earlier today).

In (5), a floating L prefix marking recent past is associated with the
subject pronoun, forming a tonal contour. In (6), it is associated with the
H of the focus marker.

(6) *Be o   bee   Ø-lí.*
     | | \\ |\   ----   /\
     H H   L   L L 'H→ L H H
     3p FOC P1 see P1 P1   C7-tree
     It was they who saw the tree (earlier today).

To recapitulate, the leftward docking of a floating L is observed only if
that tone is a tense marker. If it is a noun class prefix, it is left unassociated. On the other hand, floating Hs of all types dock left, as in (6).[2]

1.1. Association lines. Within the autosegmental model, tones and syllabic segments occur on separate tiers and are associated with each other
by rules and conventions. This means that tones are not regarded as
elements of a vowel's feature matrix. The association lines are of three
kinds: solid lines, representing lexical associations accomplished by a
general mapping rule; cross-hatched lines when a given tone is dissociated
from a vowel; and dotted lines indicating where tones are associated by
rule.

In (7), the two Ls of 'area behind the house' are always associated with
the word's two syllables by an early mapping rule. They may stay this way
in the final representation of the word if it is spoken in isolation.

In (8), however, the word is preceded by a locative preposition (LOC)
manifested by a tonal morpheme meaning 'in, at'. This H replaces the first
L of the noun.

---

[2]The convention for marking replacive tones followed in this paper is a departure
from Goldsmith's model. This convention is described in §1.2.

(7) *domo*
    | |
    L L
area^behind^the^house
an area behind the house

(8)   *Domo.*
       | |
  H→ L L
LOC area^behind^the^house
It's in the area behind the house.

1.2. Replacive tones. In Kɔɔzime, it appears necessary to posit two types of tonal morphemes—replacive and floating tones. In (8), a replacive H associates with a syllable to the right, causing detachment and deletion of a lexically-assigned L.

All replacive tones in Kɔɔzime are H. A replacive H replaces a L either to its right or to its left, depending upon the morpheme in question. This bidirectional characteristic of replacive tones constitutes a point of difference between them and floating tones in Kɔɔzime, since floating tones may be either H or L and their association lines may be drawn only to the left.

The replacing of one tone by another is described in (9). This shorthand represents the following process: a replacive H replaces an adjacent L, attaching itself to the L's syllable nucleus ($) by means of an existing association line. This means that no new association lines are added and the L is deleted entirely from the tonal tier.

(9) Replacive tones

$$\begin{array}{ccc} \$ & & \$ \\ | & \text{or} & | \\ \text{H}\rightarrow \text{L} & & \text{L} \leftarrow\text{H} \end{array}$$

This manner of presentation is seen in (10), where an initial sequence of two Ls on the object pronoun becomes a H-L sequence.

(10) *Me o   bee   mʉr.*
   | | | \   / \
   L H L L H→ L L
1s   FUT see FUT FUT person
I'm going to see a person.

It might not be clear in example (10) that the first L of 'person' has been deleted rather than being attached to the syllable along with the H and L. Support for the claim that the replaced tone is deleted is found in (11). Phonetic data show that the surface tone pattern following tonal replacement is H-H rather than H-L-H, the latter sequence also existing in the language with single, short vowels. The absence of a H-L-H sequence in (11) is, therefore, clear evidence that the L has been completely deleted.

(11)   *zɨ*
         /\
   H→ L H
   LOC trail
   (It's) on the trail.

If a replacive high tone does not, for some reason, replace the adjacent tone, the arrow accompanying it is 'stopped' by a vertical bar, as in (12), where the replacive H encounters a H. Such tones are never replaced, as seen in the study of sentence-final intonational lowering (§1.4).

(12)   *kwar*
         /\
   H→| H H
   LOC village
   (It's) in the village.

Another context where a replacive H fails to have any effect is before *e* or *le* 'with'. This preposition is unlike any other with respect to its stability in the face of replacive Hs.[3] In (13), the tonal stability of 'with' is clearly evident. The replacive suffixal H that follows the verb 'return' cannot replace the L of 'with'.

(13) *Nye   si   bula   e   me.*
    |\   \\ | \\ | |\
   L L   H H   L H→| L   L L
   3s   P1 PFV P1 return P1 P1 with 1s S^FINAL
   He brought me back (in the recent past).

Other Ls are replaced, however, as in (14), where a tonal noun class prefix becomes H and associates to the left.

---

[3]This is the case in Məkaa as well, according to Heath, personal communication.

(14)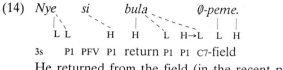
Nye   si   bula   ∅-peme.
L L   H   H   L H→L L H
3s   P1 PFV P1 return P1 P1 C7-field
He returned from the field (in the recent past).

A replacive H encountering a toneless syllable acts like a floating tone, associating with that syllable, as represented in (15). This process is observed in the case of toneless verbs, as in (16). These replacive tones, which are numerous in Kɔɔzime, are either not found or not as frequent in other Cameroonian languages.

(15) Replacive tones adjacent to toneless syllables

+ $ +   ∅   +

+   ∅   +   ←H   +

(16) Nye de-k   me-de!
     L |←H L   L   L
     3s   eat-HORT C6-food
Let him eat some food!

1.3. Floating tones. Not all tonal morphemes cause adjacent tones to be deleted. Some tones are simply added to the underlying tones of a word, coexisting with them. Such tones are more common worldwide than replacive tones and are called FLOATING TONES. In the transcription of Kɔɔzime, floating tones are shown in the tonal tier as simply H or L with no arrow, and they are glossed like any other morpheme.

It is unnecessary to specify which direction is taken by a floating tone in Kɔɔzime because all floating tones associate to their left, attaching themselves to the preceding vowel.

Two examples of floating tones are found in (17). The L following the subject pronoun and the H immediately following the verb are discontinuous parts of the morpheme marking recent past tense (P1). In both cases these tones attach to the left, associating themselves with the other

tones of their respective syllables. In the process, a contour tone H-L is
produced on the subject pronoun, and a L-H sequence on the verb.[4]

(17) Be   komo   o   bi-kwan.
      | \ | \ | | /\
      H L   L   H H→| H   L L L
      3p P1 store P1 P1 FOC C8-plaintain
      It was plantains they stored (earlier today).

In (18), the object of the verb (` *kwàǹ* 'plantain') has a floating L prefix.[5]
This tonal prefix is replaced in the construction by the suffixal tone, a
replacive H. But since the tonal prefix is floating, the H that replaces it
docks left like all Kɔɔzime floating tones. In this way, the preceding vowel
acquires a L-H contour.

(18) Be   si   komo.   ∅-kwan.
      | \   \ | \   - - - - -   / \
      H L   H   L   L   H→L   L L
      3p P1 PFV P1 store P1   P1 C7-plantain
      They have stored a plantain (earlier today).

Up to three tones have been found sharing a single short vowel in
Kɔɔzime. Note in the first word of (19) that a floating L is added to a
syllable that already has two lexically-assigned tones. After the L marking
recent past is associated with it, this one syllable has a L-H-L contour.

(19) Bih   komo   o   bi-kwan.
      / \ - - - - | \ | | /\
      L H   `L   L   H H→| H   L L L
      1s^EXCL P1 store P1 P1 FOC C8-plaintain
      It was plantains we (not you) stored (earlier today).

Additional evidence for three-tone contours is found in (20). The floating tonal prefix of the noun 'plantain' becomes H due to the replacive

---

[4]The high replacive suffixal tone is shown in (14) by analogy with other constructions like (16). It does not, in Kɔɔzime, replace lexical Hs, as seen in §1.4.

[5]For a defense of the claim for two Ls in the stem of this word, see Beavon 1984b.

suffixal H present following infinitives (INF). This H, in turn, associates itself with the tones of the preceding vowel to form the contour H-L-H.[6]

(20) *Nye lɨ   e-jam   ∅-kwan.*

  L H   L H   L   H→L   L L

  3s   LOC C5-cook INF INF C7-plantain

He is cooking a plantain.

The rule that floating Hs are associated with a syllabic segment to the left holds without exception. (The nonassociation of floating Ls indicating class membership has been noted above.) When floating Hs are found in utterance-initial position, they are unable to find a syllable to their left, as in (21). Such floating Hs do not have the option of finding a syllable to the right and, rather than associating to the right, they are left floating, without any surface result.

(21)   *∅-Peme.*

  H→ L   L H

  LOC C7-field

It's in the field.

In (22), however, the floating tone takes advantage of a third option—creating a syllable for its own use. This is a possibility only when the word begins with a prenasalized stop. As a previously nonsyllabic nasal is made syllabic, this new syllable ($) is associated with the nasal consonant and with the floating tone.

(22) Resyllabification

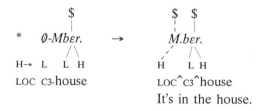

---

[6]As is common when complex tone glides occur on short syllables, the L found in a H-L-H contour is phonetically not as low in pitch as lows found elsewhere. If H is level 1 and L is usually level 4, then H-L-H would be realized phonetically as [1–2–1] or [1–3–2], but never as [1–4–1].

1.4. Intonation. Intonation, both rising and falling, plays a role in the differentiation of indicative, interrogative, and imperative moods. There are two sentence-final intonation contours, one rising (R) and the other falling (F). These are shown on a third tier, employed whenever intonation is relevant to a discussion.

Rising intonation. A rising intonation contour (R) is a mark of the interrogative mood. It is limited to those questions that lack an interrogative word, such as 'is-it?', 'what?', 'why?', 'who?', and 'when?', as illustrated in (23).

(23)

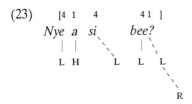

```
       [4  1    4        4 1 ]
        Nye  a  si      bee?
         |   |    \       |  \
         L   H     L     L    L
                              \
                               R
        3s   P2 PFV P2 see  P2 INT
```

Did he see (it)?

Falling intonation. The lowering of tones in ultimate and penultimate positions is dealt with by means of a rule associating the fall (F) with the tone in the penultimate position. The phonetic values reflecting the four tonal sequences (H-H, H-L, L-H, L-L) are shown in the following examples. In this section, we follow the additional convention of marking phonetic pitch with numbers, 1 for the highest pitch and 5 for the lowest.

(24)

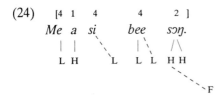

```
       [4  1    4        4      2 ]
        Me  a  si       bee    sɔŋ.
         |  |   \         | \    /\
         L  H    L       L L    H H
                                  \
                                   F
        1s   P2 PFV P2 see  P2 father IND
```

I saw (his) father.

(25)

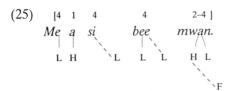

```
       [4  1    4        4      2–4 ]
        Me  a  si       bee    mwan.
         |  |   \         |  \   /\
         L  H    L       L   L  H  L
                                   \
                                    F
        1s   P2 PFV P2 see  P2 child IND
```

I saw (his) child.

If H is found in penultimate position, the fall associates itself with that tone. Examples (24) and (25) show that the penultimate H is lowered to a level of [2].

In (26), the falling intonation contour associates itself with L, and H is found in the ultimate position. The pitch of the latter is lowered to the height of the preceding L, [4]. In (27), L in the ultimate position is lowered to [5].

(26)

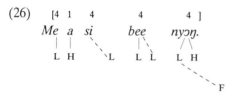

1s   P2 PFV P2 see P2   mother IND
I saw (his) mother.

(27)

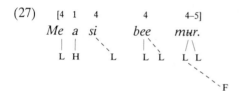

1s   P2 PFV P2 see P2 person IND
I saw a person.

Observe in (28) how falling intonation and tonal replacement interact. It was seen in §1.2 that a replacive tonal morpheme causes tonal replacement followed by deletion. The falling intonation contour has no effect on replacive Hs. In (28), the final tones are H-H, with the first H representing the result of tonal replacement. The L that had been in penultimate position has been deleted, together with the falling intonational contour which had been associated with it. The phonetic pitch of this final H-H sequence is [1] rather than [2], reflecting the deletion of the falling intonation together with the lexical L.

(28)

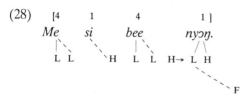

1s   P1 PFV P1 see P1 P1 mother IND
I saw (his) mother (earlier today).

In (29), the final tones are H-L, with H being a replacive high. Its phonetic value is [1–3] rather than [2–4].

(29)
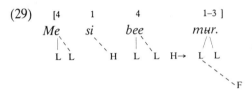

1s   P1 PFV P1 see P1 P1   person IND
I saw a person (earlier today).

In order to arrive at correct outputs, one must establish ordered rules: The intonational fall must first be associated with the penultimate L, and then replacement and deletion can take place. Reversing this order causes the replacive H in the penultimate position to be associated with the intonational fall which would produce the wrong phonetic output.

Intonational contours are not marked throughout the rest of this paper, since the effect of intonation is highly predictable.

2. Aspect

Four possibilities exist with respect to the formal marking of aspect in Kɔɔzime—perfective, imperfective, habitual, or unmarked. A verb unmarked for aspect is interpreted as being perfective, imperfective, or habitual depending upon the context.

Perfective is defined by Comrie (1976:21) as the aspectual form which "involves lack of explicit reference to the internal temporal constituency of a situation." Even if events are internally complex and last over long periods of time, they may nevertheless be viewed perfectively as constituting a single situation.

Imperfective aspect, on the other hand, draws attention to the fact that the event in question occurred over a period of time and its internal make-up is relevant.

Habitual aspect is a subtype of imperfective, describing "a situation which is characteristic of an extended period of time, so extended in fact that the situation referred to is viewed not as an incidental property of the moment but, precisely, as a characteristic feature of a whole period" (Comrie 1976:27ff). Verbs with imperfective aspectual marking can be given either an imperfective or a habitual reading while verbs with habitual marking have only the habitual reading.

2.1. Perfective. Perfective aspect is marked by the serial verb *si*, which is derived from the verb *síe* 'be done'. Lacking principled criteria for assigning either H or L to the perfective aspect marker, we represent it as inherently toneless, with its surface tone being determined by adjacent tones in a given verbal context.[7]

Perfective aspect occurs only with the past tenses, as in (30) and (31).

(30)

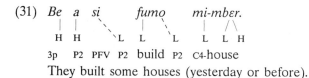

3p P1 PFV P1 build P1 P1 C4-house
They built some houses (earlier today).

(31)

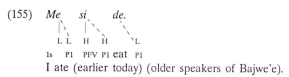

3p P2 PFV P2 build P2 C4-house
They built some houses (yesterday or before).

The perfective marker does not occur with nonpast tenses: **Bé ósí fùmò mímbĕr.* 'They are going to build (viewed perfectively) some houses'. It

---

[7]Older speakers of Bajwe'e have a different pronunciation of the perfective marker than that represented here. For these, the underlying form of the perfective marker evidently has a H, *sí*. Depending on the grammatical tone which follows, the surface tones of *sí* are either H-L or H-H, as in (154) and (155).

(154) *Me a si   de.*

```
| | | \    \
L H H  L     L
```

1s P2 PFV P2 eat P2
I ate (yesterday or before) (older speakers of Bajwe'e).

(155) *Me   si   de.*

```
\   | \   \
| \  | \   \
L L  H  H   \L
```

1s P1 PFV P1 eat P1
I ate (earlier today) (older speakers of Bajwe'e).

The surface form of (155) does not differ from that of younger speakers of Bajwe'e. This is due to the absence of contrast between one and two Hs on a single syllable. There are two associated with the perfective marker of (155), but only one in (156), which represents the speech of a younger speaker of Bajwe'e.

(156) *Me   si   de.*

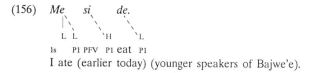

1s P1 PFV P1 eat P1
I ate (earlier today) (younger speakers of Bajwe'e).

occurs rather with the two absolute past tenses (remote past and recent past) and with the relative recent past tense.

Negating a sentence marked for perfective aspect entails the deletion of the perfective marker and the addition of the auxiliary verb, *be*, before the negation marker. A suffixal H must be added where it was lacking in the affirmative construction, as in (32), which is the negation of (31).

(32) *Be a be   a fumo   mi-mbɛr.*
    | | \\ | | \\ | /\\
   H H   L ←H L L   `L H→   L L H
   3p P2 be P2 NEG build NEG NEG C4-house
They didn't build any houses (yesterday or before).

2.2. Imperfective. Imperfective aspect is marked by a periphrastic locative construction corresponding roughly to the literal gloss, 'was at the . . . -ing'. As seen in (33), the construction in the present tense is essentially nonverbal, lacking a finite verb. The verb is grammatically an infinitive, the object of the locative preposition *lí* 'in, at'.[8]

---

[8]A verb in the infinitive is prefixed by *è* (C5) and followed by a floating L. The infinitive is syntactically distinct from nouns and verbs. On the one hand it resembles nouns, sharing with them the syntactic possibility of being the head of a noun phrase. For example, it governs agreement in possessive pronouns, as seen below:

(157) *e-to*   *lam*
      | |\\   /\\
      L H `L H→| H L
      C5-go INF INF c5^my
      my departure

The infinitive may also function as the head of an associative construction, being followed by the associative concord marker (AM).

(158) *e-gwamle*   *e*   *∅-mbɛr lo*   *e-ní*
      | | \\   \\   /\\ /\\ | \\\\
      L H `L  H→  `L L H H L L←H LH
      C5-sweep INF AM^c5 c3-house c5^your c5-that
      that way you have of sweeping the house

It differs from other nouns, however, in that it is followed by both a stem tone and a replacive H (INF) that is characteristic of most verbal constructions.

(159) *e- de*   *me-de*
      | \\ | |
      L `L H→   L L
      C5-eat INF INF c6-food
      to eat some food

(33) *Be lɨ   e-fumo   mi-mbɛr.*
   H H   L L   'L   H→   L   L H
3p LOC C5-build INF INF C4-house
They are building houses.

If past or future tense markers are present in the construction, these must be followed by the auxiliary verb, *be* 'be (at)', and the locative preposition *lɨ* before the infinitive, as in the following three examples.

(34) *Be a be   o   lɨ   e-fumo   mi-mbɛr.*
   H H   'L   H   H   L L   'L   H→   L   L H
3p P2 be P2 FOC LOC C5-build INF INF C4-house
They were building houses (in the remote past).

(35) *Be   be   o   lɨ   e-fumo   mi-mbɛr.*
   H L   H H   H   L L   'L   H→   L   L H
3p P1 be P1 FOC LOC C5-build INF INF C4-house
They were building houses (in the recent past).

(36) *Be o be   o   lɨ   e-fumo   mi-mbɛr.*
   H H   L   H   H   L L   'L   H→   L   L H
3p FUT be FUT FOC LOC C5-build INF INF C4-house
They will be building houses.

The failure to employ the auxiliary or locative verb after a segmental tense marker is ungrammatical: **Bé á lɨ̀ èfùmò mímbɛ̌r* 'They were building houses.' In the reference dialect, Upriver Bajwe'e, the auxiliary verb must be followed by the focus marker *ó* in affirmative constructions, as seen in the previous three examples. Failure to include the focus marker results in ungrammatical focus, such as: **Bé á bè lɨ̀ èfùmò mímbɛ̌r* 'They were building some houses.' In the Nzime dialect, however, both of these sentences are grammatical.

Negating an imperfective sentence entails dropping any focus marker in the main clause and introducing a negation marker followed by the auxiliary verb, as in (37).

(37) *Be a be   a be   li e-fumo   mi-mbɛr.*
   | | \ | | \ | | | \ | /\
  H H   L ←H L   L H L L   L H→ L   L H
  3p P2 be P2   NEG be NEG LOC C5-build INF INF C4-house
  They were not building houses (in the remote past).

2.3. Habitual. Habitual aspect is formed by reduplicating the auxiliary verb of a sentence marked for imperfective aspect. The habitual form corresponding to (34) is (38).

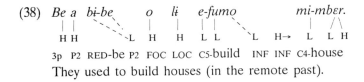

(38) *Be a bi-be   o li e-fumo   mi-mbɛr.*
  | | \ \ | | | | \ | /\
  H H   L H H L L   L H→ L   L H
  3p P2 RED-be P2 FOC LOC C5-build INF INF C4-house
  They used to build houses (in the remote past).

Reduplicating a verb may involve certain morphophonemic changes and apocopation. In the case of the auxiliary *be*, its vowel is raised from a mid front tense *e* to high-mid front tense unrounded *i* before its reduplicated counterpart.

The second tonal morpheme of the recent past tense, a floating H following the verb, spreads to both parts of the reduplicated auxiliary, as in (38) and (39).[9] The association convention for Kɔɔzime can be restated in the following way: floating tones associate themselves with one or more toneless vowels to the left.

(39) *Be   bi-be   o li e-fumo   mi-mbɛr.*
  | \   \ | | | | \ | /\
  H L   H H H L L   L H→ L   L H
  3p P1 RED-be P1 FOC LOC C5-build INF INF C4-house
  They used to build houses (during the recent past)."

It is shown in (33) that the present imperfective construction is nonverbal, lacking an auxiliary verb. The present habitual construction is fully verbal, however. The verb employed is *sâ* 'make, do'. This is reduplicated (RED) and followed by the focus marker, as in the habitual construction in other tenses. The salient verb of the sentence is no longer the head of a

---

[9]This sentence presupposes that houses of some kind can be made within the span of one day (as in the case of toy houses) and that the activity became habitual over the course of one day's activity before ceasing to be habitual.

locative prepositional phrase, as is the case in (33–39), but is instead conjugated, as in (40).

(40) Nye   si-sa   o   fumo   mi-mbɛr.

        L H   H H   H   H   L   L   H→   L   L H

        3s   PRES RED-do PRES FOC build PRES PRES C4-house

He usually builds houses.

The negation of a present habitual form is dealt with in §3.3, in connection with present tense. There is no distinct way of creating negated habitual constructions in the other tenses. In such cases, the negated imperfective form can be substituted, which acquires a habitual reading.

Future habitual employs an auxiliary verb *di*, 'remain, stay', as in (41).

(41) Nye o   di   li   e-fumo   mi-mbɛr.

        L H   L   L   H   L L   L   H→   L   L H

        3s   FUT remain FUT LOC C5-build INF INF C4-house

He will habitually build houses.

3. Absolute tenses

As indicated at the outset of this study, Kɔɔzime has both absolute and relative tenses. In the case of absolute tenses, a situation is placed in respect to a fixed reference point, the present moment. Any situation recounted which existed before the present moment is marked by one of the two past tense markers. Present tense is used to refer to situations existing at the present moment and future tense is used for those events which take place after the present moment.

The melodies of the tenses are shown in (42).

As seen in (42), Kɔɔzime tenses are marked by a number of elements (usually tonal morphemes) that together constitute the melody (Goldsmith 1976:71) for each tense. These elements are identified by Goldsmith as the tense marker, the stem tone (or stem tones, in the event that a perfective marker, adverbial, or serial verb is present), and the suffixal tone (SFX). The suffixal tone is a suffix to the entire verb phrase, associating with the following word.

The first stem tone of any tense (shown before the three dots) follows any verb that might be present, including *si* (perfective). If more than one auxiliary is present, all receive that tone. The final verb receives the second stem tone (. . . L for both past tenses.)

(42) Affirmative indicative tone melodies

	TNS	STEM	SFX
P2	á	L...L	∅
P1 (nonfocus)	L	H...L	H→
Object or subject focus	L	H	H→
PRES			
No copula	H	∅	∅
Object focus	H	H	H→
Subject focus or dependent clause			
(verb medial)	∅	←H H	H→
(verb final)	∅	←H L	∅
FUT (nonfocus)	ó	H...L	H→
Subject focus	ngá	H...L	H→
Dependent clauses	ngá	H...L	H→

3.1. Remote past. Remote past is marked by *á* and by one or more stem Ls. In affirmative constructions, no replacive suffixal H follows the verb. One is present, however, in the corresponding negative construction. These melodies are shown in (43).

(43) Remote past tense melodies

P2	TNS	NEG	STEM	SFX
AFF	á		L...L	∅
NEG	á	←H à	L...L	H →

Examples (44) and (45) give evidence of remote past forms unmarked for aspect. Such forms must be negated, have a focus-marked verb complement as in (44), or be grammatically dependent as in (45).

(44) *Nye o   a   be   bi-kwan.*

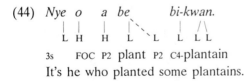

3s   FOC P2 plant P2 C4-plantain
It's he who planted some plantains.

When there are three adjacent vowels, as in (44), an epenthetical consonant appears between the second and third vowels. In the Nzime dialect the consonant is *b*, as in *nye ó b'á* . . . In the Bajwe'e dialect, it is *w*, as in *nye ó w'á* . . .

As mentioned above, the remote past tense marker may occur without any aspect marker in dependent constructions such as the relative clause in (45). At the beginning of the relative clause there is a replacive H morpheme which marks the beginning of the relative clause (Beavon 1985), though its presence is not obvious when it is followed by a morpheme which lexically has a H. It is ungrammatical to employ the perfective marker in relative clauses (*mùr á sì bè bìkwàn nywá*). (In (45), note the abbreviations SUB for subordinator, and DEF for definite article.)

(45) *m-ùr*   [*a   be*   *bi-kwan]*   *nywa*

      L L   H→| H   L   L   L L L   H

    C1-person SUB P2 plant P2 C8-plantains DEF^C1

    the person who planted some plantains (yesterday or before)

In independent affirmative past constructions, however, an aspect marker is required. In (46) both *si* (perfective) and the verb are followed by a stem tone. This supports our claim that *si* is a verb, albeit an auxiliary verb.

(46) *Be a si*   *fumo*   *mi-mbɛr.*

    H H   L   L   L   L   L H

    3p P2 PFV P2 build P2 C4-house

    They built some houses (yesterday or before).

A stem tone indicating tense also follows a serial verb occurring in a past tense form.

(47) *Be a si*   *ze*   *fumo*   *mi-mbɛr.*

    H H   L   L   L L   L   L L H

    3p P2 PFV P2 come P2 build P2 C4-house

    It was they who then built some houses.

At least four stem tones may be found in a single construction, since the perfective marker, an adverbial, and a serial verb may all exist together with the main verb and each receives a stem tone. This is L in the case of the remote past tense, as in (48).

(48) *Be a si   ka   ze   fumo   mi-mbɛr.*

    H H   L   L   L   L   L   L   L   L   L H

    3p P2 PFV P2 finally P2 come P2 build P2 C4-house

It was they who then finally built some houses.

Independent remote past tense sentences lacking a perfective marker
must either have a focus-marked complement, as in (44), or be negated, as
in (49).

(49) *Be a be   a fumo   mi-mbɛr.*

    H H   L   ←H L   L   L   H→   L   L H

    3p P2 be P2   NEG build NEG NEG C4-house

They did not build any houses (yesterday or before).

A past-tense independent sentence, therefore, must have an aspect
marker, have a focus marker, or be negated. The following sentence is
ungrammatical due to the absence of any of these markers: **Bé á fùmo
mìmbĕr* 'They built some houses.'

3.2. Recent past. Recent past tense is marked by a floating L, which
occurs after the subject noun phrase, a stem H, and a suffixal H (see (42)).
If a form includes one or more auxiliary verbs (such as perfective aspect),
the stem H follows all of these. A stem L occurs only on the final verb.

(50) Recent past tense melodies

P1		TNS	NEG	STEM	SFX
	AFF	L		H...L	H→
	NEG	L	←H à	H... L	H→

The L tense marker follows the subject noun phrase, the last constituent
of which may be *ó* (focus). The L of recent past associates with the
preceding word, as in (51).

(51) *Be o   fumo   mi-mbɛr.*

    H H   L   L   H   H→   L   L H

    3p FOC P1 build P1 P1 C4-house

It's they who built some houses (earlier today).

In (52) and (53), the tense marker associates with a subject pronoun and a noun, respectively.

(52) *Be   fumo   o   mi-mbεr.*

```
 |\    |    \     |    |   /\
 H L   L    H  H→| H    L   L H
```

3p P1 build P1 P1 FOC C4-house

It's houses that they built (earlier today).

(53) *Fwɰŋ   lεε   o   Ø-no.*

```
 /\----___      |  \     |    /\
 H  H      `L   H  H  H→| H    L H  H
```

your^father P1 say P1 P1 FOC C7-thus

It's that that your father said (earlier today).

The stem tone of recent past tense is H. Any subsequent stem tones associated with verbal auxiliaries are also H, but the stem tone associated with the final verb is L.

(54) *Be   si   ka   ze   fumo   mi-mbεr.*

```
 |\     \    |\    |\    |   \     |   /\
 H L    `H   L   `H   L  `H   L    L  H→   L   L H
```

3p P1 PFV P1 finally P1 come P1 build P1 P1 C4-house

It was they who then finally built some houses (earlier today).

In (52) and (53), the stem H combines with a L and a H verb, respectively. In (55) it associates with a verb which lacks lexical tone.

(55) *Be   be   o   Ø-mbεr.*

```
 |\    \      |   /\
 H L   H  H→| H    L   L H
```

3p P1 be P1 P1 FOC C3-house

They were at the house (earlier today).

As shown in Beavon 1990, the locative verb is atypical with respect to phonology. There are five other verbs which, like the locative verb shown above, are inherently toneless.[10] They are listed in (56), including the

---

[10]The citation form of a verb is the infinitive, which includes (1) a class 5 prefix *è-* and (2) a low stem tone following the verb. For this reason, toneless verbs spoken in citation receive a stem L.

homophonous forms of *jwe*, which means either 'die' or 'give' according to the number of arguments in the clause.

(56) *ze*   'come'
      jwe   'die'
      de   'eat'
      cwe   'stumble'
      jwe   'give'

By positing a toneless lexical form for these verbs, it is possible to account for a L in remote past forms but H in recent past forms, by attributing these changes to the grammatical tones of the respective tense melodies.

The corresponding negated form of the recent past in (55) is presented in (57). Note that the first occurrence of the locative verb represents its use as an auxiliary, while the second manifests its role as main verb.

(57) Be   be   a   be   Ø-mbɛr.
      H L   H |←H L   L   H→ L   L H
      3p   P1 be P1 NEG   be NEG NEG C3-house
      They were not at the house (earlier today).

Examples (58) and (59) illustrate affirmative and negative recent past when the verb is in sentence-final position.

(58) Be o   fumo.
      H H `L L   H
      3p FOC P1 build P1
      It's they who built (something earlier today).

(59) Be   be   a   fumo.
      H L   H |←H L   L   L
      3p P1 be P1 NEG   build NEG
      They did not build (anything earlier today).

3.3. Present. There are six contrastive tone melodies for present tense. Some include a floating H tense marker which contributes to the distinction between present and recent past. Some present-tense forms are marked by means of one or two stem Hs, although others employ stem Ls. A summary of the present-tense melodies posited is presented in (60).

(60) Present tense melodies

PRES	TNS	NEG	STEM	SFX
No copula	H		∅	∅
Object focus AFF	H		H	H→
Subject focus or dependent clause				
AFF (verb medial)	∅		←H H	H→
AFF (verb final)	∅		←H L	∅
NEG-neutral	∅	←H à	L	H→
NEG IMPF	∅	←H à	L	H→
NEG HAB (verb medial)	∅	á	←H H	H→
NEG HAB (verb final)	∅	á	←H L	∅

Two syntactic restrictions need to be mentioned. (1) Independent, present-tense forms have either a focus-marked verb complement or a negated verb. (Dependent clauses, on the other hand, can be affirmative (AFF) and yet be unaccompanied by a focus-marked complement.) (2) There is a syntactic incompatibility between the perfective aspect marker and either of the nonpast tenses.

The mark of present tense in nonverbal constructions is a floating H after the subject pronoun, as in (61).

(61) *Nye   e   mi-mbɛr*

      L H   L   L   L H

   3s   PRES with c4-house

He has/owns some houses.

This same H present-tense marker is found in the affirmative construction with an object in focus, as in (62). The high tense marker posited for affirmative present constructions has not, in preceding examples, been in an environment where its presence can be seen. It is in present-tense forms with a postverbal complement in focus that the floating H marking present time is observed. This floating tone attaches itself to the L subject pronoun as in (62). (The suffixal tone is posited in this construction by analogy, even though there is no way to confirm its presence.)

Present tense can also be indicated by one or two stem Hs appearing on the verb. These can be seen in affirmative, dependent constructions, as in (63).

(62) *Nye*   *fumo*   *o*   *Ø-mbɛr.*

     L H   L   H   H→| H L L H

    3s   PRES build PRES^HAB PRES^HAB FOC C3-house

It's a house he builds.

(63) *mi-mbɛr [*   *nye fumo*   *b-ʉr]*   *mi*

    L L H H→   L L ←H H   H→   L L   H

    C4-house SUB 3s   build PRES^HAB PRES^HAB C2-people DEF^C4

the houses he builds for people

This tone pattern on the verb is also found in affirmative independent sentences with a subject in focus, as in (64) and (65). In (64), the tone pattern on the verb is ←H . . . H, because the verb is not sentence final. In sentence-final position, the stem tone pattern for subject-focus present tense sentences becomes ← H . . . L, as in (65).

(64) *Nye o* *fumo*   *mi-mbɛr.*

    L H   L   ←H H   H→   L L H

    3s   FOC build PRES^HAB PRES^HAB C4-house

It's he who builds houses. *or* It's he who should build houses.

(65) *Nye o* *fumo.*

    L H   L   ←H L

    3s   FOC build PRES^HAB

It's he who builds. *or* It's he who should build (them).

Four negative constructions are possible in present tense, one being unmarked (neutral) in aspect, one being imperfective (progressive or habitual), and the other two indicating only habitual aspect with either a medial or a final verb.

The negated present-tense construction that lacks aspectual specification has a stem L and a suffixal H. Negation in present tense consists of a replacive H followed by the prefix *à-*. This same negation marker has already been seen in negated past tense forms (§§3.1–2).

Example (67) shows a present tense form that permits either a progressive or a habitual reading. It is more complex than (66), employing the locative verb as auxiliary and a locative prepositional phrase containing the salient verb, as seen in (33) to (36).

(66) *Nye   a   fumo   mi-mbɛr.*

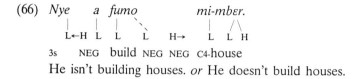

    3s   NEG   build   NEG   NEG   C4-house
He isn't building houses. *or* He doesn't build houses.

(67) *Nye   a   be   lɨ   e-fumo   mi-mbɛr.*

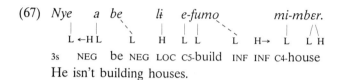

    3s   NEG   be   NEG   LOC   C5-build   INF   INF   C4-house
He isn't building houses.

Negated present habitual forms are presented in (68) and (69). Note the presence of a replacive H in the verb, followed by either a floating H or L, depending on the verb's position in the utterance. In (68), the tones are ←H…H because the verb is in utterance-medial position. In (69), on the other hand, the stem tones are ←H…L, since the verb is utterance final.

(68) *Nye   a   fumo   mi-mbɛr.*
         | | | ` ` ` | /\
         L H   L   ←H H   H→   L   L H
    3s   PRES^NEG^HAB   build   PRES^NEG^HAB   PRES^NEG^HAB   C4-house
He doesn't ever build any houses.

(69) *Nye   a   fumo.*
         | | | ` ` `
         L H   L   ←H L
    3s   PRES^NEG^HAB   build   PRES^NEG^HAB
He doesn't ever build (anything).

As seen in both of these cases, negation is expressed by *á*, together with accompanying tonal morphemes. This marker is homophonous with remote past. Negated present habitual therefore differs from affirmative remote past perfective only by the tones found on the verb and not by any difference in preverbal markers.

3.4. Future. Regular future tense refers to any event conceived of as occurring after the present moment. The affirmative future tense marker is *ó*. In negated future forms, the future marker is *ŋá* (*ngá* in the Nzime dialect), with the negation marker preceding it. The future marker *ŋgó* is found in future forms with a subject in focus, while the marker *ngá* is found in dependent future forms. For all these tonal melodies there is a stem L and a suffixal H. These facts are summarized in (70).

Keith H. Beavon

(70) Future tense melodies

FUT	NEG	TNS	NEG	STEM	SFX
Nonfocus					
AFF		ó		L	H→
NEG	a	ŋá		L	H→
Subject focus		ngó		L	H→
Dependent clauses		ngá		L	H→

Affirmative future tense is illustrated in (71).

(71) Nye o   fumo   mi-mbɛr.
　　　| | | `\ | /\
　　　L H   L   L   H→ L L H
　　 3s FUT build FUT FUT C4-house
He's going to build some houses.

The marker ŋá (future), used in negative constructions, is seen in (72), together with the negative marker appropriate to the tense.[11]

(72) Nye a   ŋa fumo   mi-mbɛr.
　　　| | | | `\ | /\
　　　L L   H L   L   H→   L L H
　　 3s NEG FUT build NEG^FUT NEG^FUT C4-house
He's not going to build (any) houses.

The future marker ngá is presented in (73) with subject in focus.

(73) Nye o   nga fumo   mi-mbɛr.
　　　| | | | `\ | /\
　　　L H   H   L   L   H→ L L H
　　 3s FOC FUT build FUT FUT C4-house
It's he who is going to build houses.

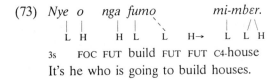

---

[11]In the Nzime dialect, the negation marker and the future tense marker form a portmanteau, á, as seen in (160).

(160) Nye a   fumo   mi-mbɛr.
　　　 | | | `\  `\ | /\
　　　 L H   L   L   H→ L L H
　　　3s NEG^FUT build NEG^FUT NEG^FUT C4-house
He's not going to build (any) houses. (Nzime dialect)

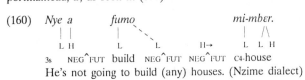

The same marker is found in dependent constructions for many speakers of Kɔɔzime. Others, primarily speakers of Băjwe'e, use ó, however, as in (74) and (75).

(74) mʉr   [nga fumo   mi-mbɛr] nywa
     |\ | | \ | /\ |
     L L   H→| H L   L   H→   L   L H   H
     person SUB FUT build FUT FUT C4-house DEF^C1
     the one who is going to build houses

(75) mʉr   [o   fumo   mi-mbɛr] nywa
     |\ | | \ | /\ |
     L L   H→| H   L   L   H→   L   L H   H
     person SUB FUT build FUT FUT C4-house DEF^C1
     the one who is going to build houses

4. Relative tenses

All the verbal constructions considered thus far have been in some direct relation to the fixed point of temporal reference represented by the present moment. In this section, attention is given to relative tenses, which have no inherent relation to this reference point. Relative tenses acquire their specific temporal meaning only in relation to a preceding clause. For this reason, relative tenses are restricted to occurrence in a discourse-medial position.

4.1. Relative recent past. Relative recent past tense indicates that an event occurs prior to some other event, which may be past, present habitual, or future. Past perfect and future perfect constructions are possible by means of this relative recent past tense. In the independent clause, a time frame is established, making use of an absolute tense. Then the clause containing relative recent past tense is introduced. This establishes what events preceded the event of the main clause. These events are presented as having occurred in the recent past with respect to the event of the main clause.

It is necessary for syntactic and phonological reasons to deal separately with two types of absolute relative constructions—those in which the verb of the independent clause is -be 'be (at)' and those in which the main clause contains some other verb. As is seen below, a locative verb in the main clause creates certain special syntactic possibilities for the clause containing the relative tense. For this reason, the presentation of the absolute relative construction begins with the normal one, that is, where the verb in the main clause is other than the locative verb.

Normal construction. In relative recent past constructions which do not contain the locative verb, the relative tense marker is ←H *o*, where *o* is toneless but takes the floating L of the normal P1 melody. The first stem tone of the P1 melody, a H, follows the PFV marker and the second stem tone, a L, follows the main verb. The tonal and segmental marks of the relative recent past tenses are summarized in (76).

(76) Relative recent past tense melodies

REL^P1	REL	TNS	NEG	STEM	SFX
AFF	←H *o*	L		H...L	H→
NEG	*le*		←H *à pà*	H...L	H→

The relative recent past tense in (77) is shown apart from any independent clause and is, therefore, grammatically incomplete. The tense-aspect marking indicates that the event in question took place in the recent past relative to some unstated reference point, and that it is viewed as a whole.

(77) nye   o   si   ba   nku
      | \   \ | ‾‾‾   /\
      L |←H L   H   L   L H→ L H
      3s   REL P1 PFV P1 cut^up P1 P1 pig
      ...he having just cut up the pig

The negative construction corresponding to (77) is (78). The relative past tense marker is not present in the negative construction. Note that the negation marker follows *e* (*le* before vowels) 'with', which here seems to function as a marker of the negative relative past construction.

(78) nye le   a pa   ba   nku
      | | |←H L L H   L ‾‾‾   /\
      L   L |←H L   L H   L   L H→   L H
      3s   REL^NEG NEG   yet P1 cut^up NEG NEG pig
      ...he not yet having cut up the pig/...prior to his having cut up the pig

The event referred to in a relative recent past clause, such as the cutting up of the pig in (78), is relegated to past, present, or future time by the tense of the independent clause. In (79), the relative tense acquires a

remote past orientation from its context. This means that the pig butcher-
ing occurred in the remote past (yesterday or before), just prior to the
event (also in the remote past) of the main clause. A pause is present
between the two clauses, which is indicated by a comma.

(79) Nye a jebe bur o, nye o si ba nkʉ.

    L H H L L L   H   L|←H L   H   L   L H→ L H

  3s   P2 call P2 people FOC 3s   REL   P1 PFV P1 cut^up P1 P1 pig

He called the people (in the remote past) after having just cut up
the pig.

In (80), the first verb is in the recent past. This influences the possible
readings of the second clause. Both the action of cutting up the pig and
the action of calling the people occurred earlier today.

(80) Nye jebe bur o,

    L L H H H→L L   H

  3s   P1 call P1 P1 people FOC

nye o si ba nkʉ.

    L ←H   L   H L   L H→ L H

  3s   REL   P1 PFV P1 cut^up P1 P1 pig

He called the people (earlier today) having just cut up the pig.

In (81), the first clause is marked for future tense. This gives a future
reading to the relative recent past tense of the second clause. The cutting
up will occur in the future, but just prior to the calling of the people.

(81) Nye o jebe bur o,

    L H H L   H→ L L   H

  3s   FUT call FUT FUT people FOC

nye o si ba nkʉ.

    L ←H L   H L   L H→ L H

  3s   REL   P1 PFV P1 cut^up P1 P1 pig

He is going to call the people just after cutting up the pig.

In (82), the main clause is marked as present imperfective. Depending upon the context, the reading of this verb may be either progressive or habitual. In the event that the former is chosen, the relative tense refers to a single action in the recent past. If the main verb is interpreted as indicating habitual aspect, then the action in the second clause is repeated. Both of these readings are appropriate to (82).

(82) *Nye lɨ   e-jebe   bur   o,*
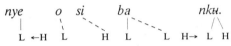
     L H   L H   L   H→   L L   H
     3s   LOC C5-call PRES PRES people FOC

      nye   o   si   ba   nkʉ.

       L ←H L   H   L   L H→ L H
       3s   REL P1 PFV P1 cut^up P1 P1 pig
       He is calling the people having just cut up a pig. *or* He calls the people just after cutting up pigs.

The choice of subjects in the two clauses is not restricted. As seen in (83), different subjects can appear in the two clauses.

(83) *Nye a jebe   bur   o,   me   o   si   mɛkle.*
     L H H L   L L   H   L|←H L   H   L   L
     3s   P2 call P2 people FOC 1s   REL P1 PFV P1 consent P1
     He called the people just after I consented.

Either or both of the clauses in an absolute relative construction can be negated, as in (84)–(86). Note in (85) and (86) that when the main clause is negated, the focus marker no longer occurs at the end of the main clause. This is because the *ó* (focus) and negation are mutually exclusive within a clause.

(84) *Nye a jebe   bur   o,   me le   a pa   mɛkle.*
     L H H L   L L   H   L L |←H L   L H   L   L
     3s   P2 call P2 people FOC 1s REL^NEG NEG yet NEG consent NEG
     He called the people without my consent.

(85) *Nye a be   a jebe   bʉr,*

L H   L ←H L H L   H→ L L

3s   P2 be P2 NEG   call NEG NEG people

me   o   si   kamle.

L ←H L   H L   L

1s   REL P1 PFV P1 forbid P1

He didn't call the people after I had forbidden it.

(86) *Nye a be   a jebe   bʉr,*

L H   L ←H L H L   H→ L L

3s   P2 be P2 NEG   call NEG NEG people

me le   a pa   kamle.

L L |←H L   L H   L   L

1s   REL^NEG NEG   yet NEG forbid P1

He called the people in spite of my just having forbidden it.

Locative construction. This section considers a special case in which the verb of the main clause is the locative verb *be*. Although these constructions conform in general with what has been seen above, they are distinct from a syntactic and phonological point of view. When the first verb in an absolute relative construction is the locative verb, deletion of the subject and the relative marker ←H *o* of the second clause is allowed. It is also necessary in this case to delete the floating L recent past tense marker. These constructions constitute the past and future perfect constructions in Kɔɔzime.

In (87) and (88), absolute relative constructions have the same subjects throughout, and the first clause contains the locative verb. In (88), the subject of the relative clause is deleted along with the markers of recent past and relative tense. The pause between the two clauses in (88) is so minimal that it has been left unmarked.

(87) *Nye a be   o, nye   o   si   kamle.*

L H   L H   L |←H L   Ḣ L   L

3s   P2 be P2 FOC 3s   REL P1 PFV P1 forbid P1

He had just finished forbidding it.

(88) *Nye a be   o   si   kamle.*
         | | \ | \   \
         L H   L H   H L   L
      3s   P2 be P2 FOC PFV P1 forbid P1
      He had just forbidden (it).

Negating these perfect constructions is possible only in the second clause, as in (89). It is ungrammatical to attempt to negate the main clause: **Nye á bé abe sí kamle* 'He had not forbidden (it).'

(89) *Nye a be   o,   le   a pa   kamle.*
         | | \ | | | | \ | \
         L H   L H   L |←H L   L H   L   L
      3s   P2 be P2 FOC REL^NEG NEG yet NEG forbid NEG
      He had not yet forbidden (it).

The locative verb in the independent clause may be given any absolute time reference. In (90) and (91), the main verb is in the present tense. Note that the present tense form of the locative verb is suppletive: *mʉ* 'be (PRES)'. Example (91) is a transformation of (90), illustrating deletion of the subject, the recent past tense marker, and the relative tense marker.

(90) *Nye mʉ   o,   nye   o   si   kamle.*
         | /\ | | \   \ | \
         L H L   H   L |←H L   H L   L
      3s   be^PRES FOC 3s   REL P1 PFV P1 forbid P1
      He has just forbidden (it).

(91) *Nye mʉ   o   si   kamle.*
         | /\ | \   \
         L H L   H   H L   L
      3s   be^PRES FOC PFV P1 forbid P1
      He has just forbidden (it).

A future perfect construction, making use of the relative recent past tense, is seen in the next two examples. The second shows the result of subject and tense deletion in the second clause.

(92) Be o be   o,   be   o   si   kamle.
     | | \ | | \ | \
     H H   L   H   H|←H L   H   L   L
     3p FUT be FUT FOC 3p REL P1 PFV P1 forbid P1
     They will have just forbidden (it).

(93) Be o be   o   si   kamle.
     | | \ | \ | \
     H H   L   H   H   L   L
     3p FUT be FUT FOC PFV P1 forbid P1
     They will have just forbidden (it).

When an absolute relative construction is transformed into a dependent clause, the focalizer in the first part of the construction must be deleted. The verb 'be' may also be deleted. Both of these changes are seen in (94). The optionality of the locative verb is shown by means of parentheses. The subjects of the two clauses can differ, as seen in (95). It is not possible to delete the second subject in this case, however. (The final L indicates sentence final (S^FINAL).)

(94) Be o (be)   si   kamle   wa, . . .
     | | \   \ | \ |
     H H   L   H   L   L   H
     3p FUT (be FUT) PFV P1 forbid P1 if/when
     If/when they will have just forbidden (it) . . .

(95) Me a be   o,   nye o   si   bene   me.
     | | \ | | \ | \ | \
     L H   L   H   L|←H L   H   L   L   H→ L L
     1s P2 be P2 FOC 3s REL P1 PFV P1 reject P1 P1   1s S^FINAL
     I had just been rejected by him.

4.2. Consecutive relative. In the preceding section, relative tenses all relate to events or situations existing prior to the action of main verbs. In this section, relative tense refers to a subsequent action.

When a sequence of activities is in view, the preferred way of referring to them is by use of the consecutive relative tense. Verbs in this tense acquire a past, present, or future reference depending on the tense of the verb that initiates the sequence of verbs. The essential meaning of the consecutive relative tense is 'next' or 'then'. There is no negated form of this tense. The structure of the consecutive relative tense is simple, as indicated in (96).

(96)   Consecutive relative tense melodies

CONS^REL	TNS	STEM	SFX
Third person plural subjects			
Following P2	∅	H . . . -ɔ̂ɔ̂	H→
Elsewhere	∅	H . . . L	H→
Other person and number subjects	∅	H . . . L	H→

The second clause in (97) contains an example of the consecutive relative tense. It has a remote past orientation due to the tense of the preceding verb.

(97)   *Nye a si   lolo   me-jwii me,*

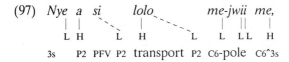

L H   L H   L   L LL H

3s   P2 PFV P2 transport P2 C6-pole C6^3s

ntɔk fumo   ∅-mbɛr.

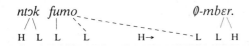

H L L   L   H→   L L H

then build CONS^REL CONS^REL C3-house

He carried his poles in and then built his house.

In (97), it is evident that the verb in the consecutive relative tense is unmarked with respect to person and number of subject. In the case of the remote past consecutive relative tense, however, a suffix exists to indicate that the subject is third person, plural, and human. The suffix is -ɔɔ after disyllabic stems and monosyllabic CVC stems; it is -ŋɔɔ after CV stems.[12] This plural suffix is illustrated in (98).

---

[12]This suffix is formally identical to the passive suffix. There is no confusion between the two, however, due to other aspects of passive voice marking, such as fronting of the promoted object.

(98) *Be a si   lolo   me-jwii mɔɔ,*
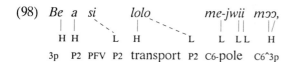
    H H   L H   L   L LL   H
    3p P2 PFV P2 transport P2 C6-pole C6^3p

    fum-ɔɔ   Ø-mbɛr.
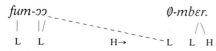
    L   L   H→   ⁻L   L H
    build-CONS^REL^3p CONS^REL C3-house

They carried their poles in and then built a house.

The consecutive relative tense acquires a future reading when it follows a future-tense main verb.

(99) *Be o   lolo   me-jwii mɔɔ,*
    H H   H   ⁻L   H→ L LL   H
    3p FUT transport FUT FUT C6-pole C6^3p

    fumo   Ø-mbɛr.
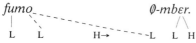
    L   L   H→   ⁻L   L H
    build CONS^REL CONS^REL C3-house

They will carry their poles in and then build a house.

The tense melodies in (96) state that, if there are serial verbs preceding the main verb, they are accompanied by high stem tones. This is illustrated in (100) on the serial verb *ze* 'then', derived from *ze* 'come'.

(100) *Be lɨ   e-ze   wa,*
     H H   L   L   H→| H L
     3p LOC C5-come INF INF here

     ze   fumo   mi-mbɛr.

     L   H   L   L   H→   L   L H
     then CONS^REL build CONS^REL CONS^REL C4-house

They come here and then build houses.

4.3. Consecutive future purpose. Consecutive future purpose differentiates between two future events that are logically linked such that the first event is done in order that the second might take place. There is no negative counterpart to the affirmative form. This construction exists only following a future-tense clause. Its form is presented in (101).

(101) Consecutive future purpose melody

	TNS	STEM	SFX
CONS^FUT^PURP	←H ò	L	H→

This construction is similar to that of future, except that the tone of consecutive future purpose is L rather than H. In addition, there is a replacive H in the consecutive future that brings about tonal change in L subject pronouns, as seen in (102).

(102)
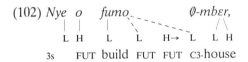

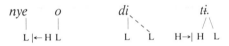

He's going to build a house in order to live in it.

4.4. Present perfect. Present perfect is the only absolute relative tense. It relates a present situation to a past event. This means that it has an absolute time orientation, since the situation exists at the present moment. It also has a relative time orientation, since the past event in question may be either remote or recent past, depending on the larger context. There is no negated counterpart to present perfect. Its tone melody is presented in (103).

(103) Present perfect tense melody

	TNS	STEM	SFX
PRES^PRF	←H [+1Ht]	L	H→

This tense is also unique with respect to vowel-raising, which occurs on the subject pronoun. The vowel of the subject pronoun is raised one level. Given the vowels of Kɔɔzime pronouns, examples are limited to e and o. These become i and u, respectively. These changes are illustrated in (104) and (105). The feature [+1 Height] (abbreviated [+1Ht]) is used to represent the closure of the oral cavity. This is employed in the examples on a separate tier. (Note: *i̵* refers to a mid high front unrounded tense vowel, and *u̵*, to a mid high back rounded tense vowel.)

(104)

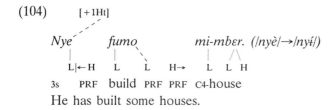

3s   PRF   build   PRF PRF C4-house
He has built some houses.

(105)

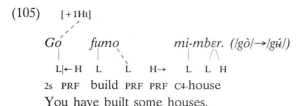

2s   PRF   build   PRF PRF C4-house
You have built some houses.

Present perfect tense is semantically distinct from the relative recent past constructions discussed in §4.1. In the latter case, it is possible to cancel the implicature created by the tense. With the present perfect tense, however, this is not possible. For example, it must be true, in the case of the present perfect construction in (105), that houses exist. This is not necessarily the case with the relative recent past construction in (106). One can go on to say after (106) "but they have all been destroyed."

(106)

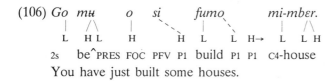

2s   be⌃PRES FOC PFV P1 build P1 P1 C4-house
You have just built some houses.

This concludes the proposed analysis of tense in Konzime. An overview of negation is presented in the following section, drawing together elements included in the preceding description and adding details which were not in focus there.

5. Negation

The principal negation markers are shown in (107), which incorporates information given throughout the paper with reference to negation. In certain cases, therefore, it is helpful to refer to the relevant section for more detail and examples.

(107) Negation markers

	NEG	TNS	NEG	STEM	SFX
P2		á	←H à	L...L	H→
P1					
(verb medial)		L	←H à	H...L	H→
(verb final)		L	←H à	H...L	∅
PRES					
Neutral		∅	←H à	L	H→
IMPF		∅	←H à	L	H→
HAB (verb medial)		∅	á	←H H	H→
(verb final)		∅	á	←H L	∅
FUT	a	ŋá		L	H→
REL ('with...yet')		le	←H à pà	H...L	H→
HORT		∅	àyí	L	H→
IMP		∅	à	L	H→
INF		∅	à	L	H→

One common mark of negation is *a*. Other additional marks of negation vary according to the tense and aspect of the construction. These additional markers are tonal morphemes, many of them being replacive. These tones have the effect of encoding tense and aspect information on the negation marker.

The negation marker has a dual function as a class 1a noun prefix. When it is present on a verb, the result can be interpreted as a verbal noun capable of governing the agreement of modifiers. In (108), the negated verb *atô* 'not going' is the head noun of a noun phrase. The possessive pronoun and the subject pronoun are in class agreement with *atô*.

(108) A-   to   i   ∅-peme we,   nye   i   bebe.
      | |\ | | | | | |\\ | | |
      L   H L   H   L L H   H   L H   H   H L
      C1aˆNEGˆINF go NEG LOC C7-field C1ˆhis C1ˆ3s PRES LOC bad
      His (habit of) not going to the field is bad.

Several of the negative morphemes in (107) merit special attention. Present habitual employs a H negation marker *á* as discussed in §3.3. This is homophonous with the remote past marker discussed in §3.1. The two are distinct, however, since their tonal melodies differ in other respects. The melody for negated habitual is |←H H or |←H L, while it is L for affirmative remote past.

A frequent variant of the negation marker is |←H *à-*, which is used in past and present (nonhabitual) tenses, among others. In (109), it can be seen in recent past, and a comparable example in remote past is seen in (110).

(109) *Nye   be   a   be   bi-kwan.*

    L L   H |←H L L   L   H→ L L L

    3s P1 be P1 NEG plant NEG NEG C8-plantain

He did not plant (any) plantains (in the recent past).

(110) *Nye a be   a be   bi-kwan.*

    L H   L ←H L L L H→ L L L

    3s   P2 be P2 NEG plant NEG NEG C8-plantain

He did not plant (any) plantains (in the remote past).

Negating nonverbal constructions such as the present imperfective is done by introducing the locative verb *be* 'be (at)' in its role as auxiliary verb, followed by the primary stem tone, as in (111).

(111) *Nye   a   be   lɨ e-fumo   mi-mbɛr.*

    L|←H L   L H L L   L H→ L L H

    3s PRES^NEG be NEG LOC C5-build INF INF C4-house

He is not building houses.

Another nonverbal construction is given in (112). This lacks a verb in the surface structure due to the mandatory deletion of the locative verb in independent, affirmative, present-tense constructions (see Beavon 1990). This is negated in example (113), in which the locative verb resurfaces.

(112) *Nye o   ngbɛl.*

    L H   L L

    3s   FOC hunter

He is a hunter.

(113) *Nye   a   be   ngbɛl.*
          | |
      L|←HL   L   H→   L L
      3s   NEG   be NEG NEG hunter
      He is not a hunter.

The negated future imperfective also requires the locative verb *be* in its role as auxiliary verb, as seen in (114).

(114) *Be   a   ŋa   be   lɨ   e-fumo   mi-mbɛr.*
         | | | | | | | /
      H L   H   L   H   L L   L   H→   L   L H
      3p   NEG FUT^NEG be NEG LOC C5-build INF INF C4-house
      They're not going to be building houses.

Nonpresent imperfective constructions are negated by adding a second auxiliary verb following the negation morpheme, as in (115) and (116).

(115) *Nye a   be   a   be   lɨ   e-fumo   mi-mbɛr.*
          | | | | | | | /
       L H   L ←H L   L   H   L L   L   H→   L L H
       3s   P2 be P2 NEG   be NEG LOC C5-build INF INF C4-house
       He was not building any houses (in the remote past).

(116) *Nye   be   a   be   lɨ   e-fumo   mi-mbɛr.*
          | | | | | | /
       L L   H |←H L   L   H   L L   L   H→   L L H
       3s   P1 be P1 NEG   be NEG LOC C5-build INF INF C4-house
       He was not building any houses (in the recent past).

The perfective aspect marker *si* can occur with negation, but only in the case of rhetorical questions (by which one calls to mind a piece of generally-shared truth). This is encountered in greetings, as in (117).

(117) *Go   a   si   bwak   a?*
          | | |
       L |←H L   H   L   ~L   H
       2s   NEG PFV NEG become^big NEG INT
       Haven't you grown!

6. Focus

Although focus is most often treated in the context of the noun phrase, it merits discussion alongside verb phrase constituents since focus marking and perfective aspect are in complementary distribution in Kɔɔzime. As already noted in §3.1, independent affirmative past tense sentences must either mark perfective aspect or focalize a nominal, but not do both. This seems to indicate that focus and perfective aspect occupy the same syntactic postition, and that one or the other may be selected, but not both.

Focus markers in Kɔɔzime are either assertive or counterassertive. These are syntactically distinct, as will be shown.

6.1. Assertive focus. Assertive focus is marked by *ó*. Any noun phrase may be focalized regardless of its grammatical relation to the verb. *ó* (focus) follows a nominal that precedes a verb, but precedes one that follows the verb. Postverbal noun phrases not selected for focus are generally deleted if another verb complement is focussed. If an object is focussed, however, the subject is usually pronominalized rather than deleted.

Sentences with focussed complements are generally construed as responses to questions or counterassertions in which a speaker is asserting slightly different information from that which someone else has just asserted. That part of the response regarded as most salient (new information) is focussed. This noun phrase often corresponds to the interrogative word in a previous question. If a question is polar (a yes/no question), the response lacks a focussed nominal.

The epenthetic consonant /w/ is automatically inserted between the second and third vowels of any three vowel sequence, as in the first answer of (118) . This consonant is enclosed in parentheses and shown without a gloss because it has no semantic or syntactic content.

(118) Question   Answer

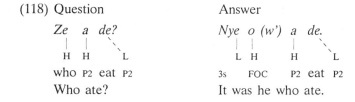

(119) *Nye a de nkoo?*

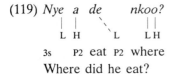

      L H   L   L H

3s   P2 eat P2 where

Where did he eat?

Nye a de o, ɨ ∅-mbɛr wam.

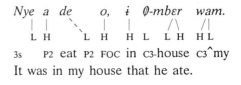

    L H   L H   H L L H H L

3s   P2 eat P2 FOC in c3-house c3^my

It was in my house that he ate.

(120) *Nye a de ye?*

      L H   L   H

3s   P2 eat P2 what

What did he eat?

Nye a de o, bi-kwan.

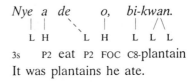

    L H   L H   L L L

3s   P2 eat P2 FOC c8-plantain

It was plantains he ate.

It is ungrammatical in Kɔɔzime to use the affirmative focus marker in a perfective sentence: *Nyè á sì dè ó mede.* 'It was food he (perfectively) ate.' The affirmative focus marker may be used together with negation only if it is the subject that is focussed, as in (121).

(121) *Nye o be a de me-de.*

     L H L   H́ |←H L   L H→ L L

3s   FOC P1 be P1 NEG eat P1 P1 c6-food

It was he who did not eat any food (in the recent past).

6.2. Negative focus. Negative focus is marked by *ntʉk* H→ 'it's not' where the H is replacive. This focus marker may also occur sentence medially, in which case the stem tone is also H: *ntʉ́k* H→ 'it's not'. In either case, however, it precedes the focussed noun. It can be used together with the assertive focus marker in successive sentences to give counterassertive focus to a noun phrase. This enables the speaker to isolate and correct a mistake found in another speaker's statement. In (122) and (123), a noun is the head of a relative clause. The fact that the noun it focusses must be relativized is peculiar to the negative focus marker.

Example (122) demonstrates that the clause following a negative focus marker is a relative clause, due to the occurrence of *nywá*, the specific definite article which can only follow such constructions. There is a tone change in the first tone to the right of the negative focus marker which affects the pronoun *me* 'I'.

(122) *Ntʉk me [a fumo ∅-mbɛr] nywa.*

    L H H→ L H→| H L   L L L H   H

FOC^NEG 1s SUB P2 build P2 c3-house DEF^c1

It was not I who built the house (in the remote past).

Marking a noun phrase with the negative focus marker precludes marking the verb with perfective aspect: *Ntŭk mé á si fumo mbĕr nywá. 'It's not I who built the house'. This reinforces another restriction that the verb in a dependent or relative clause may not be marked as perfective.

A further restriction is that negative focus cannot occur with negation of the verb: *Ntŭk nyé á bé ade méde nywá. 'It's not he who didn't eat any food.' However, a double negative may occur, as in (123), where both the relative clause and the main clause are negated.

(123) Ø-mbɛr [me a be a fumo] wɨ
　　　/\　　| |　　　　| |　　　　|
　　L　L H　H→　L H　L ←H L L　L　　H
　　C3-house SUB 1s P2 be P2 NEG build NEG DEF^C3
　　the house that I did not build

Any sentence beginning with ntŭk can be preceded by the class 7 subject pronoun yé which gives the sentence a dummy subject and moves the negative focus marker from sentence-initial position. Its tone then changes to H-H, as in (124).

(124) Ye ntuk me-de [nye a de] ma.
　　| /\　　| |　　| |　　\　|
　　H H H H→　L L H→　L H　L　H
　　3s^C7 FOC^NEG C6-food SUB 3s P2 eat P2 DEF^C6
　　It's not food that he ate (in the remote past).

7. Mood

There are five moods in Koozime—indicative, hortative, imperative, consecutive imperative, and interrogative. No formally distinct subjunctive mood exists. In the place of a subjunctive, hortative is used, which acquires a subjunctive reading in certain contexts.

7.1. Indicative. Indicative mood, treated in considerable detail in preceding sections, needs little further comment. In contrast with nonindicative moods, indicative encodes statements of fact. It is syntactically distinguished from other moods by the possibility of focussing its noun phrases.

There are, however, a number of indicative constructions which may receive an extended pragmatic reading which is usually triggered by the context. A present indicative with an object marked for assertive focus can be given a near-future reading, as in (125), if it is obvious the man has not yet commenced building.

(125) *Nye   fumo   o   Ø-mbεr.*

       L H   L   H   H→| H   L   L H

       3s PRES build PRES PRES FOC C3-house

It's a house he's building. *or* He's going to build a house soon.

A negated present equative form has a paradoxically affirmative reading when the complement is a verbal noun, shown by the nominalizer suffix (NOM) -*a*, as in (126).

(126) *Ye   a   be   n-dim-a!*

      H |←H L   L   H→`L H H

      3sˆC7 NEG   be NEG NEG C3-deep-NOM

It was really deep!

There is an unusual modal use of the future indicative which can be seen in (127).

(127) *Me nteme o   to   Ø-nkana.*

      L H H H   H L   H→ L   L L

      1s   also   FUT go FUT FUT C7-city

I would like to go to the city too.

7.2. Nonindicative. Hortative (HORT) and imperative (IMPV) moods are both marked by verbal suffixes, a given verb usually having similar forms for both. For the most part, the morphology of these suffixes is regular, being governed by the phonological attributes of the verb stem. In a few cases, however, the form of the verb stem changes in the hortative or imperative, as in (128).

(128) *e-ze*   →   *Nta-k!*

      L |← `L   H

      C5-come INF   come^IMP-IMP

      to come   Come!

In general, regular rules generate the appropriate hortative or imperative forms. The selection of the right suffix is based on the number and type of stem syllables and on vowels in the syllable nuclei. (129) gives an idea of the regularities observed in the morphophonemics of these moods.[13]

(129) Imperative and hortative suffix formation

Stem	Affix	IND	HORT	IMPV	Gloss
ce, o, a	-k	bà	bâk	bǎk	'plant'
		bá	bâk	bák	'marry'
ci, ɨ	-ke	bì	bíkè	bìké	'receive'
		bí	bíkè	bíké	'beat'
cu, ʉ	-ko	dú	dúkò	dúkó	'follow'
		sʉ	súkò	súkó	'pour out'
CVC	'v-copy'	cìk	cíkì	cìkí	'save'
		cík	cíkì	cíkí	'be cut'
CVCV	-a	fùmo	fúmà	fùmá	'build'
		lúmo	lúmà	lúmá	'pierce'
caa	-ŋ-	ntàa	ntáŋà	ntàŋá	'cross over'
		sáa	sáŋà	sáŋá	'seek'

Although hortative and imperative moods resemble each other with respect to the verb suffix required, they differ in their tonal melodies. The hortative melody, ←H-L, follows the verb, with the replacive tone neutralizing tonal distinctions between lexically H and L verbs. There is no replacive suffixal H following the verb in the hortative mood, even when an object is present.

In contrast, the imperative melody is a floating H following the verb. This associates to the left, becoming a tone of the verb in its final pronunciation. In addition, a suffixal replacive H does follow an imperative verb, causing detachment and deletion of an immediately-following L on a following complement.

In addition to this regular imperative, there is also a sequential imperative that follows a previous command. It is formally distinct from either hortative or the regular imperative, consisting of a stem ←H-L and a suffixal H.

[13]'V-copy' means that the vowel of the verb stem is copied as the suffix.

Interrogative mood is not indicated by any distinctive tonal melody on the verb. It is usually marked by an interrogative word; but in the absence of one of these, it is indicated by an intonational rise at the end of the question.

(130) Tonal melodies for nonindicative moods

	MOOD	STEM	SFX
Hortative	$\emptyset$	←H L	$\emptyset$
Imperative (verb medial)	$\emptyset$	H	H→
(verb final)	$\emptyset$	H L	$\emptyset$
Consecutive imperative (verb final)	$\emptyset$	←H L	$\emptyset$
(verb medial)	$\emptyset$	←H H	H→

Hortative. Hortative is used to express an intention, permission, a wish, or a prohibition. The subject of the verb may be first, second, or third person, in contrast with the imperative.

The affirmative hortative mentioned above has a different tonal melody than the negated counterpart, as seen in (131).

(131) Hortative tonal melodies

HORT	MOOD	NEG	STEM	SFX
AFF PFV	$\emptyset$		←H L	$\emptyset$
IMPF	$\emptyset$		←H L	H→
NEG	$\emptyset$	àyí	L	H→
or	lè	à	L	H→

Affirmative hortatives have a H-L melody regardless of the lexical tone of the verb, as seen in (132).

(132) *Nye fum-a   mi-mbɛr.*
```
     |   |   |        |   /\
     L  L←HL          L   L H
```
3s   build-HORT C4-house
He should build some houses!

This tone melody is maintained for monosyllabic verbs as well, since Kɔɔzime allows for the association of multiple tones with a single, short vowel. This is seen in (133).

(133) *Nye to-k   θ-mbɛr!*
　　　 |　 |⌐``、 　 /\
　　　 L　 H|←H L L　 L H
　　 3s　　go-HORT c3-house
　　 He should go home!

Negating hortative constructions is done in one of two ways—either through the use of the negative hortative marker *àyí* or by using *le* 'with' and the negated infinitive. Stem L and suffixal H accompany both of these constructions. In negated hortative constructions there is no suffix to the verb indicating hortative mood. These are shown in (134) and (135).

(134) *Nye ayi   fumo   mi-mbɛr.*
　　　 |　| |　　　　　|　 、　　　　 |　 /\
　　　 L　L H　　　　 L　 L　H→　　 L　L H
　　 3s　NEG^HORT build NEG NEG c4-house
　　 He should not build any houses. *or* Don't let him build any houses!

(135) *Nye le   a-fumo   mi-mbɛr.*
　　　 |　 |　　　　|　|　 `、　　　　　|　 /\
　　　 L　L |←H L L　 L　　 H→　　　 L　L H
　　 3s　 with NEG^INF-build NEG^INF NEG^INF c4-house
　　 He should not build any houses. *or* Don't let him build any houses!

The hortative in (136) shows progressive or habitual action through the use of the imperfective auxiliary *di* 'stay'.

(136) *Nye di-ke   fumo   mi-mbɛr.*
　　　 |　 |　\　　　 |　 、　　　　 |　 /\
　　　 L　 L←H L　　 L　 L　H→　　 L　L H
　　 3s　 stay-HORT build HORT HORT c4-house
　　 He should continuously build houses.

Imperative. Affirmative imperative involves a single floating H added to the verb and a replacive suffixal H following the verb. The tense marker for negative imperative is *à* followed by a stem L and a suffixal H, as summarized in (137).

(137) Tonal melodies for the imperative mood

IMP		MOOD	NEG	STEM	SFX
AFF	(verb medial)	$\emptyset$		H	H→
	(verb final)	$\emptyset$		HL	$\emptyset$
NEG		$\emptyset$	à	L	H→

In (138)–(140), H verbs are seen to become H-H (138) after the addition of this stem tone, while L verbs become L-H (139) and toneless verbs become H (140).

(138) Jam-a   bi-kwan   bi!
   | | | /\   /\
   H H   H→   L L L   H L
   cook-IMP IMP C8-plantains C8^these
   Cook these plantains!

(139) Be-k   bi-kwan   bi!
   | \ | /\   /\
   L H   H→   L L L   H L
   plant-IMP IMP C8-plantains C8^these
   Plant these plantains!

(140) De-k   me-de   ma!
     \ | | /\
     H   H→   L L H L
   eat-IMP IMP C6-food this^C6
   Eat this food!

Sentence-final verbs, which have the segmental imperative suffix -a, receive an additional L, as in (141).

(141) Jam-aa!
   | |\
   H   H L
   cook-IMP^VERB^S^FINAL
   Cook (it)!

Prohibitions are expressed as a negative imperative, which employs the negation marker à followed by the verb, a stem L, and a suffixal H, as in (142). In negative commands, the verb does not include the segmental suffix encountered in affirmative commands.

(142) *A   fumo   mi-mbɛr!*

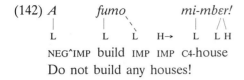

```
 |           |    \          |    /\
 L          L    L    H→    L    L H
```
NEG^IMP build IMP IMP C4-house
Do not build any houses!

Commands addressed to two or more persons use the plural marker (PL) *gá*, which becomes *gâ* word-finally, and occurs after the suffixal H, as in (143). This plural morpheme is also encountered in prohibitions, as in (144). Once again, because the negative marker is present, the segmental imperative suffix is not present.

(143) *Fum-a   ga mi-mbɛr!*
```
 |   |        |     |    /\
 L   L    H→|  H    L    L H
```
build-IMP IMP PL C4-house
Build houses (you plural)!

(144) *A   di   ga kʉl!*
```
 |    |  \          |   /\
 L    L  L    H→|   H  L  H
```
NEG stay IMP IMP PL outside
Don't stay outside (you plural)!

Imperfective aspect in the imperative mood is conveyed by the auxiliary *di* 'stay' rather than by the locative verb *be*, as seen in (145).

(145) *Di-ke   de   me-de ma!*
```
 |  |     \           |   |    /\
 L  H      L    H→    L   L   H L
```
stay-IMP eat IMP IMP C6-food C6^this
Keep on eating this food!

Consecutive imperative. Consecutive imperatives exist only in the affirmative. There are two tonal melodies, presented in (146), which depend upon the location of the verb in the sentence.

(146) The consecutive imperative construction

Consecutive imperative	MOOD	NEG	STEM	SFX
(verb medial)	-à		←H H	H→
(verb final)	-à		←H L	∅

This mood is used noninitially in a chain of commands. It occurs in nonfinal position in (147), where it is reflected in the H-H melody of the verb.

(147) *Go-a*   *fumo*   *mi-mbɛr!*

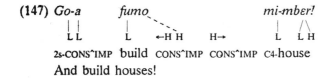

    L L   L   ←H H   H→   L   L H

2s-CONS^IMP build CONS^IMP CONS^IMP C4-house

And build houses!

In (148), it occurs in utterance-final position, where the verb has a H-L melody.

(148) *Go-a*   *fumo!*

    L L   L   ←H L

2s-CONS^IMP build IMP

And build!

Interrogative. Interrogative mood is distinguished from imperative and hortative by the possibility of marking tense. It is distinguished from indicative by the incompatibility between focussing a verb complement and addressing a question. It is also distinguished from the other moods by the presence of an overt interrogative marker—interrogative word or a distinctive, rising intonation.

On the other hand, there is a structural resemblance between indicative and interrogative moods. A yes/no question can be derived from a statement simply by adding rising intonation, as in (149), which is derived from (30). The tone on *mbɛr* 'house' rises to a height equal to that of the H at the beginning of the sentence.

(149) *Be a si   fumo   mi-mbɛr?*

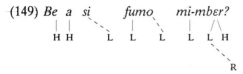

3p P2 PFV P2 build P2 C4-house INT
So they built some houses (yesterday or before)?

In other interrogative constructions, the slightly falling utterance-final intonation of the indicative occurs along with an interrogative word somewhere in the construction. In (150), the interrogative word *zê* 'is it?', is used to ask a yes/no question similar to that of (149). Note the presence of falling intonation with the question word instead of the rising intonation for questions without such a word. The difference between these two questions is that (149) occurs in the context of an assertion's having been made 'they built some houses', while (150) can occur more freely.

(150) *Ze   be a si   fumo   mi-mbɛr?*

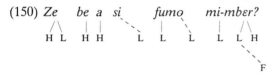

is^it? 3p P2 PFV P2 build P2 C4-house INT
Is it true that they built some houses (in the remote past)?

Interrogative words other than *zê* 'is it true?' cannot occur in a construction with *si* (perfective). This indicates that other interrogative words are in the same syntactic class as the focus marker, which is likewise incompatible with the perfective marker. See examples (118–120) above, where interrogative morphemes meaning 'who?', 'where?', and 'what?' are used.

Rhetorical questions are discussed in §5 and illustrated by (117), which is clearly rhetorical due to the occurrence together of negative, interrogative, and perfective markers. Any real question may also be used rhetorically. When a 'normal' question is asked, it is necessary to decide whether or not it should have a rhetorical or nonrhetorical reading. This is done on the basis of pragmatic considerations. The constellation of interrogative, negative, and perfective markers removes such ambiguity since such a construction is capable of bearing only a rhetorical reading.

8. Conclusion

This study of the Kɔɔzime verbal system has detailed a rich and varied verb-marking system. It has been seen that an extensive inventory of tense and aspect markers exists, which enables its speakers to refer contrastively and with precision to events that are distinct with regard to time and internal consistency. There is, alongside the basic tense-marking system, a parallel system of relative tenses, as well as numerous possibilities for indicating mood and negation.

In the course of this study, we have examined in detail the multiple tonal markers which play an important role in distinguishing the verbal constructions from each other. The numerous replacive tones found among Kɔɔzime grammatical markers, some of which occur alongside of and in contrast with the more normal floating tones common in autosegmental descriptions, show the need for an autosegmental convention to indicate replacive tones. We have suggested as one possible means of notation the use of an arrow on the tonal tier with no change to existing association lines.

In conclusion, three lists follow which summarize many of the numerous tonal melodies found in the Kɔɔzime verbal system.

(151) Relative tense summary

CONS REL tense	REL	TNS	NEG	STEM	SFX
3p subjects					
Following P2	∅			H . . . -ɔ́ɔ̀	H→
Elsewhere	∅			H . . . L	H→
Other subjects	∅			H . . . L	H→
REL P1					
AFF	←H *o*	L		H . . . L	H→
NEG 'with' + 'yet'	*le*		←H *à pà*	H . . . L	H→

(152) Absolute tense summary

	NEG	TNS	NEG	STEM	SFX
P2					
AFF		á		L...L	∅
NEG		á	←H à	H...L	H→
P1					
AFF		L		H...L	H→
NEG		L	←H à	H...L	H→
PRES					
No copula		H		∅	∅
Object focus AFF		H		H	H→
Subject focus or dependent clause					
AFF (verb medial)		∅		←H H	H→
AFF (verb final)		∅		←H L	∅
NEG neutral		∅	←H à	L	H→
NEG IMPF		∅	←H à	L	H→
NEG HAB (verb medial)		∅	á	←H H	H→
NEG HAB (verb final)		∅	á	←H L	∅
PRF		←H		L	H→
		[+Ht]		L	H→
FUT					
Nonfocus					
AFF		ó		H...L	H→
NEG	a	ŋá		H...L	H→
Subject focus		ngá		H...L	H→
Dependent clauses		ngá		H...L	H→
CONS FUT		←H ò		H...L	H→

(153) Nonindicative mood summary

INF	MOOD	NEG	STEM	SFX
AFF	è-		H . . . L	H→
NEG	∅	à	H . . . L	H→
HORT				
AFF			←H L	∅
AFF (HAB)			←H L	H→
NEG		àyí	L	H→
IMP				
AFF (verb medial)			H	H→
AFF (verb final)			HL	∅
NEG		à	L	H→
CONS IMP				
(verb medial)	-à		←H H	H→
(verb final)	-à		←H L	∅

References

Barreteau, Daniel and Keith H. Beavon. 1989. Les catégories grammaticales en koozime. In Daniel Barreteau and Robert Hedinger (eds.), Descriptions de langues camerounaises, 333–408. Paris: Agence de Coopération Culturelle et Technique et ORSTOM.

Beavon, Keith H. 1978. A comparative analysis and historical reconstruction of Konsime noun class prefixes and consonantal phonemes. ms.

———. 1983a. A phonology of Konzime. Africana Linguistica IX. Annales, Sciences Humaines, 110:110–36. Tervuren: Musée Royal de l'Afrique Centrale.

———. 1983b. Expressions of location in Kɔɔzime. Journal of West African Languages 13(2):33–51.

———. 1984a. A partial typology of Konzime (Bantu) discourse. In Robert E. Longacre (ed.), Theory and application in processing texts in non-Indoeuropean languages, 211–71. Hamburg: Helmut Buske Verlag.

———. 1984b. Tone and intonation in Konzime. Cahiers du Département des Langues Africaines et Linguistique 3:23–37. Yaoundé, Cameroon: University of Yaoundé.

———. 1985. Two relativization strategies in Kɔɔzime discourse. Journal of West African Languages 15(1):31–56.

————. 1986. Pronominal systems: Konzime. In Ursula Wiesemann (ed.), Pronominal systems, 163–84. Continuum Schriftenreihe Zur Linguistik 5. Tübingen: Gunter Narr Verlag.

————. 1990. The locative verb in Kɔɔzime: Its semantic, phonological, morphological and syntactic attributes. ms.

Comrie, Bernard. 1976. Aspect. Cambridge: Cambridge University Press.

Goldsmith, John A. 1976. Autosegmental phonology. Bloomington: Indiana University Linguistics Club.

Guthrie, Malcolm. 1971. Comparative Bantu 2. Farnborough, England: Gregg International Publishers.

Le système temporel et aspectuel de la langue nɔmaándɛ

Patricia Wilkendorf

Résumé

Dans la langue nɔmaándɛ du Cameroun, on trouve un système verbal caractérisé par un chevauchement de temps et d'aspect. Certaines variations de tons et de segments dans le complexe pronominal indiquent un changement temporel. L'aspect perfectif est caractérisé par des tons grammaticaux sur le radical verbal, tons qui indiquent à la fois l'aspect et le temps du verbe. En plus, au futur proche (FI) on relève un suffixe -Vk qui s'ajoute au radical verbal pour le rendre distinct du présent. Ce système amène à l'emploi de plusieurs marques temporelles qui semblent redondantes dans certains cas, mais qui par contre ne permettent qu'une opposition minimale dans d'autres cas. L'aspect imperfectif se divise en deux catégories: les actions et les états habituels et les actions progressives. Des morphèmes segmentaux distinctifs au niveau du complexe pronominal (au présent et au futur) et l'auxiliaire ɔbá 'être' (aux temps passé) s'emploient pour exprimer une action habituelle. Les actions progressives sont caractérisées par la présence d'une phrase locative qui comprend la particule locative, un ton flottant haut, et le verbe à l'infinitif. Les fonctions du parfait en nɔmaándɛ font aussi partie de cette étude, ainsi que les formes de l'énoncé verbal au négatif, aussi bien au perfectif qu'à l'imperfectif.

Abstract

The Nɔmaándɛ language of Central Cameroon has a verbal system characterized by an overlapping of temporal and aspectual markings. In the pronominal complex, which precedes the verb, various segmental and suprasegmental changes denote distinctions in tense only. Perfective aspect makes use of grammatical tones on the verb stem which indicate both the aspect and the tense of the verb. The today future (FI) makes use of a suffix -Vk on the verb stem in order to distinguish it from the perfective present.

105

This system leads to redundancy in the case of certain tenses but it allows only minimal contrast in others. Imperfective aspect is divided into two categories: habitual and progressive. Habitual actions and states are marked by distinctly habitual morphemes in the pronominal complex (in the present and future tenses) or by the auxiliary verb ɔbá 'to be' (in the past tenses). Progressive actions are denoted by the use of a locative phrase which consists of the locative particle, a high floating tone and the infinitive form of the verb. The uses of the perfect form in Nɔmaándé are also discussed, as well as the negative forms of the verb phrase in both the perfective and imperfective aspects.

Cette étude[1] qui porte sur le système temporel et aspectuel du nɔmaándé[2] est une révision des études antérieures sur l'aspect (Wilkendorf 1985) et sur le temps (Wilkendorf 1986), ayant pour but d'examiner les rapprochements qui existent entre les deux systèmes. Nous avons profité en même temps d'apporter à notre première analyse certaines modifications nécessaires. Cette révision s'est rendue possible grâce aux données supplémentaires, ainsi qu'à une meilleure compréhension du système tonal.

Le système des temps verbaux en nɔmaándé est caractérisé par des tons grammaticaux, aussi bien au niveau du complexe pronominal, qu'au niveau

---

[1]La présente étude se base sur un corpus recueilli lors des séjours à Tchekos entre 1983 et 1987, dans le cadre d'un accord de coopération entre le Ministère de l'Enseignement Supérieur, de l'Informatique et de la Recherche Scientifique (MESIRES) et la Société Internationale de Linguistique (SIL) (Permis de recherche N°. 21/87). Le principal dialecte étudié est celui de Tchekos. Le corpus sur lequel est basée cette étude comporte aussi bien des conjugaisons fournies par nos aides linguistiques que des récits enregistrés sur cassette, entre autres des contes, des descriptions, etc. C'est grâce à nos deux aides linguistiques MM. Emmanuel Atoko et Cosmas Babouaken que ce corpus a pu être revu, contrôlé et traduit. Nous aimerions exprimer notre reconnaissance à ces deux hommes en particulier pour l'aide précieuse qu'ils nous ont apportée. Nous voulons aussi remercier Professeur Bernard Comrie pour ses conseils sur le temps et l'aspect, et nos collègues Dr. Stephen Anderson (pour des conseils sur le ton), Dr. Carol Stanley (pour toute l'aide qu'elle a donnée sur la terminologie française), et Mme Carolyn Taylor (pour des discussions concernant le système verbal du nɔmaándé).

[2]La langue nɔmaándé est le parler d'un groupe linguistique assez restreint (entre 4000 et 5000 locuteurs), connu officiellement sous le nom 'lemandé'. Ce groupe habite au Cameroun dans la province du Centre, au département du Mbam, à l'arrondissement de Bokito. Les Lemandé habitent 7 villages, plus un quartier de la ville de Bokito et ils se comprennent mutuellement entre eux. La langue nɔmaándé est une langue bantu classifiée A.46 par Guthrie (1971:32) et N° 512 dans l'ALCAM (Dieu et Renaud 1983:53). On y trouve de l'harmonie vocalique, des voyelles longues, des diphtongues et une opposition de deux tons lexicales (H et B).

du verbe lui-même.[3] Le temps est aussi marqué par des morphèmes segmentaux, qui se trouvent dans le complexe pronominal. Ce système sera présenté ci-dessous à la §1.2.

Il y a amalgame des systèmes aspectuel et temporel au niveau du radical verbal. Les formes qui comportent à la fois des marques aspectuelle et temporelle seront décrites à la §2.1. Il y a toutefois des cas où on ne relève que des marques aspectuelles. Ceux-ci seront traités à la §4.

Pour que notre description du système temporel et aspectuel du nɔmaándɛ soit la plus compréhensive que possible, nous avons tenu à aborder brièvement trois autres sujets, à savoir: le suffixe -*Vk* qui apparaît assez souvent (cf. §3), le sens du parfait (cf. §5), et finalement, le négatif (cf. §6).

1. Le temps

Nous opérons une distinction entre le temps absolu et le temps relatif. En nous basant sur le travail de Comrie, nous employons le terme TEMPS ABSOLU comme perspectif (optique) du temps qui établit le présent comme point de référence (Comrie 1985:36). Les temps absolus peuvent être définis indépendamment d'un certain contexte (Comrie 1985:26). La présente étude ne traite que le temps absolu en nɔmaándɛ.

1.1. Degrés d'éloignement sur le plan temporel. Comme dans la plupart des langues bantu, le nɔmaándɛ distingue plusieurs temps au passé (passé immédiat—P0, passé premier degré—P1, passé deuxième degré—P2, et passé troisième degré—P3), un temps au présent (PR), et plusieurs temps au futur (futur immédiat—F0, futur premier degré—F1, futur deuxième degré—F2, et futur troisième degré—F3).

Il faut tout d'abord souligner que le futur immédiat (F0) utilise un calque linguistique de français qui le distingue des autres temps. Les pronoms indépendants sans marque temporelle (Taylor 1983) se combinent avec l'infinitif du verbe ɔcɔba 'aller,' suivi d'un syntagme locatif qui consiste en un morphème locatif en plus que l'infinitif du verbe principal, pour former

---

[3]Les tons sont marqués sur les voyelles de la manière suivante:
   ton haut (ʜ) = ´
   ton bas (ʙ) = pas de marque
   et ton haut abaissé (ꜝʜ) = ꜝ´
(voir (31) pour l'occurrence de ce dernier ton).

ce futur. Les règles tonales qui opèrent sur ce syntagme locatif sont
présentées à la §4.2.[4]

(1)   Mí   ɔ-cɔb-a   o-o-!búm-e.
      1s   cl5^INF-aller-VF LOC-cl5^INF-chasser-VF
      Je vais (les) chasser (tout de suite).

(2)   Tú   ɔ-cɔb-a   ɔ-ɔ-cábɛn-a.
      1p   cl5^INF-aller-VF LOC-cl5^INF-courrir-VF
      Nous allons courrir (tout de suite).

Les règles tonales qui opèrent sur ce syntagme locatif sont présentées à
la §4.2. Les formes qui nous intéressent ici sont surtout celles où on relève
le complexe pronominal et le radical verbal. Or, le futur immédiat a une
forme particulière en ce qu'elle est constituée d'un calque. Il n'est donc
pas question d'essayer d'intégrer cette forme dans le système verbal du
nɔmaándé tel qu'il est présenté ici.

Le tableau (4) servira à montrer quand et, de quelle manière, chaque
temps s'emploie. Les restrictions d'occurrence avec les adverbes temporels
donnés à titre d'exemple montrent plus précisément les limites des temps
en langue nɔmaándé (Wilkendorf 1986:66).

En nɔmaándé, comme dans la plupart des langues où on relève des
degrés d'éloignement (Comrie 1985:85), le point de référence est le présent. En regardant le tableau (4) à droit, on constate un chevauchement
de temps à deux endroits, à savoir, au niveau des formes P1 et P0 et celui
des formes P3 et P2. Les limites entre ces deux dernières formes du passé,
(P3 et P2), semblent ne pas être très fixes pour les locuteurs de la langue.
Quant au chevauchement entre P1 et P0, il est intéressant à noter que le
passé immédiat (P0) peut être utilisé pour la même étendue du temps que
le passé premier degré (P1), à condition que l'action a encore des répercussions au moment de l'énoncé. Certains locuteurs insistent que P0 ne
peut être utilisé avec *ne buutúé* 'dans la nuit' sauf avant 7 heures du matin.

(3)   Í-me-mí búm-ék-e   ne   buutúé.
      1s-P0-1s chasser-DUR-VF avec nuit
      J'ai chassé pendant la nuit (et je suis encore fatigué).

---

[4]Dans cet article les exemples en paires représentent les verbes à tons haut et bas
respectivement.

(4) Degrés d'éloignement temporels et leurs restrictions d'occurrence

ADVERBES TEMPORELS	DEGRES D'ELOIGNEMENT DE TEMPS							
	P3	P2	P1	P0	PR	F1	F2	F3
buáya il y a longtemps	X		.		.		.	.
oolí ɔwɔ́ ŋa hɔ́la le mois passé	X		.		.		.	.
hɛnaánɔ sɔndɛ ífendí ... X		X	.		.		.	. il y a deux semaines
hɛnaánɔ ahanyɛ ahé ŋa hɔ́la la semaine passée		X	.		.		.	.
nyióffónyínyí avant hier		X	.		.		.	.
buóci nanyiɔ́fɔ́ .... X hier soir			.		.		.	.
ne buutúé dans la nuit			X	X	.		.	.
nɔ́ɔnɔyá ce matin			X	X	.		.	.
wayáŋa injéŋí ífendí il y a deux heures			X	X	.		.	.
híambaya .... X tout à l'heure (passé)				X	.		.	.
aámbaya/ekúlú eéye maintenant					X		.	.
híambaya tout de suite (futur)						X	.	.
nanyiɔ́fɔ́ .... X ce soir						X	.	.
nɔyá nɔ́ɔnɔyá demain matin							X	.
oolí awɔ́ ŋa fáakɔna le mois prochain							X	.
a tuɔ́ŋɔ túfendí .... X dans deux ans								.
buɔ́sé un jour (indéterminé)								X
te nyiényí .... X n'importe quand								

Il faut aussi souligner que la différence entre les temps du futur F2 et F3
n'est pas une différence du degré d'éloignement du temps, mais plutôt une
différence de certitude concernant *si*, ou *quand*, l'action va se réaliser. Le
temps du futur F2 indique que l'action est plus ou moins sûre de se passer
dans un futur à partir du demain. Par contre, le futur F3 s'emploie pour
exprimer un futur indéterminé où on n'est pas du tout sûr de la réalisation
de l'action.

1.2. Marques temporelles au complexe pronominal. Le complexe pronominal est employé comme pronom sujet d'un énoncé. Il est susceptible
d'avoir trois composants.

(5)   un pronom sujet initial
        une marque temporelle
        un pronom sujet final

Le premier élément est le pronom sujet initial qui s'accorde toujours
avec la classe nominale du sujet. (Il est à noter que dans nos exemples, les
référants étant des noms du genre humain, c'est-à-dire des classes 1 et 2,
les pronoms substituts sont donc ceux de ces deux classes). Ce pronom
initial du complexe disparaît au moment où le nom sujet est présent.

(6)   *U-ŋɔ-ɔ́ tɔ́lí-ák-a   tu-áyé   tú-koli.*
        3s-P3-3s tendre-DUR-VF c13-3s^PS c13-corde
        Il avait tendu ses pièges.

(7)   *Ɔ-ɔcɔ   ŋɔ-ɔ́ tɔ́lí-ák-a   tu-áyé   tú-koli.*
        c1-homme P3-3s tendre-DUR-VF c13-3s^PS c13-corde
        L'homme avait tendu ses pièges.

Ensuite, le complexe pronominal comporte une marque de temps qui se
présente sous trois formes segmentales différentes, qui restent invariables,
quelle que soit la personne.

(8)   *ŋa* marque les temps du passé P1, P2, et P3, ainsi que le présent
              (PR) et le futur F1.
        ka marque les temps du futur F2 et F3.
        ma marque le passé immédiat, ce qui implique souvent le parfait
              (§4).

Il nous semble qu'on pourrait bien considérer ces marques temporelles
comme étant le noyau du complexe pronominal; ceci, du fait que la

marque temporelle est le plus stable des trois composants du complexe. Pour une description plus détaillée du complexe pronominal, voir §4.1.

A la fin du complexe pronominal se trouve un pronom sujet final. A la différence du pronom sujet initial, ce pronom final ne change pas de forme selon la classe nominale du sujet. Il est à souligner que ce pronom final est susceptible de disparaître. Quand la voyelle finale de ce pronom porte un ton haut, elle disparaît devant un verbe à ton bas. Pourtant, le ton haut reste pour dominer le ton bas lexical de la première syllabe du verbe.

(9)   *U-ŋa fá!n-ák-a   nu-fule.*
      3s-P3 lire-DUR-VF cl1-livre
      Il/Elle a lu le livre.

Dans le cas des verbes à ton haut, un pronom final portant un ton haut ne peut pas disparaître parce qu'il n'y aurait aucune trace de ce pronom dans le syntagme verbal, étant que le verbe suivant porte déjà un ton haut.

(10) *U-ŋe-é búm-ék-e.*
      3s-P3-3s chasser-DUR-VF
      Il/Elle a chassé.

Quant au pronom initial du complexe, sa disparition, comme nous l'avons déjà vu, est aussi prévisible, la présence du nom sujet imposant forcément la disparition de ce pronom. Les voyelles du complexe pronominal sont régies par le système d'harmonie vocalique de la langue.[5] Mais le système d'harmonie vocalique ne régit pas seulement les voyelles d'un seul et même mot. Son influence est susceptible de dépasser les frontières morphologiques. Il faut dire que ce phénomène est limité au syntagme verbal ou, le cas échéant, au pronom objet direct.

Une liste des pronoms sujet en positions initiale et finale pour toutes les personnes se trouvent au tableau (11) (voir Wilkendorf 1986:67).

---

[5]Pour une description détaillée de ce système d'harmonie vocalique en nɔmaándɛ, voir Scruggs 1983:72. Les voyelles du complexe pronominal changent selon celles du verbe qui suit. Font exception les cas où il y a un pronom objet qui intervient; là, les voyelles du complexe pronominal s'accordent avec celles de ce pronom objet.

(11) ɛ- TMP -amɛ (1s)[6]   tɔ- TMP -asɔ (1p)
      ɔ- TMP -ɔɔ   (2s)   nɔ- TMP -anɔ (2p)
      u- TMP -aa   (3s)   bá- TMP -abɔ (3p)

Le pronom sujet initial de la troisième personne du pluriel *bá* porte un
ton haut qui reste invariable, quel que soit le temps du verbe. Or, comme
tous les autres segments pronominaux du complexe n'ont pas de tons
lexicaux, le ton de ceux-ci varie donc selon le schéma tonal imposé par la
marque temporelle. Ce schéma est susceptible de changer selon le temps
qu'on veut exprimer. Ils s'étendent sur tous les trois segments du complexe.
Le tableau (12) montre les schémas tonaux des différentes marques temporelles (voir Wilkendorf 1986:68).

(12)

TEMPS	COMPLEXE PRONOMINAL[7]	TEMPS	COMPLEXE PRONOMINAL
(P3)	*x-ŋa-x* B B H	(PR)	*x-ŋa-x* B B H
(P2)	*x-ŋa-x* H B B	(F1)	*x-ŋa-x* B B H
(P1)	*x-ŋa-x* B H B	(F2)	*x-ka-x* B H B
(P0)	*x-ma-x* H B H/s B/p	(F3)	*x-ka-x* B B H

Les distinctions temporelles manifestées dans le complexe pronominal
sont les suivantes:

(a) Les temps du passé P3, P2, et P1 se distinguent entre eux par des
    schémas tonaux distincts. Les temps du passé, P2 et P1, se distinguent
    du présent et du futur premier degré (F1) par la même chose.

(b) Les temps du futur F2 et F3 se distinguent entre eux par des schémas
    tonaux distincts aussi. Les deux ne se confondent jamais avec les autres

---

[6]Les marques du temps varient selon le temps de l'action décrite (cf. (8)). La
première voyelle du pronom final (*a* pour toutes les personnes sauf 2s) s'élide avec la
voyelle de la marque temporelle. Cette première voyelle du pronom final se
réapparaîtra quand la marque temporelle est absente (cf. §4.1).

[7]Le symbole *x* dans ce tableau signifie l'emplacement des pronoms sujets en
positions initiale et finale qui changent selon le nombre et la personne du sujet (voir
(11)).

temps à cause de la marque temporelle *ka*, qui n'est révélée que dans ces temps.

(c) Le temps du passé immédiat (P0) est distinct de toutes les autres formes par sa marque temporelle *ma*. Le schéma tonal sur le complexe pronominal au passé immédiat est H-B-H au singulier et H-B-B au pluriel. Toutefois même si le schéma tonal n'est pas invariable, la présence de *ma* montre clairement de quel temps il est question.

Le temps du passé troisième degré (P3), le présent (PR), et le temps du futur premier degré (F1) ont tous le même schéma tonal sur le complexe pronominal, ainsi que la même marque temporelle *ŋa*, ce qui prêterait à la confusion quand il s'agissait d'identifier le temps du verbe. Il faut cependant souligner que ces complexes pronominaux ne suffisent pas à eux-mêmes à exprimer le temps verbal. Il doivent être toujours suivis d'un radical verbal qui porte, lui aussi, un ton propre au temps exprimé. L'ambiguïté sera donc enlevée par le radical verbal au perfectif (cf. §2) et par des changements segmentaux au niveau du complex pronominal lorsqu'il s'agit de l'imperfectif (cf. §4).

2. Le perfectif

Dans le système aspectuel du nɔmaándɛ il y a lieu d'opérer une distinction trinaire, à savoir: perfectif (PF), imperfectif (IPF), et parfait (PAR). En empruntant notre terminologie à Comrie (1976), nous accordons à ces trois catégories les définitions suivantes:

(13) perfectif   le procès est envisagé dans sa totalité
     imperfectif le procès est envisagé sous l'angle de son déroulement
     parfait   le procès est envisagé comme accompli mais toutefois, continuant, au moins dans ses conséquences, au moment de l'acte de la parole

Il y a en nɔmaándɛ un chevauchement entre l'aspect et le temps. Nous voyons ce chevauchement en examinant l'aspect perfectif. Cet aspect se différencie en huit valeurs aspectuelles selon la relation temporelle du procès au moment de l'énoncé:

(14)   perfectif passé immédiat
        perfectif passé premier degré
        perfectif passé deuxième degré
        perfectif passé troisième degré
        perfectif futur premier degré
        perfectif futur deuxième degré
        perfectif futur troisième degré
        perfectif présent[8]

Avant d'entrer dans les détails de l'analyse du perfectif, nous voulons décrire la structure du radical verbal qui existe en nɔmaándɛ. Comme dans presque toutes les langues bantu (Greenberg 1948:200), la langue nɔmaándɛ a deux classes verbales principales: l'une qui comporte les verbes à ton haut et, l'autre, les verbes à ton bas. Le schéma syllabique canonique pour la racine verbale semble être -CVC- avec un suffixe vocalique obligatoire en tant qu'extension de la racine. Cette combinaison explique la structure dissyllabique du radical verbal. En examinant les radicaux verbaux, nous avons laissé de côté toutes les extensions verbales déjà identifiées (Taylor 1984), sauf ce suffixe vocalique qui se trouve toujours en finale du syntagme verbal après toutes autres extensions éventuelles.

Nous continuons maintenant la description des marques à la fois aspectuelle et temporelle dans le radical verbal en donnant d'abord un aperçu global des réalisations tonales dans le tableau (15) ci-dessous. Il est à noter que les réalisations tonales au P3 et au P2 sur le radical des verbes à ton bas diffèrent de celles décrites dans l'étude antérieure sur le temps en nɔmaándɛ (Wilkendorf 1986:69). Toutes les réalisations tonales seront discutées aux sections suivantes.

---

[8]Ces termes sont empruntés à Stanley (1986).

(15)

TEMPS	COMPLEXE PRONOMINAL (du 1p)	RADICAL VERBAL	
		TON H	TON B
P3	tɔ-ŋa-sɔ	HH	H!H
	B B H		
P2	tɔ-ŋa-sɔ	HH	HB
	H B B		
P1	tɔ-ŋa-sɔ	HH	BB
	B H B		
P0	tɔ-ma-sɔ	HB	BB
	H B B/p (H/s)		
PR	tɔ-ŋa-sɔ	BB	HB
	B B H		
F1	tɔ-ŋa-sɔ	H!H	HB
	B B H		
F2	tɔ-ka-sɔ	HH	BB
	B H B		
F3	tɔ-ka-sɔ	HH	HB
	B B H		

Perfectif passé immédiat. En formulant ces schémas de réalisation tonale, nous avons suivi la méthode autosegmentale de Goldsmith (1976). Pour le nɔmaándɛ́ les règles suivantes se montrent nécessaires:

(a) certains des morphèmes en nɔmaándɛ́ portent des tons lexicaux,

(b) un ton flottant haut (seulement) cherche à s'associer avec la première syllabe à droit et il dissocie tout autre ton déjà y associé,

(c) toute syllabe pas encore associée avec un ton s'associe avec le premier ton à gauche sans dissocier ce ton d'une autre syllabe,

(d) un ton flottant bas ne cherche pas de syllabe pour s'y associer, et

(e) comme règle phonétique tardive, l'abaissement tonal constaté qu'il y a un abaissement du registre tonal chaque fois qu'un ton haut suit un ton bas (voir aussi (31)).

L'aspect perfectif au passé immédiat se présente sous la forme d'un ton flottant bas qui domine le ton de la deuxième syllabe du radical verbal (RAD), donnant ainsi le schéma suivant:

(16)   PF-P0: RAD-B$(-Vk)$-V

Le radical verbal est suivi de trois suffixes; le premier n'étant qu'un ton bas, le suffixe -*Vk* étant sans ton et la voyelle finale qui porte un ton bas. La réalisation tonale de ce schéma se présente de la manière suivante:

(17)   PF-P0:

$$
\begin{array}{ccccccc}
\text{S} & + & & + & (Vk) & + & \text{V} \\
| & & & & & & | \\
\text{H/B} & + & \text{B} & + & & + & \text{B}
\end{array}
$$

ce qui donne: HB(B) pour les verbes à ton H
                BB(B) pour les verbes à ton B

Le symbole S représente la syllabe de la racine au niveau segmental. Le symbole plus (+) représente une limite morphologique. Comme nous l'avons déjà vu ci-dessus à la §2, le radical verbal du nɔmaándé est dissyllabique où la voyelle finale suit toutes les extensions verbales éventuelles. Le fait que -*Vk* est entre parenthèses signifie que ce suffixe (à valeur de duratif) est facultatif. Il est susceptible de s'ajouter au radical (entre la racine et la voyelle finale) dans certains cas que nous examinerons en détail ci-dessous à la §3. Le symbole H/B dénote le ton lexical du verbe, soit ton haut (H), soit ton bas (B). Le ton flottant sera toujours noté soit comme préfixe, avec le ton mis devant le ton lexical, soit comme suffixe, avec le ton mis après le ton lexical. Le suffixe -*Vk*, n'ayant pas de ton, cherche un ton à gauche. Ainsi ce suffixe s'associe avec le ton flottant bas. Mais si le suffixe -*Vk* n'est pas présent, le ton flottant bas reste flottant. En bas du schéma se trouve sa réalisation phonétique selon le ton lexical du verbe.

(18)   *Tɔ́-ma-sɔ lɔ́ŋ-ɔk-ɔ.*
       1p-P0-1p   appeler-DUR-VF
       Nous (les) avons appelé (tout à l'heure).

(19)   *É-ma-mɛ́ hɛŋ-a   ma-kɛ́lɛ́.*
       1s-P0-1s   remplacer-VF   c6a-sel
       J'ai remplacé le sel (tout à l'heure).

Perfectif passé premier degré. Cet aspect sert à exprimer une action qui s'est passée assez récemment, dans la journée même. Le principe de réalisation tonale pour le radical verbal au perfectif passé premier degré s'emploie aussi au perfectif futur deuxième degré. Ce principe peut être représenté par le schéma suivant.

(20)   PF-P1/F2: RAD-ç(-*Vk*)-V

Le radical verbal est suivi d'un ton flottant qui copie (imite) le ton lexical du radical. Ce ton flottant copié est représenté par le symbole (Ç). La possibilité existe dans certains cas d'avoir le suffixe -*Vk* ajouté au radical après le ton flottant. La voyelle finale du radical reste toujours en dernière position. Sa réalisation tonale sur le radical est la suivante:

(21)   PF-P1:   S   +   +   (*Vk*) +   V
        (PF-F2) | ＿＿＿＿ |
                       H/B   +   H/B ＿ +   +   B
                                 (Ç)

        ce qui donne: HH(B) pour les verbes à ton H
                       BB(B) pour les verbes à ton B

Le ton flottant copié (Ç) est associé soit avec le suffixe -*Vk* (s'il est présent) soit avec la voyelle finale. Dans le dernier cas, un ton haut dominera le ton bas de la voyelle finale. Si le suffixe -*Vk* est présent, la voyelle finale prendra son ton bas.

(22)   *Ɛ-ŋá-mɛ táŋ-ák-a.*
       1s-P1-1s   parler-DUR-VF
       Je (leur) ai parlé (ce matin).

(23)   *Tu-ŋé-su ket-i.*
       1p-P1-1p   croire-VF
       Nous (y) avons cru (ce matin).

Perfectif passé deuxième degré. Dans le perfectif passé deuxième degré, l'action ou le fait se situe dans un passé plus ancien que la journée même: la veille ou quelques jours auparavant, la limite n'étant pas très claire entre ce temps et celui du passé troisième degré pour les locuteurs de la langue. Le principe de réalisation tonale peut-être représenté par le schéma suivant:

(24)   PF-P2/F3: H-RAD-∅(-*Vk*)-V

Il est à noter que ce même schéma s'emploie également au perfectif futur troisième degré. Sa réalisation tonale sur le radical verbal est la suivante:

(25)   PF-P2:   +   S   +   (Vk) +   V
       (PF-F3)
                         H   +   H/B   +   +   B

ce qui donne: HH(B) pour les verbes à ton H
              HB(B) pour les verbes à ton B

Le ton flottant haut a tendance à chercher la syllabe à droit et ainsi, il domine ici le ton de la première syllabe du radical verbal, pendant que la deuxième syllabe prend le ton lexical du verbe, qui est dissocié du radical. Comme pour le temps du passé P1 et pour le futur F2, la voyelle finale prend un ton bas, sauf lorsque le suffixe -*Vk* n'est pas present. Dans ce cas, elle prend le ton lexical du verbe.

(26)   *Ú-ŋa bét-á.*
       3s-P2 penser-VF
       Il a pensé (là-dessus) (hier).

(27)   *Nɔ́-ŋa-nɔ námb-ak-a   é-sɔmbɔlɔ.*
       2p-P2-2p cacher-DUR-VF c4-termites
       Vous avez caché les termites (hier).

Perfectif passé troisième degré. A la §1.2 ci-dessus, le problème de différencier entre les temps P3, F1 et PR a déjà été soulevé. Là, nous avons proposé que la solution se trouverait au niveau du radical verbal. Dans le perfectif passé troisième degré, nous proposons qu'il y a deux tons flottants, l'un qui précède étant un ton flottant haut, l'autre qui suit le radical verbal étant un ton flottant polarisé (P̥). Ici aussi, le suffixe -*Vk* est susceptible d'apparaître. Ce principe est représenté par le schéma suivant:

(28)   PF-P3: H-RAD-P̥(-*Vk*)-V

Sa réalisation tonale sur le radical étant complexe, nous la montrons en deux parties:

(29) PF-P3:   +   S   +   +   (Vk) +   V
                  H   +   H   +   B   +   +   B
                                    (P̥)

ce qui donne: HH(B) pour les verbes à ton H

Ce schéma signifie que le ton flottant haut domine le ton de la première syllabe du radical verbal. Ainsi, les verbes à ton bas, aussi que ceux à ton haut, auront un ton haut sur la première syllabe. Le ton lexical haut du radical s'associe alors avec la première syllabe à droit qu'elle soit le suffixe -*Vk* ou la voyelle finale. Dans le cas où ce ton haut doit s'associer à la voyelle finale, le ton bas de cette voyelle sera dissocié. Ici le ton flottant polarisé (c'est à dire un ton bas pour les verbes à ton haut) ne s'associe pas selon la règle établie ci-dessus pour un ton flottant bas.

(30) PF-P3:

ce qui donne: H!H(B) pour les verbes à ton bas

Ce schéma signifie qu'après la domination du ton flottant sur la première syllabe du radical, le ton lexical bas devient flottant lui-même et il ne cherche pas à s'associer. Le ton flottant polarisé, étant un ton haut pour les verbes à ton bas, s'associe avec la syllabe suivante, soit avec le suffixe -*Vk*, soit avec la voyelle finale. A cause du ton flottant bas qui précède le ton haut, le ton sur cette deuxième syllabe du verbe se réalise comme un ton haut abaissé. Ce fait exige alors la formulation de la règle suivante, qui explique la présence de ce ton haut abaissé:

(31) L'abaissement tonal: H → !H/ HB _____

Selon cette règle donc, quand il y a une séquence tonale H-B-H au niveau d'une phrase phonologique, un abaissement du registre tonal a lieu. Ainsi, un ton haut qui suit un ton bas se réalise comme un ton haut abaissé. Pour illustrer la réalisation du schéma H-RAD-P̥(-*Vk*)-V sur des verbes au perfectif passé troisième degré, les phrases suivantes serviront à titre d'exemple:

(32) *Tɔ-ŋa-sɔ́ sɔ́mb-ák-a   o-nyike.*
       1p-P3-1p   couper-DUR-VF   c3-viande
       Nous avons coupé la viande (le mois passé).

(33) *Bá-ŋa-bɔ́ kɔ́!c-ák-a   ɛ-sɔ́mbɔ́lɔ́.*
       3p-P3-3p   ramasser-DUR-VF   c4-termites
       Ils ont ramassé les termites (le mois passé).

En comparant ces exemples avec ceux du perfectif futur premier degré et ceux du perfectif présent, nous constatons que ce n'est qu'au niveau du radical verbal que toutes ces formes temporelles se distinguent.

Perfectif futur premier degré. En empruntant la définition du futur proche de Dugast pour le tunən (1971:183), nous constatons que le perfectif futur premier degré s'emploie lorsqu'on veut parler d'une action qui s'accomplira, ou d'un état qui "existera, dans la journée même, bientôt après le moment où l'on parle; en tout cas avant le lendemain." Le principe de réalisation pour ce temps en nɔmaándé postule qu'une suite de deux tons flottants (HB) existent comme préfixes du radical. Il est à noter que pour ce temps du futur premier degré, le radical verbal est toujours accompagné d'un suffixe -*Vk*. Il est intéressant à noter que Dugast (1971:184) constate un phenomène pareil en tunən. Pour une discussion plus détaillée sur ce suffixe, voir §3. Cette construction est représentée par le schéma suivant:

(34)   PF-F1: H-B-RAD-∅-*Vk*-V

Ces tons flottants se réalisent sur le radical verbal de la manière suivante:

(35)   PF-F1:

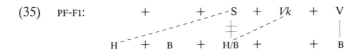

ce qui donne: H!HB pour les verbes à ton H
              HBB pour les verbes à ton B

Le premier ton flottant, c'est-à-dire le ton haut, domine le ton de la première syllabe du radical. Dans le cas des verbes à ton haut, le ton lexical haut, étant dissocié de la première syllabe du radical, cherche à s'associer avec la prochaine syllabe à droit, c'est-à-dire le suffixe -*Vk*. La présence du ton flottant bas précédant ce ton haut fait passer le ton haut au ton haut abaissé. Ce phénomène est semblable à celui dont il a déjà été question dans le cas du perfectif passé troisième degré (P3). La règle (31) déjà formulée ci-dessus s'applique dans les deux cas. En ce qui concerne les verbes à ton bas, le ton flottant bas se confond avec le ton lexical bas de la deuxième syllabe. La voyelle finale prend toujours son ton bas au futur F1.

(36) *Tɔ-ŋa-sɔ́ lɔ́!ŋ-ɔ́k-ɔ.*
      1p-F1-1p appeler-FIS-VF
      Nous allons (les) appeler (ce soir).

(37) *Nɔ-ŋa-nɔ́ cákɔn-ak-a.*
      2p-F1-2p jouer-FIS-VF
      Vous allez (le) jouer (ce soir).

Ainsi, nous constatons dans ces exemples que le temps du perfectif futur premier degré est marqué de trois manières: au complexe pronominal, au radical verbal (le schéma tonal), et par la présence obligatoire du suffixe *-Vk* au radical.

Perfectif futur deuxième degré.

En empruntant la définition du futur déterminé de Dugast pour le tunən, qui convient assez bien, semble-t-il, de définir le perfectif futur deuxième degré en nɔmaándɛ̀, nous constatons que "l'action aura lieu à un moment qui est précisé, à partir de la journée du lendemain, et jusqu'à un futur qui peut être lointain (se plaçant l'année suivante, ou plus loin encore), mais à condition que l'époque en soit précisée" (1971:187). Il y a toutefois lieu de raffiner cette définition en ce qui concerne le nɔmaándɛ̀, puisqu'il y a plus de certitude dans l'esprit du locuteur que l'action va se passer quand il se sert du F2 que lorsqu'il s'exprime en utilisant le F3.

(38) PF-F2: RAD-∅(-*Vk*)-V

Ce schéma donne la même réalisation tonale que celui du perfectif passé premier degré (19).

(39) *U-ká-a námb-ák-a.*
      3s-F2-3s préparer-DUR-VF
      Elle (le) préparera (demain).

(40) *Ɔ-kɔ́-ɔ lat-a.*
      2s-F2-2s coudre-VF
      Tu (le) coudras (demain).

Perfectif futur troisième degré. Lorsqu'une action s'accomplira dans un futur indéterminé (exprimé en nɔmaándɛ̀ par des adverbes temporels tels que *buɔ́sé* 'un jour' ou *te nyiényí* 'n'importe quand'), le locuteur se sert du futur troisième degré. Comme nous l'avons déjà dit, le locuteur s'avère moins certain quant à la réalisation de l'action quand il se sert du F3 que lorsqu'il se sert du F2.

La réalisation tonale sur le radical verbal peut être représentée par le schéma (41).

(41)   PF-F3: H-RAD-∅(-*Vk*)-V

Ce schéma est identique à celle du perfectif passé deuxième degré (26).

(42)   *Tu-ke-sú búm-ék-e.*
        1p-F3-1p   chasser-DUR-VF
        Nous (les) chasserons (un jour).

(43)   *U-ka-á kɔ́c-ak-a   i-bíle.*
        3s-F3-3s ramasser-DUR-VF c4-noixˆdeˆpalme
        Elle ramassera les noix de palme (un jour).

Perfectif présent. Le nɔmaándé semble avoir un présent au perfectif qui signifie un présent ponctuel. La définition de ce perfectif présent est identique à celle du présent ponctuel donnée par Dugast pour le tunən: "Ce présent énonce un état ou un fait contemporain du moment où l'on parle: le sujet est en train de ... dans le moment présent" (1971:175). Ce présent au perfectif est aussi employé pour exprimer des idées telles que: 'je conduis' avec le sens de 'je sais conduire' ou bien 'l'intelligence dépasse la force'. Pour répondre à la question "Qu'est-ce qu'il fait maintenant?", etc. le locuteur se sert du perfectif présent dans des circonstances normales. Mais, le perfectif présent n'est pas utilisé pour exprimer un présent inchoatif. Pour exprimer une action qui est sur le point de se produire, le nɔmaándé emploie soit le verbe ɔwaamba 'vouloir' plus un verbe à l'infinitif, soit le verbe otúme 'commencer' plus un verbe à l'infinitif.

En examinant notre corpus de textes, nous avons constaté que dans la majorité des cas où l'on relève la forme du perfectif présent, il s'agit des verbes d'état, tels que omenyi 'savoir', olíkíme 'avoir peur', ɔkɔnɔ 'être malade', ɔwaamba 'vouloir', oketi 'croire', et olimine 'être, s'asseoir'. Ces verbes d'état n'apparaissent que dans la forme perfective et elle ne permet pas le suffixe duratif, parce que ces verbes sont lexicalement duratifs. La notion de la durée est donc toujours présente. Notre étude des formes imperfectives au progressif (cf. §4.2) a relevé le fait que les verbes d'état en général n'apparaissent pas à la forme progressive. Le principe de réalisation tonale sur le radical verbal pour le perfectif présent est formulée en (44).

(44)   PF-PR: P-RAD-V

Ce schéma peut être représenté de la manière suivante:

(45)   PF-PR:

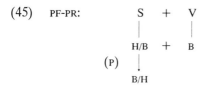

ce qui donne: BB pour les verbes à ton H
HB pour les verbes à ton B

La flèche dans le schéma signifie qu'il y a une polarisation (P) du ton lexical. Tout ceci veut dire que le ton lexical des verbes à ton haut devient ton bas et le ton lexical des verbes à ton bas devient ton haut. Le ton qui résulte de cette polarisation s'associe à la première syllabe du radical verbal. La voyelle finale du verbe porte toujours un ton bas. Il est à souligner que -Vk n'apparaît jamais avec le perfectif présent, parce que le présent au perfectif a toujours un sens duratif. Ainsi, le suffixe duratif -Vk serait superflu. Dugast a constaté le même phénomène en tunən (1971:175).

(46)   *U-ŋa-á sɔmb-a   o-nyike.*
       3s-PR-3s couper-VF   c4-viande
       Il coupe la viande.

(47)   *Tu-ŋe-sú két-i   anyía . . .*
       1p-PR-1p   croire-VF que
       Nous croyons que . . .

Récapitulation. Le tableau (48) résume les différentes marques du temps au perfectif dans un énoncé à valeur affirmative.

(48)

	COMPLEXE PRONOMINAL	RADICAL VERBAL	VERBE H	VERBE B
(P3)	x-ŋa-x B B H	H-RAD -p̥($-Vk$) -V	HHB	H!HB
(P2)	x-ŋa-x H B B	H-RAD $(-Vk)$ -V	HHB	HBB
(P1)	x-ŋa-x B H B	RAD $(-Vk)$ -V	HHB	BBB
(P0)	x-ma-x H B H/s B/p	RAD -B($-Vk$) -V	HBB	BBB
(PR)	x-ŋa-x B B H	P-RAD -V	BB	HB
(F1)	x-ŋa-x B B H	HB-RAD $-Vk$ -V	H!HB	HBB
(F2)	x-ka-x B H B	RAD $(-Vk)$ -V	HHB	BBB
(F3)	x-ka-x B B H	H-RAD $(-Vk)$ -V	HHB	HBB

Le tableau (49) compare un verbe à ton haut (ɔlɔ́ŋɔ 'appeler') à un verbe à ton bas (oketi 'mesurer, croire') selon les différentes catégories de temps en nɔmaándé. Les formes sont présentées sous leur aspect perfectif à la première personne du pluriel.

(49)

	ɔlɔ́ŋɔ 'appeler'	oketi 'mesurer, croire'
(P3)	tɔŋasɔ́ lɔ́ŋɔ́(kɔ)	tuŋesú ké!tí(ki)
(P2)	tɔ́ŋasɔ lɔ́ŋɔ́(kɔ)	túŋesu kéti(ki)
(P1)	tɔŋásɔ lɔ́ŋɔ́(kɔ)	tuŋésu keti(ki)
(P0)	tɔ́masɔ lɔ́ŋɔ́(kɔ)	túmesu keti(ki)
(PR)	tɔŋasɔ́ lɔŋɔ	tuŋesú kéti
(F1)	tɔŋasɔ́ lɔ́!ŋɔ́kɔ	tuŋesú kétiki
(F2)	tɔkásɔ lɔ́ŋɔ́(kɔ)	tukésu keti(ki)
(F3)	tɔkasɔ́ lɔ́ŋɔ́(kɔ)	tukesú kéti(ki)

3. Le suffixe -Vk

Le suffixe $-Vk$, dont il a déjà été question (§2), sera examiné maintenant sous l'angle de ses plusieurs fonctions dans le système verbal du nɔmaándé.

Nous donnons le plus souvent à ce suffixe la rubrique DURATIF (DUR) comme terme général[9]. Le morphème -*Vk* se suffixe à la racine verbale et précède tout autre suffixe eventuel. A. E. Meeussen, en parlant des éléments verbaux en proto-bantu, constate qu'un élément pénultième du verbe, *-ag-* "is largely attested; its meaning, ranging from 'imperfective' to 'repetitive' or 'habitual', is difficult to state more exactly for the proto-period" (1967:110). Le *g* du proto-bantu est devenu *k* en nɔmaándɛ́ pour être conforme au système phonologique. La voyelle du suffixe est toujours identique à celle de la voyelle finale du verbe. Ainsi, la voyelle du suffixe -*Vk* peut être *i, e, a, ɔ,* ou *o.* Exemples avec *ɛ* ou *u* n'ont pas été relévés ici parce que l'extension *-ɛ* ne s'emploie qu'avec les noms ou les adjectifs and l'extension *-u* n'existe que pour exprimer un adjectif en nɔmaándɛ́.

Le suffixe -*Vk* s'emploie dans le système verbal du nɔmaándɛ́ et comporte parfois un sens itératif comme une variante du sens duratif. On le trouve donc:

(a) lorsque l'action se fait sur plusieurs objets.

(50)   *U-ŋá-a   kɔc-ak-a   i-bíle.*
       3s-P1-3s ramasser-DUR-VF c4-noix^de^palme
       Elle a ramassé des noix de palme.

(b) lorsque l'action se répète plus d'une fois.

(51)   *Tɔ-ká-sɔ   sɔ́ɔn-ák-a   bi-kúlú bi-éɲí.*
       1p-F2-1p   descendre-DUR-VF c8-fois c8-beaucoup
       Nous descendrons plusieurs fois (demain).

(c) lorsque l'action continue à se dérouler pendant un certain moment. Ceci semble être surtout le cas pour un inventaire assez limité de verbes dont le caractère intrinsèque a une valeur de duratif.

(52)   *Ɛ-ŋá-mɛ   nyí-ák-a   o-nyiké.*
       1s-P1-1s   manger-DUR-VF   c3-viande
       J'ai mangé de la viande (ce matin).

(53)   *Ú-ŋa-a   bɛ́-ákáb-ák-a.*
       3s-P2-3s RE-laver-DUR-VF
       Il s'est lavé (hier).

---

[9]Appelé INTENSIF par Taylor (1984).

(d) Comme nous avons déjà souligné, ce même suffixe -*Vk* semble avoir une autre fonction qui est propre au perfectif futur premier degré. La présence obligatoire du -*Vk* au perfectif futur premier degré (F1) à l'affirmatif, aussi bien qu'au négatif (§6), sert, semble-t-il, à distinguer la forme du futur F1 de la forme du présent au perfectif. Autrement, ces deux formes se confondraient lorsqu'il s'agissait des verbes à ton bas (13). Puisque le présent au perfectif ne peut jamais prendre le suffixe -*Vk*, cette forme reste distincte de celle du perfectif futur premier degré. Nous proposons que nous avons affaire à deux morphèmes homophones: le suffixe -*Vk* qui apparaît au perfectif futur premier degré et le suffixe -*Vk* à valeur de duratif.

La question qui nous est parfois posée est de savoir si le suffixe -*Vk* en nɔmaándɛ́ reste en quelque sorte une marque de l'imperfectif comme elle est proposée pour le proto-bantu. A cause des occurrences de ce suffixe au perfectif (cf. §2), il est difficile de le considérer comme étant rattaché à l'imperfectif. En plus, à l'imperfectif (cf. §4) ce suffixe n'est pas toujours relevé. Ainsi, il semble assez clair qu'une des formes homophones -*Vk* fait partie du système temporel en nɔmaándɛ́, c'est-à-dire le suffixe qui sert à distinguer le perfectif futur premier degré du perfectif présent, et que l'autre forme homophone -*Vk* a une valeur de duratif/itératif. On suppose qu'au moins le suffixe duratif -*Vk* en nɔmaándɛ́ est venu du suffixe imperfectif proto-bantu mais qu'il a subi un petit changement au niveau sémantique (de l'imperfectif au duratif) au cours des années.

4. L'imperfectif

L'imperfectif envisage un procès "sous l'angle de son déroulement (Stanley 1986:83)." Comrie définit l'imperfectif comme l'aspect qui donne "explicit reference to the internal temporal structure of a situation, viewing a situation from within" (1976:24). En nɔmaándɛ́, l'imperfectif est constitué des formes qui expriment les actions et les états habituels et celles qui expriment les actions progressives.

Les actions et états imperfectifs se différencient en sept valeurs aspectuelles selon la relation temporelle du procès au moment de l'énonciation:

(54)   imperfectif présent
        imperfectif passé immédiat
        imperfectif passé premier degré
        imperfectif passé deuxième degré
        imperfectif passé troisième degré
        imperfectif futur premier degré
        imperfectif futur deuxième degré

Bien que dans le perfectif, on fait la distinction entre le futur deuxième degré et le futur troisième degré, dans l'imperfectif une telle distinction n'est pas relevée. Ceci fait que la même forme aspectuelle s'emploie pour exprimer ces deux degrés d'éloignement dans le futur à l'imperfectif (57).

Le locuteur nɔmaándɛ peut choisir entre une multiplicité de formes quand il s'agit de l'aspect imperfectif. Les sept imperfectifs cités ci-dessus ont chacun une forme habituelle et deux autres formes progressives sauf pour l'imperfectif présent qui n'a qu'une seule forme progressive et l'imperfectif passé immédiat (où le sens habituel est exclu) qui n'a que deux formes progressives. En plus, les trois autres passés ont aussi trois formes: une qui ne signifie qu'un sens progressif et deux autres formes qui peuvent signifier soit un sens progressif soit un sens habituel.

Le tableau (55) montre les différentes marques aspectuelles et temporelles à l'imperfectif dans un énoncé à valeur affirmative. Nous avons indiqué les tons pour toutes les formules, pour démontrer les différentes formes, surtout au passé (voir les tons au complexe pronominal et à l'auxiliaire). A la différence des tableaux (57) et (67) plus bas, nous avons supprimé le symbole Ø pour ce tableau, ne laissant que les éléments du complexe pronominal présents dans chaque cas. La voyelle finale est présente pour chaque schéma et ainsi, le symbole VF est aussi supprimé pour ce tableau.

(55)

TEMPS	HABITUEL	PROGRESSIF
F2/(F3)	x-*ka-bule*-x H-RAD B H B B H	x-*ka*-x AUX LOC+INF B HB H x-*ka*-x AUX X-X RAD-*Vk* B HB H
F1	x-*ŋa-bule*-x RAD B B B B H	x-*ŋa*-x AUX LOC+INF B BH H x-*ŋa*-x AUX X-X RAD-*Vk* B BH H
PR	x-*na-ŋa* X-X RAD-*Vk* B B B	x-x-*ŋa* LOC+INF B H B
P0	———————	x-*ma*-x AUX LOC+INF H B H H x-*ma*-x AUX X-X RAD-*Vk* H B H H
P1	———————	x-*ŋa*-x AUX LOC+INF B HB H
P1	x-*ŋa*-x AUX X-X RAD-*Vk* B HB H x-*ŋa*-x AUX X-*ŋa*-x RAD B HB H B HB	
P2	———————	x-*ŋa*-x AUX LOC+INF H B B H
P2	x-*ŋa*-x AUX X-X RAD-*Vk* H B B H x-*ŋa*-x AUX X-*ŋa*-x RAD H B B H H B B	
P3	———————	x-*ŋa*-x AUX LOC+INF B BH H
P3	x-*ŋa*-x AUX X-X RAD-*Vk* B BH H x-*ŋa*-x AUX X-*ŋa*-x RAD B BH H B B B H	

4.1. Actions et états habituels. Les marques de l'habituel s'emploient pour exprimer un fait qui se produit habituellement. Bien que les actions habituelles se différencient en six valeurs aspectuelles selon les relations temporelles du procès au moment de l'énonciation, il n'y a que cinq formes distinctives pour décrire les actions ou faits habituels. A l'imperfectif, le futur premier degré et le futur deuxième degré, ainsi que le présent, ont chacun une formule particulière. Quant à l'imperfectif passé quoique soit le degré, on peut choisir entre deux formules pour décrire une action habituelle ou un état habituel. Les distinctions de degré dans les passés imperfectifs sont faites à l'aide des mêmes schémas tonals sur le complexe pronominal que ceux que nous avons vus au tableau (12).

Avant de procéder aux formules du syntagme verbal à l'imperfectif, il semble nécessaire de proposer une règle de succession des éléments qui peuvent apparaître dans le complexe pronominal à l'affirmatif. Nous proposons ainsi le schéma et les règles suivants:

(56)   x   - * -   *bule* - na -   ŋa
                         - x -
         1   2   3   4   5

1. Pronom initial: obligatoire si le nom sujet n'est pas présent; supprimé si le nom sujet est présent
2. Marque temporelle (cf. §1.2): supprimé si le suffixe *-na* (élément 4) est présent
3. Marque du futur habituel: *-bule*
4. Le suffixe *-na*: présent habituel; le pronom final (x) est présent pour tout autre temps/aspect
5. Marque de l'imperfectif au présent: *-ŋa*; sa présence supprime celle de la marque temporelle (élément 2)

Pour voir comment ces éléments du complexe pronominal figurent dans les différentes formules de l'imperfectif, on doit se référer aux tableaux (57) et (67) ci-dessous. La justification principale de décrire le suffixe *-ŋa* (élément 5 ci-dessus) comme une forme homophone avec la marque du temps *ŋa* est la construction à l'imperfectif au progressif présent (§4.2 ci-dessous).

Le tableau (57) ci-dessous montre les marques de l'habituel en nɔmaándɛ avec les quatre formules qui les distinguent.

(57)   COMPLEXE PRONOMINALE   AUX   PRO-RED   RADICAL VERBALE[10]

(F1)   x- * -*bule* -x -∅   RAD

(F2/3)   x- * -*bule* -x -∅   H-RAD

(PR)   x- ∅ -∅   -*na* -*ŋa*   x- ∅ -x   RAD-Vk

(P1/2/3) x- * -∅   -x -∅   AUX   x- ∅ -x   RAD-Vk
                                        x- * -x   RAD

Les schémas tonals au complexe pronominal sont identiques aux schémas présentés au tableau (12) ci-dessus. Les tons grammaticaux relevés au niveau du radical verbal au perfectif n'apparaissent pas à l'imperfectif. Toutes les syllabes du verbe retiennent leur ton lexical dans les phrases imperfectives, sauf au futur deuxième degré. Dans ce futur, un ton flottant haut domine le ton de la première syllabe du radical verbal. Ce ton ressemble beaucoup au ton haut qui domine le verbe dans le perfectif au futur troisième degré (41), même que le complexe pronominal garde les tons du futur deuxième degré.

Comme ces schémas au tableau (57) le montrent, les pronoms du complexe pronominal sont souvent répétés à l'habituel, tout de suite avant le radical verbal (représenté au tableau (57) par la forme x-∅-x). Il est à souligner que ce n'est pas tout le complexe pronominal qui est répété, mais uniquement les pronoms; toutefois avec certains changements d'ordre phonétique. Nous allons constater une chose pareille en ce qui concerne le progressif (67). Le tableau suivant (58), en reprenant les pronoms du complexe pronominal tels qu'ils ont été présentés au tableau (11), montre les formes qu'ont ces pronoms répétés, qui se trouvent à l'imperfectif. Une explication plus détaillée de ces formes sera donnée à la §4.1.

(58) | PRONOM | TEMPS | PRONOM | | PRONOMS REPETES | |
|---|---|---|---|---|---|
| ɛ- | TMP | -*amɛ́* | → | *yamɛ́* | (1s) |
| ɔ- | TMP | -*ɔɔ́* | → | *ɔɔ́* | (2s) |
| *u-* | TMP | -*aá* | → | *waá* | (3s) |
| *tɔ-* | TMP | -*asɔ́* | → | *tɔasɔ́* | (1p) |
| *nɔ-* | TMP | -*anɔ́* | → | *nɔanɔ́* | (2p) |
| *bá-* | TMP | -*abɔ́* | → | *bábɔ́* | (3p) |

---

[10]x = pronoms; * = *ŋa* au F1 et au passé, et *ka* au F2; AUX = *bá* 'être'; ∅ = absence d'un élément segmental.

L'habituel au futur

$$F1 = x\text{-}*\text{-}\textit{bule}\text{-}x\text{-}\emptyset \quad \text{RAD}$$
$$F2 = x\text{-}*\text{-}\textit{bule}\text{-}x\text{-}\emptyset \quad \text{H-RAD}$$

Un fait qui sera habituel dans l'avenir, c'est-à-dire un fait qui n'est pas encore habituel au moment où on parle, mais qui le sera, est distingué en nɔmaándɛ́ par:

(a) l'adjonction au complexe pronominal d'un suffixe *-bule-* après la marque temporelle. Ce suffixe porte deux tons bas;

(b) l'absence de perturbations tonales au niveau du radical verbal au futur premier degré et la présence d'un ton flottant haut qui domine le ton de la première syllabe du radical verbal au futur deuxième degré;

(c) l'absence du suffixe duratif.

Il est à noter que l'harmonie vocalique du complexe pronominal à l'imperfectif futur pour les actions habituelles est assez compliquée. Les voyelles du pronom initial et de la marque temporelle du complexe pronominal sont déterminées par la première voyelle du suffixe habituel du futur *-bule-*, mais les voyelles du pronom final du complexe sont déterminées plutôt par les voyelles du radical verbal suivant. En plus, la première voyelle du pronom final s'élide avec la dernière voyelle du suffixe *-bule-* laissant seulement la première voyelle du pronom final (*a/e* ou bien *ɔ/o*, selon l'harmonie vocalique avec le radical verbal).

(59) *Tu-ŋe-bul-asɔ́ lɔ́ŋ-ɔ.*
      1p-F1-HAB/F-1p appeler-VF
      Nous allons (les) appeler (habituellement) (plus tard aujourd'hui).

(60) *Tu-ké-bul-esú kín-e.*
      1p-F2-HAB/F-1p refuser-VF
      Nous (les) refuserons (habituellement) (demain).

L'habituel au présent

$$x\text{-}\emptyset\text{-}\emptyset\text{-}na\text{-}\eta a$$
$$x\text{-}\emptyset\text{-}x \quad \text{RAD-}Vk$$

Un fait qui est habituel au présent est exprimé en nɔmaándɛ́ par une forme qui dénote une action habituelle ou un état habituel qui commençait dans le passé et qui va continuer dans l'avenir. La forme du présent habituel est distinguée par:

(a) l'adjonction au complexe pronominal d'un suffixe -na après le pronom initial. Ce suffixe est suivi d'un suffixe marquant l'imperfectif au présent -ŋa, qui est homophone à une des marques temporelles (12). Les fonctions de ces deux formes homophones sont distinctes et elles s'opposent également l'une à l'autre par leur position dans le complexe pronominal. En présence du suffixe -na, le pronom final du complexe disparaît. Les voyelles du complexe pronominal au présent habituel ne sont pas régies par le système d'harmonie vocalique à travers les frontières morphologiques;

(b) la séquence immédiate des deux pronoms qui apparaît à la suite du complexe pronominal; c'est-à-dire la marque temporelle fait défaut. Dans ce cas, la première voyelle du pronom final ne tombe pas (58). Par contre, cette voyelle disparaît lorsqu'elle se trouve entre deux autres voyelles, dans le cas de la deuxième personne du singulier et, lorsqu'elle entre en contact avec une autre voyelle a, dans le cas de la troisième personne du pluriel. Les voyelles de cette séquence de pronoms sont conditionnées par les voyelles du radical verbal. Dans tous les exemples relevés jusqu'à présent, la dernière syllabe du deuxième pronom de cette séquence porte toujours un ton haut. Ce ton haut indique le fait qu'il s'agit ici d'un redoublement partiel, c'est-à-dire que la marque temporelle fait défaut;

(c) le fait que le ton du radical verbal ne subit jamais de perturbations tonales;

(d) la présence obligatoire du suffixe duratif -Vk.

Les énoncés suivants au présent habituel serviront à titre d'exemple:

(61)   *U-na-ŋa*   *w-aá*   *nyí-ák-a.*
        3s-HAB/PR-IPF/PR   3s-3s   manger-DUR-VF
        Il mange (habituellement).

(62)   *Ɛ-na-ŋa*   *y-amé*   *ket-ik-i.*
        1s-HAB/PR-IPF/PR   1s-1s   croire-DUR-VF
        Je crois (habituellement).

A propos de la marque de l'imperfectif au présent -ŋa en nɔmaándɛ, et son emplacement particulier dans le complexe pronominal, voir (57).

L'habituel au passé

$$\text{P1/2/3} = \begin{array}{l} \text{x-*-}\emptyset\text{-x-}\emptyset \;\; \text{AUX} \;\; \text{x-}\emptyset\text{-x} \quad \text{RAD-}Vk \\ \text{x-*-}\emptyset\text{-x-}\emptyset \;\; \text{AUX} \;\; \text{x-}\eta a\text{-x} \quad \text{RAD} \end{array}$$

Une action qui se déroulait dans le passé, mais qui ne se fait plus au moment de l'énoncé, est exprimée en nɔmaándɛ par des formes avec deux fonctions. Elles s'emploient aussi bien pour exprimer une action habituelle au passé que pour exprimer une action progressive, c'est-à-dire une action qui était en train de se dérouler à un moment donné dans le passé (cf. §4.2). Il y a en fait deux formules presque identiques qui peuvent être employées pour décrire ces actions habituelles ou progressives dans le passé. L'auditeur nɔmaándɛ ne saura quel sens entre ces deux possibilités est en vue qu'à partir du contexte.

Dans ces deux formules, le complexe pronominal est identique aux complexes déjà décrits ci-dessus à la §1.2 pour exprimer le temps en nɔmaándɛ. Dans le cas des formes à valeur d'habituel et de progressif, le complexe pronominal est suivi d'auxiliaire *bá* 'être'. Cet auxiliaire a un ton lexical haut, mais, au passé P1 et P2, ce ton subit un abaissement automatique. Ceci vient du fait que le complexe pronominal qui précède l'auxiliaire se termine avec un ton bas.

C'est dans ce qui suit l'auxiliaire que l'on constate une différence dans les deux formules, aussi bien dans la suite des pronoms que du côté des composants du verbe. La première formule de l'habituel/progressif au passé contient une suite de deux pronoms sans la marque temporelle et le radical verbal porte toujours son ton lexical, avec la présence obligatoire du suffixe duratif *-Vk*.

Quant à la deuxième formule de l'habituel/progressif au passé, elle contient une répétition de tout le complexe pronominal (12). Dans ce cas aussi, le radical verbal garde toujours son ton lexical, mais le suffixe duratif n'apparaît jamais. Ces deux formules ont déjà été présentées au tableau (57). Les exemples suivants serviront à illustrer les deux formules dans chacun des trois passés:

(63a) *Bá-ŋa-bɔ́ bá   bá-bɔ́ nyí-ák-a.*
        3p-P3-3p   AUX   3p-3p manger-DUR-VF
        Ils mangeaient (habituellement).

(63b) *Bá-ŋa-bɔ́ bá   bá-ŋa-bɔ́ nyí-á.*
        3p-P3-3p   AUX   3p-P3-3p manger-VF
        Ils étaient en train de manger.

(64a) *Nɔ́-ŋa-nɔ bá   nɔ-anɔ́ cɔ-cɔb-ak-a.*
       2p-P3-2p   AUX   2p-2p   RED-aller-DUR-VF
       Vous alliez (habituellement)(hier).

(64b) *Nɔ́-ŋa-nɔ bá   nɔ́-ŋa-nɔ cɔb-a.*
       2p-P3-2p   AUX   2p-P3-2p   aller-VF
       Vous étiez en train d'aller (hier).

(65a) *U-ŋá-a bá   w-aá   fan-ak-a.*
       3s-P1-3s   AUX   3s-3s   lire-DUR-VF
       Il lisait (habituellement)(ce matin).

(65b) *U-ŋá-a bá   u-ŋá-a fan-a.*
       3s-P1-3s   AUX   3s-P1-3s   lire-VF
       Il était en train de lire (ce matin).

Il faut souligner que les formules de l'imperfectif passé premier degré
(IPF-P1) seront le plus souvent comprises comme exprimant une action
progressive plutôt qu'habituelle. Ceci semble être dû au fait que le passé
premier degré s'emploie uniquement pour décrire une action qui s'est
passée dans la journée même de l'énoncé. Pour que le fait soit vu comme
habituel, plus de temps devrait normalement se dérouler.

La question se pose quant à l'interprétation de ces deux formules
possibles pour exprimer l'imperfectif passé, si elles ont vraiment le même
sens ou non. Selon plusieurs locuteurs de la langue nɔmaándé, la différence serait une distinction entre une action prolongée et une action brève
dans le passé. La formule qui emploie le suffixe duratif semble exprimer
plutôt une action prolongée, tandis que celle où il n'y a pas de suffixe
duratif semble signifier une action brève. Une personne suggère qu'il y a
une distinction ici entre l'habitude et le fait d'être en train de faire quelque
chose. D'autres locuteurs suggèrent que les formules sont en variation libre
et que c'est l'idiolecte de chacun qui décide quelle formule sera employée.
C'est cette dernière interprétation que nous avons gardée parce qu'elle
nous semble la plus répandue.

4.2. Actions progressives. Malgré le fait que les formules pour les actions progressives au passé sont identiques à celles des actions habituelles,
tel n'est pas le cas dans le présent et le futur. Là, le progressif est marqué
d'une manière distinctive, avec encore une autre construction possible qui
comporte un syntagme locatif. Bien que, comme nous l'avons déjà dit (§4),
l'imperfectif passé immédiat (PF-P0) ne puisse pas exprimer une action
habituelle, il est toutefois susceptible d'exprimer une action progressive.

Le progressif en nɔmaándɛ est distingué tout d'abord par un syntagme locatif trouvé à chaque niveau temporel. Avant de procéder aux autres formes, nous regarderons de plus près ce syntagme locatif. La marque locative est une voyelle qui est identique à la voyelle qui la suit. Dans nos exemples la marque locative est toujours suivie d'un infinitif. Les infinitifs en nɔmaándɛ ont le préfixe o/ɔ selon les règles d'harmonie vocalique du verbe. Ainsi, la marque locative dans ces phrases sera aussi toujours o/ɔ. Cette marque a un ton bas, mais elle porte aussi un ton flottant haut qui s'attache à l'infinitif de la manière suivante:

(66)   Construction locative + infinitif:

    ɔ + H + ɔ-RAD-V → ɔ ɔ-HB (pour les verbes à ton bas)
    ɔ + H + ɔ-RAD-V → ɔ ɔ́-!HB (pour les verbes à ton haut)

Il est à noter que, en règle générale, la deuxième syllabe d'un verbal dissyllabique à l'infinitif porte un ton bas. Le comportement du ton flottant haut dans le syntagme locatif s'explique en deux parties. Dans le cas des verbes à ton haut, le ton flottant haut de la marque locative domine le ton lexical bas du préfixe de l'infinitif. Ainsi, le ton flottant bas qui résulte de la dissociation du ton lexical bas de ce préfixe provoque un abaissement tonal du ton lexical haut du radical verbal. Dans le cas des verbes à ton bas, le ton bas lexical de la marque locative domine aussi le ton du préfixe de l'infinitif verbal, et ainsi, le ton flottant haut du syntagme locatif domine le ton lexical bas de la première syllabe du radical verbal. Nous n'avons pas encore trouvé de raison pour cette différence de comportement.[11]

Le tableau (67) montre toutes les formes utilisées pour exprimer le progressif en nɔmaándɛ. Il est à souligner que deux des trois formes du passé progressif en nɔmaándɛ sont identiques à celles du passé habituel (cf. (57)).

---

[11]Nous pouvons constater le schéma suivant pour les verbes à ton haut:

    ɔ +   + ɔ - RAD -V → ɔ - ɔ́ - !HB
    | ‡ | |
    B + H + B + H + B

Le ton bas qui est dissocié du préfixe de l'infinitif provoque l'abaissement tonal au niveau du radical pour les verbes à ton haut. La voyelle finale du verbe à l'infinitif prend toujours un ton bas.
Pour les verbes à ton bas, nous constatons le schéma suivant:

    ɔ +   + ɔ - RAD -V → ɔ - ɔ - HB
    | ‡ |
    B + H + B + B B

(67)

	COMPLEXE PRONOMINAL	AUX	PRO-RED	RADICAL VERBAL[12]
(F1/2)	X- TMP -$\emptyset$ -X -$\emptyset$	AUX		LOC-INF-RAD
	X- TMP -$\emptyset$ -X -$\emptyset$	AUX	X- $\emptyset$ -X	RAD-Vk
(PR)	X- $\emptyset$ -$\emptyset$ -X -ηa			LOC-INF-RAD
(P0)	X- TMP -$\emptyset$ -X -$\emptyset$	AUX		LOC-INF-RAD
	X- TMP -$\emptyset$ -X -$\emptyset$	AUX	X- $\emptyset$ -X	RAD-Vk
	X- TMP -$\emptyset$ -X -$\emptyset$	AUX		LOC-INF-RAD
(P1/2/3)	X- TMP -$\emptyset$ -X -$\emptyset$	AUX	X- $\emptyset$ -X	RAD-Vk
	X- TMP -$\emptyset$ -X -$\emptyset$	AUX	X- TMP -X	RAD

Le progressif au futur

X-*-$\emptyset$-X-$\emptyset$ AUX LOC-INF-RAD
X-*-$\emptyset$-X-$\emptyset$ AUX X-$\emptyset$-X   RAD-Vk

Une action qui va se dérouler dans l'avenir est exprimé en nɔmaándɛ en employant premièrement le complexe pronominal de la même manière que pour les actions habituelles; ensuite, il y a l'auxiliaire *bá* 'être' et finalement, le syntagme locatif.

(68)   *Tɔ-ŋa-sɔ́ bá   ɔ-ɔ́-!nyí-á.*
       1p-F1-1p   AUX   LOC-c15^INF-manger-VF
       Nous allons être en train de manger.

(69)   *Tɔ-ká-sɔ bá   ɔ-ɔ-fán-a.*
       1p-F2-1p   AUX   LOC-c15^INF-lire-VF
       Nous serons en train de lire.

Il y a toutefois aussi la possibilité d'exprimer le progressif au futur avec une construction qui ressemble à celle du passé habituel/progressif (cf. §4.1, tableau (57)).

(70)   *Tɔ-ká-sɔ bá   tɔ-asɔ́ námb-ák-a.*
       1p-F2-1p   AUX   1p-1p   préparer-DUR-VF
       Nous serons en train de (le) préparer (demain).

(71)   *Bá-ŋa-bɔ́ bá   bá-bɔ́ lat-ak-a.*
       3p-F1-3p   AUX   3p-3p   coudre-F1S-VF
       Ils seront en train de coudre (ce soir).

---

[12] X = pronoms; * = marque du temps; AUX = *bá*, 'être'; LOC = o/ɔ (selon l'harmonie vocalique avec le préfixe de l'infinitif).

Le progressif au présent

      x-∅-∅-x-ŋa LOC-INF-RAD

Une action qui se déroule encore au moment de l'énoncé s'exprime au moyen du présent progressif en nɔmaándɛ. Cette formule est caractérisée par une forme distinctive du complexe pronominal, suivie d'un syntagme locatif identique aux autres syntagmes locatifs employés au progressif. La forme du complexe pronominal est distinctive en ce qu'elle comporte les deux pronoms, c'est-à-dire le pronom initial et le pronom final, sans l'interposition de la marque temporelle. Par contre, la marque de l'imperfectif au présent se trouve après ces deux pronoms répétés pour compléter le complexe pronominal.

(72)   *Y-amé-ŋa   ɔ-ɔ́-!námb-a.*
       1s-1s-IPF/PR   LOC-cl5^INF-préparer-VF
       Je suis en train de (le) préparer.

(73)   *Bá-bɔ́-ŋa   ɔ-ɔ-fán-a.*
       3p-3p-IPF/PR   LOC-cl5^INF-lire-VF
       Ils sont en train de lire.

Ce genre de complexe pronominal (x-x-ŋa) est appelé le "pronom invariable" par Taylor (1983:3), parce qu'il ne change pas de voyelle selon les règles d'harmonie vocalique qui régissent habituellement le pronom et le verbe en nɔmaándɛ. Le progressif au présent peut être employé pour exprimer l'insistance ou la mise en relief d'une action. Par exemple, pour répondre à des questions telles que "Pourquoi ne viens-tu pas?" et "Qu'est-ce qu'ils font là?" le locuteur nɔmaándɛ se sert de cet aspect.

Le progressif au passé

      x-*-∅-x-∅ AUX LOC-INF-RAD
      x-*-∅-x-∅ AUX x-∅-x   RAD-*Vk*
      x-*-∅-x-∅ AUX x-ŋa-x RAD

Un fait qui se déroulait déjà à un certain moment dans le passé peut être exprimé en nɔmaándɛ avec les mêmes formules décrites ci-dessus pour exprimer l'habituel au passé (cf. §4.1). Au lieu de donner d'autres exemples de ces mêmes formules, nous procéderons directement à une troisième possibilité pour exprimer l'idée de déroulement au passé. Comme au futur et au présent, le syntagme locatif est susceptible d'être employé au passé progressif. Bien que cette forme au passé apparaisse moins fréquemment que les deux autres formes du progressif au passé (63) dans le corpus de textes enregistrés, le syntagme locatif au passé reste néanmoins acceptable pour les locuteurs de la langue.

(74)   *Ahé   bá-ŋa-ka-bɔ   hám-á,*
       quand 3p-P2-DIR-3p sortir-VF

       tɔ́-ŋa-sɔ   bá   ɔ-ɔ́-!nyí-á.
       1p-P3-1p AUX LOC-c15^INF-manger-VF
       Quand ils sont arrivés, nous étions en train de manger.

(75)   *Ɛ-ŋá-am*[13] *bá   ɔ-ɔ-lát-a.*
       1s-P1-1s   AUX LOC-c15^INF-coudre-VF
       J'étais en train de coudre (ce matin).

Le syntagme locatif s'emploie aussi à l'imperfectif passé immédiat.

(76)   *É-má-am bá   ɔ-ɔ́-!lɔ́ŋ-ɔ.*
       1s-P0-1s   AUX LOC-c15^INF-appeler-VF
       J'étais en train de (les) appeler.

(77)   *Ú-má-á bá   ɔ-ɔ-fán-a.*
       3s-P0-3s   AUX LOC-c15^INF-lire-VF
       Il vient d'être en train de lire.

L'imperfectif passé immédiat peut aussi s'exprimer en employant la formule: x-*-∅-x-∅ AUX x-∅-x RAD-*Vk*.

---

[13]Le complexe pronominal à la première personne du singulier subit des changements segmentaux dans les contextes suivants:
- lorsque le schéma tonal au complexe est BBH;
- devant un verbe à ton haut;
- devant un verbe qui commence avec /b/ ou /m/.
Il y a deux sortes de changements, à savoir:
(1) la première voyelle du pronom final apparaît. Ceci provoque l'allongement de la voyelle de la marque temporelle. C'est la voyelle longue qui prend le ton haut du schéma tonal BBH et la voyelle finale du complexe pronominal sera munie d'un ton bas. Par exemple: *ɛ-ŋa-ámɛ*.
(2) Dans le cas des verbes qui commencent avec /b/ ou /m/, la dernière voyelle du complexe pronominal tombe.

(78) *Tɔ́-ma-sɔ bá tɔ-asɔ́ fan-ak-a.*
      1p-P0-1p   AUX 1p-1p   lire-DUR-VF
      Nous étions en train de lire (tout à l'heure).

5. Le sens du parfait

Comme nous avons déjà mentionné ci-dessus à la §2,

> le parfait sert à exprimer un procès qui est envisagé comme accompli
> mais toutefois, continuant … dans ses conséquences, au moment de
> l'acte de parole. Ce procès a eu lieu dans le passé et … ses
> répercussions continuent dans le présent (Stanley 1986:116).

En nɔmaándɛ le sens du parfait est un sens étendu du passé immédiat
et il est marqué par la même marque du passé immédiat *ma*. Cette marque
apparaît dans le complexe pronominal entre le pronom initial et le pronom
final dans les deux cas. Selon les fonctions du parfait détaillées par Comrie
(1976:56–60), le nɔmaándɛ semble employer *ma* pour exprimer

(a) le passé immédiat—employé lorsque les répercussions du procès sont
    dues simplement à la proximité temporelle de l'action au moment de
    l'acte de parole;

(b) un résultat—employé lorsqu'un état actuel est dénoté comme étant le
    résultat d'une situation dans le passé si la situation est proche ou loin.

En parlant du complexe pronominal (11), nous avons constaté la présence de la marque *ma* pour exprimer le passé immédiat (P0). Le sens du
parfait est tiré tacitement du sens du passé immédiat comme un sens
étendu.

(79) *Ú-me-é we.*
      3s-P0-3s   mourrir
      Il est mort (vient de mourrir).

(80) *Ɔ́-mɔ-ɔ́ bɔ́ŋ-ɔ   nu-fule.*
      2s-P0-2s   recevoir-VF c11-lettre
      Tu as reçu (viens de recevoir) une lettre.

(81) *Bé-me-bú suet-e.*
      3p-P0-3p   partir-VF
      Ils sont déjà partis (viennent de partir).

(82)   Ɔ́-mɔ-ɔ́ hányu-a   e?
       2s-P0-2s   réveiller-VF   Q
       Tu t'es réveillé? (salutation)

(83)   Nú-me-nú   límín-e   e?
       2p-P0-2p   s'asseoir-VF   Q
       Vous êtes assis? (salutation)

(84)   Í-me-émi eéc-e.
       1s-P0-1s   se^rassasier-VF
       Je me suis rassasié.

L'exemple suivant montre une situation qui n'a qu'un sens (celui du passé immédiat) parce que le résultat (de l'achat) n'est plus valable au moment où on parle:

(85)   É-ma-mé ɔ́nd-ɔ́   ɔ-sɔŋɔ   mbá í-ma yaáti-a.
       1s-P0-1s   acheter-VF c3-huile mais c9-P0 casser-VF
       Je viens d'acheter de l'huile mais elle (la calebasse) s'est cassée.

Cet exemple montre que le sens du P0 est à la base et que le sens du parfait est tiré de ce sens de base. Noter l'ambiguïté de la fonction de *ma* dans la deuxième proposition du même énoncé (85). Le sens du parfait du résultat aussi bien que la fonction du passé immédiat sont possibles dans ce contexte. Nous relevons les exemples suivants qui nous semblent moins ambigus que les exemples précédents parce que les situations se sont passées plus loin dans le passé, ce qui rend un sens du parfait du résultat la seule fonction possible.

(86)   A-mbányɛ yí   ó-líhe ma-á ká-hám-a.
       c7-bon   c7^MG c3-vie PAR-3s DIR-sortir-VF
       La bonne vie est arrivée.

(87)   A-mbányɛ yí   e-lilé   ma-∅   fáay-a.
       c7-bon   c7^MG c7-esprit PAR-3s venir-VF
       Le Saint Esprit est venu.

(88)   E-bítúlúle   ma-∅   cáŋi-a.
       c7-voiture   PAR-3s gâter-VF
       La voiture est gâtée.

Tous les exemples de cette section montrent que la marque *ma* a deux fonctions. C'est-à-dire que la distinction entre un parfait du résultat et un passé immédiat qu'on trouve dans beaucoup de langues est neutralisée en nɔmaándé.

6. Le négatif

La marque du négatif en nɔmaándé n'a qu'une seule forme au mode indicatif, à savoir: *tɛ-/ti-* selon les règles d'harmonie vocalique. Le ton lexical de ce préfixe est ton bas. Cette marque du négatif se trouve dans le complexe pronominal au perfectif et à l'imperfectif, sauf dans le cas de l'habituel. Là, la marque du négatif se manifeste seulement entre les deux pronoms répétés qui précèdent directement le verbe (cf. §6.2). Nous commencerons la description de la marque du négatif en parlant de son emplacement canonique au complexe pronominal. Le tableau (89) montre la forme des complexes pronominaux à valeur de négatif (cf. (11)).

(89)

PRONOM	NEGATIF	TEMPS	PRONOM	(avec *ŋa*)	
ɛ-	tɛ-	ŋa	-amɛ	→ ɛtɛŋamɛ	(1s)
ɔ-	tɛ-	ŋa	-ɔɔ	→ ɔtɛŋɔɔ	(2s)
u-	tɛ-	ŋa	-aa	→ utɛŋaa	(3s)
tɔ-	tɛ-	ŋa	-asɔ	→ tɔtɛŋasɔ	(1p)
nɔ-	tɛ-	ŋa	-anɔ	→ nɔtɛŋanɔ	(2p)
bá-	tɛ-	ŋa	-abɔ	→ bátɛŋabɔ	(3p)

6.1. Le négatif au perfectif. La marque du négatif se place toujours entre le pronom initial du complexe et la marque temporelle.

(90) *I-ti-ké-mi   búm-e.*
      1s-NEG-F2-1s chasser-VF
      Je ne chasserai pas (demain).

(91) *Tu-ti-ŋé-su   ket-i.*
      1p-NEG-PR-1p mesurer-VF
      Nous ne mesurons pas.

Les schémas tonals au négatif sont différents des schémas tonals à l'affirmatif, mais les règles tonales au négatif restent à être elucidées. Ces règles tonales sont le sujet d'une autre étude.[14] Nous limitons notre présente description aux morphèmes segmentaux.

Il y a un changement de morphème dans le complexe pronominal aux temps du passé P0, P1, et P2, quand l'énoncé est au négatif. La marque temporelle qui s'y trouve à l'affirmatif (*ma* au passé P0 et *ŋa* au passé P1 et P2) est remplacée par le morphème *omo/ɔmɔ* pour P0 et P2 et par le morphème *mo/mɔ* pour P1. Ainsi, il n'y a pas de distinction entre le passé immédiat et le passé deuxième degré au négatif, c'est-à-dire les formes sont neutralisées. Au singulier, le pronom final (élément pronominal) devient *-ó/-ɔ́* pour toutes les personnes dans ces trois temps du passé. Ce pronom final disparaît devant un verbe à ton bas. Au pluriel, les pronoms finals restent comme d'habitude pour chaque personne dans les temps du passé P0 et P2.

(92) *I-ti-ómo-ó   bum-e.*
      1s-NEG-P0/2-EP chasser-VF
      Je ne (l')ai pas chassé.

(93) *Tɔ-tɛ-ɔ́mɔ́-sɔ́ hít-e.*
      1p-NEG-P0/2-1p prendre-VF
      Nous ne (l')avons pas pris.

Le passé premier degré emploie le pronom final *-ó/-ɔ́* pour toutes les personnes, mais ce pronom final disparaît devant un verbe à ton bas. Ainsi, le ton haut du pronom final domine le ton lexical bas du radical verbal.

(94) *Nɔ-tɛ-mɔ-ɔ́   taŋ-a.*
      2p-NEG-P1 -EP parler-VF
      Vous n'avez pas parlé (ce matin).

(95) *Tɔ-tɛ-mɔ námb-a   tabɔkɔ.*
      1p-NEG-P1 cacher-VF rien
      Nous n'avons rien caché (ce matin).

Il est à souligner que le suffixe *-Vk* ne peut pas apparaître au négatif au perfectif sauf au futur premier degré (F1).

(96) *U-ti-ŋé-e   ket-ik-i.*
      3s-NEG-F1-3s mesurer-F1S-VF
      Il ne va pas mesurer.

---

[14]Voir Wilkendorf 1988.

Ce fait semble confirmer la fonction grammaticale du suffixe -*Vk* au futur F1 et il montre que ce suffixe n'est qu'un homophone du suffixe duratif (cf. §3), parce qu'il se trouve dans les constructions du futur proche (F1) là où les règles générales disent que le suffixe duratif est exclu.

6.2. Le négatif à l'imperfectif. L'habituel au présent emploie la même marque du négatif qu'au perfectif, c'est-à-dire *tɛ-/ti-*, mais, au lieu de se trouver au sein du complexe pronominal, cette marque apparaît au milieu de la séquence de deux pronoms répétés qui vient après l'auxiliaire *bá* et avant le verbe lui-même.

(97) *Ɛ-na-ŋa   i-ti-émi   lén-é   hɛ-maka.*
    1s-HAB-IPF/PR 1s-NEG-1s aimer-VF c19-fusil
    Je n'aime pas du tout les armes.

De même, au passé de l'habituel, la marque du négatif ne se trouve que dans la séquence de pronoms répétés avant le radical du verbe.

(98) *Ɔ́-ŋɔ-ɔ bá ɔ-tɛ-ɔ́   kuán-a.*
    2s-P3-2s AUX 2s-NEG-2s trouver-VF
    Tu n'avais pas l'habitude de trouver.

En regardant l'habituel au futur à valeur négatif, nous constatons que la marque du négatif se trouve de nouveau au sein du complexe pronominal.

(99) *I-ti-ŋé-búl-émi   lén-é   ba-násé   a   bá-abé.*
    1s-NEG-F1-HAB/F-1s aimer-VF c2-enfant MA c2-mauvais
    Je n'aurai pas l'habitude d'aimer les mauvais enfants (ce soir).

(100) *Tu-ti-ké-búl-asɔ́   fán-a.*
    1p-NEG-F2-HAB/F-1p lire-VF
    Nous n'aurons pas l'habitude de lire (dès demain).

Le progressif au présent place la marque du négatif dans le complexe pronominal, mais la forme de celui-ci change. Au lieu de garder la forme *x-x-ŋa* comme à l'affirmatif (67), le progressif au présent place le négatif *tɛ-/ti-* entre les deux pronoms et laisse tomber la marque de l'imperfectif au présent *-ŋa*. La forme du complexe devient ainsi parallèle à la suite de pronoms répétés dans l'habituel au présent et au passé à valeur de négatif (cf. (97) et (98)).

(101) *Nɔ-tɛ-anɔ́   bá   ɔ-ɔ-wáamb-a   bɛnyɛma bi-ɔ́nyia.*
2p-NEG-2p   AUX LOC-c15ˆINF-chercher-VF choses   c8-manger
Vous n'êtes pas en train de chercher de nourriture.

La forme du complexe pronominal au négatif dans le progressif au passé est identique à celle du complexe au négatif du perfectif (cf. §6.1). Ainsi, aux temps du passé P0, P1, et P2 le morphème *omo/ɔmɔ* suit la marque du négatif *tɛ-/ti-* dans le complexe pronominal. Le pronom final est *-ó/-ɔ́* pour toutes les personnes au singulier. Le passé troisième degré garde sa marque temporelle *ŋa* après la marque du négatif.

(102) *Tɔ-tɛ-ŋá-sɔ́   bá   o-ó-!wéénd-e   i-bíle.*
1p-NEG-P3-1p   AUX LOC-c15ˆINF-piétiner-VF c4-noix
Nous n'étions pas en train de piétiner des noix.

(103) *Nɔ-tɛ-ɔ́mɔ-nɔ́   bá   ɔ-ɔ-wáamb-a   i-búnyí.*
2p-NEG-P0/1/2-EP   AUX LOC-c15ˆINF-chercher-VF c9-chèvre
Vous n'étiez pas en train de chercher la chèvre.

Dans le progressif au futur, la marque du négatif se trouve toujours au sein du complexe pronominal aussi bien au futur premier degré qu'au futur deuxième degré.

(104) *Tɔ-tɛ-ŋá-sɔ   bá   ɔ-ɔ́-!nyí-á.*
1p-NEG-F1-1p   AUX LOC-c15ˆINF-manger-VF
Nous ne serons pas en train de manger (ce soir).

(105) *Ɛ-tɛ-ká-mɛ   bá   ɔ-ɔ-nyí-ɔ   buóli.*
1s-NEG-F2-1s   AUX LOC-c15ˆINF-travailler-VF travail
Je ne serai pas en train de travailler (demain).

7. Conclusions

Le système temporel et aspectuel de la langue nɔmaándé semble du premier coup beaucoup trop complexe et même redondant. Le perfectif seul emploie plusieurs marques segmentales et tonales pour indiquer le temps du verbe et il y ajoute un suffixe verbal pour le futur premier degré. Pour cinq des huit temps présentés ici, les marques temporelles au niveau du complexe pronominal suffisent déjà pour distinguer ces temps. Les tons verbaux sont redondants dans ces cas, mais ils aident à indiquer l'aspect perfectif. Pour les trois autres temps (P3, PR, F1), les tons verbaux sont nécessaires chaque fois pour parvenir à une opposition minimale entre ces temps. Il y a quand même la nécessité d'employer le suffixe verbal -*Vk* au futur premier degré pour le rendre distinct du présent pour les verbes à ton bas.

En parlant du suffixe -*Vk*, nous avons découvert deux formes homophones en nɔmaándɛ: l'une qui indique le perfectif futur premier degré et l'autre qui marque les actions duratives et itératives. La forme qui marque duratif/itératif ne semble pas distinguer l'aspect imperfectif du perfectif. Ce suffixe peut apparaître dans des syntagmes verbaux à l'imperfectif aussi bien qu'au perfectif.

L'emploie de la méthode autosegmentale de Goldsmith nous aide à comprendre le phénomène de l'abaissement tonal, qui donne un ton haut abaissé. En plus, cette méthode nous donne la possibilité de bien expliquer l'emplacement de tous les tons verbaux.

A l'imperfectif nous avons constaté plusieurs syntagmes possibles, surtout au progressif. Le syntagme locatif semble suffire pour marquer le progressif dans tous les cas, mais aux temps du passé deux autres syntagmes sont également employés. Ceux-ci indiquent aussi bien l'habituel que le progressif. L'opposition entre ces deux catégories d'imperfectif semble être neutralisée au passé, et la distinction entre ces syntagmes n'est pas manifeste même pour les locuteurs de la langue. Peut-être que leurs distinctions se trouvent dans les domaines du discours, de la mise en relief, ou dans d'autres considérations pragmatiques. Nous n'avons pas encore aborder ces domaines en détail.

La marque *ma* en nɔmaándɛ est employée pour exprimer le passé immédiat. Elle s'emploie aussi dans un sens étendu pour exprimer le résultat d'une situation dans le passé. La forme de la marque pour ces deux fonctions reste la même.

Au perfectif la marque du négatif *tɛ-/ti-* se trouve toujours dans le complexe pronominal. La forme de ce complexe devient identique aux temps du passé P0 et P2. Mais à l'imperfectif, l'emplacement de la marque du négatif varie selon le temps du verbe et selon l'aspect—s'il s'agit d'une action habituelle ou d'une action progressive.

Le syntagme verbal en nɔmaándɛ est visiblement bien complexe avec plusieurs marques disjonctives et d'autres qui sont redondantes. En plus, il y a des morphèmes sans tons et d'autres qui ne consistent qu'en ton flottant. On trouve aussi dans le syntagme verbal une seule fonction exprimée par plusieurs syntagmes aussi bien que la neutralisation de plusieurs fonctions sur un seul syntagme.

Les règles tonales décrites ici forment aussi un domaine assez complexe dans l'étude du système temporel et aspectuel en nɔmaándɛ. Dans une étude plus approfondie nous aborderons la question des autres règles tonales pour les constructions négatives.

References

Comrie, Bernard. 1976. Aspect. Cambridge: Cambridge University Press.

———. 1985. Tense. Cambridge: Cambridge University Press.

Dieu, Michel et Patrick Renaud. 1983. Situation linguistique en Afrique Centrale, Inventaire préliminaire: le Cameroun. Paris/Yaoundé: ACCT CERDOTOLA DGRST (Atlas linguistique de l'Afrique Centrale: Atlas linguistique du Cameroun). cartes.

Dubois, J. et al. 1973. Dictionnaire de linguistique. Paris: Larousse.

Dugast, I. 1971. Grammaire du tunən. Langues et Littératures de l'Afrique Noire, VIII. Paris: Editions Klincksieck.

Goldsmith, John. 1976. Autosegmental phonology. Bloomington: Indiana University Linguistics Club.

Greenberg, Joseph. 1948. The tonal system of Proto-Bantu. Journal of the Linguistics Circle of New York 4:196–208.

Guthrie, Malcolm. 1967. The classification of Bantu languages. London: Dawsons of Pall Mall.

———. 1971. Comparative Bantu 2. Farnborough, England: Gregg International Publishers.

Hedinger, Robert. 1985. The verb in Akɔɔse. Studies in African Linguistics 16(1):1–55.

Meeussen, A. E. 1967. Bantu grammatical reconstructions. Africana Linguistica III, Annales, Sciences Humaines, 61:79–121. Tervuren: Musée Royal de l'Afrique Centrale.

Nissim, Gabriel. 1975. Grammaire bamiléké. Yaoundé: Université de Yaoundé. Cahier du Département 6.

Pulleyblank, Douglas. 1986. Tone in lexical phonology. Dordrecht: D. Reidel Publishing Company.

Scruggs, Terri. 1983. Phonological analysis of the Nɔmaándé language. ms.

Stanley, Carol. 1986. Description phonologique et morpho-syntaxique de la langue tikar (parlée au Cameroun). Thèse présentée en vue du doctorat d'état. Université de la Sorbonne Nouvelle, Paris III.

Taylor, Carolyn. 1983. Notes et observations. ms.

———. 1986. Extensions du radical en nɔmaánté. Journal of West African Languages 16(1):53–62.

Wilkendorf, Patricia. 1985. Nɔmaánté aspect. ms.

———. 1986. The marking of tense in nɔmaánté. Journal of West African Languages 16(1):63–74.

———. 1988. Negation in Nɔmaándé. Journal of West African Languages 18(2):49–70. ms.

Relative Time Reference in Nugunu

Carol Orwig

Abstract

This paper briefly outlines the constructions used to mark tense and aspect in Nugunu before it focuses on their interaction in constructions where the present moment is not the basic reference point. While some constructions allow tense markers to retain their reference to various degrees of remoteness, others do not. Most noteworthy in this regard is the symmetrical restrictions which allow only the near past marker to occur in past and future perfect constructions and only the near future marker to occur in constructions referring to actions which follow other future actions. In these constructions, where certain tense markers are not allowed, the permitted markers lose their reference to near past and near future and refer instead to just past or future in general. By describing these relative time constructions, this paper helps to extend our understanding of Nugunu as it has been described by previous authors.

Résumé

Cet article présente brièvement les structures employées pour marquer le temps et l'aspect en nugunu; puis leur comportement dans des constructions où le moment de l'énonciation n'est pas le point de référence. Un grand nombre de structures sont examinées. Bien que quelques constructions permettent que les marques de temps retiennent leur référence à de divers degrés d'éloignement, il y a d'autres constructions qui ne le permettent pas. Notées particulièrement sont les restrictions symétriques qui permettent que seule la marque du P1 apparaisse dans les constructions du perfectif passé et du perfectif futur; que seule la marque du F1 apparaisse dans des constructions où il y a référence aux actions postérieures à d'autres actions futures. Dans ces constructions, où certaines marques de temps ne sont pas permises, celles qui le sont (P1 ou F1) perdent leur référence au temps passé récent et au futur proche et se réfèrent plutôt au temps du passé ou du futur en général. En décrivant toutes ces constructions au temps relatif, cet article aide à approfondir notre connaissance du nugunu tel qu'il a été décrit par des auteurs précédents.

The object of this paper is to examine the various constructions in Nugunu which refer to the relative marking of time. In order to clearly understand the various options and restrictions of these relative constructions, we first briefly summarize the more basic absolute-time constructions. The similarities and differences of the relative constructions can then be seen in detail.

Geographical location. Nugunu is spoken in the Central province of Cameroon in the subdistricts of Ombessa and Bokito of the district of Mbam. There are two dialects, Nugunu North and Nugunu South. Though differing somewhat both lexically and phonologically, these dialects are mutually intelligible and are considered to be the same language by their speakers. It is difficult to estimate the number of speakers, given the lack of a recent census, but considering the increase in population in the area and the significant number of speakers living outside the language area, we may say with some assurance that there are currently more than the 30,000 speakers estimated by Robinson in the introduction to his phonology (1984:13).

Language name and classification. The name Nugunu is used by the speakers themselves to refer to their language. This name contains the prefix *nu-*, the classifier used for languages, and the root *gunu*, which refers to the ethnic and linguistic identity of the people. They refer to themselves, the people, as *bégunu*. Some earlier descriptions of this language use the name Gunu, or Yambassa. The latter name appears to have been given by German colonial authorities to a group of peoples of the Mbam who speak related but distinct languages and who consider themselves to have different cultural identities. The *bégunu* are among these people. As they themselves prefer the name Nugunu, and as the Linguistic Atlas of Cameroon has now adopted this name, we employ it here.

Phonemes. In his phonology of Nugunu, Robinson (1984:38) established the following consonant phonemes: *p, b, mp, mb, m, f, t, d, nt, nd, n, s, l, c, nc, ny, y, k, g, nk, ng,* + and *h*. There are seven vowels: *i, e, ε, a, ɔ, o, u*, which are arranged into two sets according to vowel harmony: the close set consists of *i, e, u,* and *o*; the open set of *ε, a, ɔ,* and *o*. Note that *o* may occur with either set (Robinson 1984:55).

Phonetically, there are five lexical pitch patterns in Nugunu—high, low, mid, rising, and falling. They are analyzed, however, as phonemically high or low tones, the pitch glides being sequences of high and low or low and high. The phonetic mid pitch comes from lexical downstep or from tone perturbations. In the orthography, high tone (H) is marked. All unmarked vowels therefore carry low tone (L). All rising and falling tones are marked by a series of high and low tones over vowel sequences, even if the tone glide is realized phonetically as a short vowel.

1. Basic tense and aspect systems

Nugunu has a typically Bantu spectrum of tense oppositions. In addition to present tense (PRES), there are three degrees of remoteness in both past and future tenses. The tense hereafter referred to as P1 is a HODIER-NAL PAST TENSE, that refers to an event or state occurring earlier the same day as the speech event. P2 normally refers to situations or events occurring the day preceding the speech event, although it may extend further into the past. P3 is the most remote past tense, typically referring to things which happened long ago or at least earlier than the preceding day.

Future tenses are symmetrical with those of the past. F1 refers to something which will happen later today, F2 to something which will happen tomorrow or in the relatively near future, and F3 to something which will occur in the distant future. The difference between F2 and F3 is also one of certainty; if the speaker is more certain that something will happen in the future—in say, a year's time—he is more likely to use F2 than F3. For a more complete description of absolute tense in Nugunu, see Gerhardt 1989.

1.1. Tense. Tense is marked in the Nugunu verb phrase by an overt form accompanied by an additional tone realized on a noninitial syllable of the verb. This overt form follows the subject marker and precedes the verb root. The tense markers are presented in (1) and a sample paradigm follows in (2).

(1) Tense markers

P3	*mba*	+	H following the verb root
P2	*á*	+	H following the verb root
P1	*báa*	+	L following the verb root
PRES	$\emptyset$	+	L following the verb root
F1	*gaá*	+	H following the verb root
F2	*ná*	+	L following the verb root
F3	*nga*	+	H following the verb root

(2) Sample paradigm of *go dɔ́mba* 'to leave/pass'

	SUBJ	TNS	ROOT	
P3	*A*	*mba*	*dɔ́mbá.*	'He left (long ago).'
P2	*A*	*á*	*dɔ́mbá.*	'He left (yesterday).'
P1	*A*	*báa*	*dɔ́mba.*	'He left (earlier today).'
PRES	*A*		*dɔ́mba.*	'He is about to leave.'
F1	*A*	*gaá*	*dɔ́mbá.*	'He will leave (later today).'
F2	*A*	*ná*	*dɔ́mba.*	'He will leave (tomorrow).'
F3	*A*	*nga*	*dɔ́mbá.*	'He will leave (someday).'

The perfective form of the present tense is used to signal imminent action.

1.2. Aspect. In each tense it is possible to mark the distinction between perfective and imperfective (IMPF) aspect. Some verbs take a verbal suffix *-an* (or its reduplicated form *-anan*) in their imperfective forms; others, like *go bana* 'to read', do not. The most frequent way to show imperfectivity is by a periphrastic construction using the verb *go bémba* 'to be'. Paradigms of imperfective forms of the verbs *go dúe* 'to sell' and *go bana* 'to read' follow in (3) and (4), where *lɛ* (BE) is the suppletive form of *go bémba* found in present and past tenses. When the tense marker precedes the form of the verb 'to be', the subject marker *a* is repeated before the verb root. The form of the verbal suffix showing imperfectivity for *go dúe* is *-enen* because of vowel harmony.

(3) Paradigm of imperfective forms of *go dúe* 'to sell'

	SUBJ	TNS	BE	SUBJ	IMPF^ROOT	
P3	*A*	*mba*	*lɛ́*	*a*	*dúenene.*	'He was selling (long ago).'
P2	*A*	*á*	*lɛ́*	*a*	*dúenene.*	'He was selling (yesterday).'
P1	*A*	*báa*	*lɛ́*	*a*	*dúenene.*	'He was selling (today).'
PRES				*A*	*dúenene.*	'He is selling.'
F1	*A*	*gaá*	*bémbá*	*a*	*dúenene.*	'He will be selling (today).'
F2	*A*	*ná*	*bémba*	*a*	*dúenene.*	'He will be selling (tomorrow).'
F3	*A*	*ŋga*	*bémbá*	*a*	*dúenene.*	'He will be selling (someday).'

(4) Paradigm of imperfective forms of *go bana* 'to read'

	SUBJ	TNS	BE	SUBJ	IMPF^ROOT	
P3	*A*	*mba*	*lέ*	*a*	*bana.*	'She was reading (long ago).'
P2	*A*	*á*	*lέ*	*a*	*bana.*	'She was reading (yesterday).'
P1	*A*	*baá*	*lέ*	*a*	*bana.*	'She was reading (today).'
PRES				*A*	*bana.*	'She reads.'
F1	*A*	*gaá*	*bémbá*	*a*	*bana.*	'She will be reading (today).'
F2	*A*	*na*	*bémba*	*a*	*bana.*	'She will be reading (tomorrow).'
F3	*A*	*ŋga*	*bémbá*	*a*	*bana.*	'She will be reading (someday).'

Although the phrases in (3) and (4) are given progressive glosses, they are general imperfective forms and can equally well express habitual meaning. Except for the frequently used present tense, the imperfective verb suffix is redundant in that the construction as a whole marks imperfective aspect. On the other hand, for verbs which do not allow the imperfective suffix, such as *go bana* 'to read', the contrast between present perfective (i.e., imminent action) and present imperfective is neutralized. For more detailed discussion of aspectual distinctions in Nugunu, see Gerhardt 1989.

1.3. Other verbal constructions. Nugunu has a number of other common verbal constructions, some of them periphrastic. Several of these enter into this study and are mentioned here. First, two variations on the present progressive are illustrated in (5) and (6). (Note in the examples following the abbreviations INF for infinitive, NEG for negative, and DEP for dependent marked on verbs in dependent clauses.)

(5) *A   gá   dúenene.*
     he still sell^IMPF
     He is still selling.

(6) *A   ná   lέ   go   dúenene.*
     he already BE INF sell^IMPF
     He is already selling./He is in the process of selling.

Another construction indicates past perfective action.

(7)   *A báa go dúe.*
      he P1 INF sell
      He already sold.

Yet another construction shows imminent future.

(8)   *A ná lé ba go dúe.*
      he already BE of INF sell
      He is about to sell.

1.4. Subject marker repetition. We saw above, in the discussion of the imperfective constructions, that the subject marker is repeated. There seems to be a limit to the amount of information that can be packed into the verb phrase before the repetition of the subject marker becomes necessary. Take the constructions with present progressive meaning in examples (5) and (6). These constructions, in past or future tense, require separate sections for marking tense and aspect, respectively. This is accomplished by use of the auxiliary verb *ŋá*, which in its independent form is the verb meaning 'to do'. The tense marker occurs before the verb *ŋá*, then the subject pronoun is repeated before the marking of progressive aspect.

(9)   *A mba ŋá a gá   dúenene.*
      he P3   do he still sell^IMPF
      He was still selling.

(10) *A mba ŋá a ná   lé go dúenene.*
      he P3   do he already BE INF sell^IMPF
      He was already selling.

If the form in (9) is negated, yet another section must be added to the verb phrase to mark the negation, as in (11). It is not possible to negate the form in (10) containing *ná*, because it seems to indicate something that actually is going on.

(11) *A mba ŋá a gá lé a dɛ   dúé.*
      he P3   do he still BE he NEG sell
      He had not yet sold.

In (11) both *ŋá* and *lé* are used as auxiliaries. The first section of the phrase, using *ŋá* and the tense marker, sets the time of the situation. The second section, using *lé*, shows that progressive or habitual action is in focus, while the final section indicates both the nature of the action and the fact that the action was not taking place. It should be noted that the imperfective suffix drops out in this negative construction.

2. Relative time reference

The purpose of this study is to indicate how Nugunu uses tense and aspectual systems to locate events relative to each other in time. As a basis for discussing time reference, we use the framework set out by Comrie (1985:36,56), in which he defines absolute tense as locating situations in time relative to the present moment (moment of speech), and relative tense as relating situations in time relative to a reference point which may or may not coincide with the present moment. We now consider the constructions Nugunu uses to describe simultaneous actions as well as those anterior to or posterior to another state or event.

2.1. Simultaneity. The term SIMULTANEOUS is used to refer in general to actions or situations which occur at the same time. Within this definition, however, we distinguish included situations from those which are coextensive. Included situations are those which occur completely within the time span of another situation, e.g., 'It was raining when I arrived'. Here there may well have been a period of time when it was raining and I did not arrive, but no time at which I arrived and it was not raining. Coextensive situations are those which occupy roughly the same time span, as in 'The woman chatted with her neighbor while she sold doughnuts'.

Included situations. Nugunu typically expresses the INCLUDING situation with the imperfective form of a given tense and the INCLUDED situation by the perfective form of the same tense. Any tense may be used. It is irrelevant to tense marking whether the subjects of the two clauses are identical or different.

(12) Ɔkɔ́dɔ a   bá lɛ́ a   foanana mbasa,
      woman she P1 BE she grill^IMP corn

           gɔ́ɔgɔ a   bá ná ɔ́bɔ́ boóma.
           then   she P1 DEP hear thing
      The woman was grilling corn, then she heard something.

(13)   *Nobólá nó á lé nó náanana,*
       rain it P2 BE it fall^IMPF

       aŋa   ŋga á ná bolá   iyo.
       when   I   P2 DEP arrive yesterday
       The rain was falling when I arrived yesterday.

(14)   *Gɛcamɛna gimmée géɛgɛ mbolamɔ́   naá   isekúle,*
       time   every   that   I^arrive^DEP at   school

       nobóla   nó náanana.
       rain   it fall^IMPF
       Every time I go to school, it is raining.

(15)   *A gaá bémbá a   dúenene makala   méhé naá nyonyí,*
       she F1 BE   she sell^IMPF doughnuts her   at   market

       aŋa   kaá ná bolá.
       when   I^F1 DEP arrive
       She will be selling her doughnuts at the market when I arrive.

We see from (12)–(15) that there is no relative use of tense markers in
included situations, rather both clauses are overtly marked for tense and
there is overt concord between them. The aspectual difference is marked
overtly and is the key for determining which clause expresses the including
and which the included situation. To stress progressive meaning in the
including situation a verb phrase begins with a section using the verb *ŋá*
to mark tense, as in the constructions discussed in §1.4, and indicates
aspect in a second section, as in (16).

(16)   *A ná ŋá a ná   lé go dúenene fɛa   séhé,*
       she F2 do she already BE INF sell^IMPF avocados her

       gɛcamɛna géɛgɛ o   ná bolamɔ́.
       time   which you F2 arrive^DEP
       She will already be selling her avocados when you arrive.

In narrative discourse, there are two other forms which may be used in
the second clause of such sentences in place of fully specified verbs—the
narrative past (NP) or the infinitive. The narrative past is similar in form
to P1, using the same marker, *báa*, but causing H instead of L on syllables
in the verb which follow the root. The infinitive is marked the same as the

present tense but is preceded by the infinitive marker *go* instead of by a subject pronoun. The infinitive may have either a noun as subject or may be preceded by a possessive pronoun in place of a subject pronoun. For further discussion of these forms and the conditions under which they are used, see Robinson 1980. For the purposes of this study, we simply note here that these forms may be substituted for perfective verbs of any of the three past tenses in certain discourse settings, once the time setting has been established. An example is presented in (17).

(17)   *Kɔ́ɔ, aŋa a ná   lé go éda,*
        so, when he already BE INF go

        géhé go gɔ́lɛnɔ   naá bɛasé.
        his INF be^caught in   trap
        So, when he is already going along, he is caught in a trap.

Coextensive situations. Coextensive situations are those which extend over roughly the same period of time. In Nugunu, these situations are expressed by specifying the first clause overtly for tense and using the present imperfective in the second clause to indicate an action taking place at the same time as the first. Depending on whether or not the verb takes an imperfective suffix (§1.2), it may or may not be overtly marked as imperfective. This, therefore, is a relative use of the present, since it is 'present' only in relation to the time frame of the first clause and not in relation to the moment of speaking.

(18)   *A ná ŋá a ná   lé go dúenene makala,*
        she F2 do she already BE INF sell^IMPF doughnuts

        a   ménɛgana na   begúle béhɛ.
        she visits^IMPF with friends her
        She will be in the market selling doughnuts and visiting with her friends.

(19)   *Ɔkɔ́dɔ a báa lé ndukíi naá busío bá nnyaŋá,*
        woman she P1 BE seated at   front of house

        a   ná   lé go bana.
        she already BE INF read
        The woman was seated in front of the house reading.

(20) *Ompɔ́nyɛ   yó   mba   lɛ́   badɛ́mánáalú naá   gɛcaba,*
      mosquito   it   P3   BE   perched   on   wall

          yó   mo   núune.
          it   him   watch
      The mosquito was perched on the wall, watching him.

It is also possible in Nugunu to refer to the first verb in the perfective
aspect and describe the coextensive situation by the present imperfective
following the expression *ɛ éda* meaning 'as he goes'.

(21) *A   mba   yɔgɔ́nɔ́   naá   ntɛ́mɛ́,*
      he   P3   work   in   field

          ɛ   éda   a   agana   ɛsɔgɔ́.
          he   go   he   sing^IMPF   songs
      He worked in the fields, singing songs as he worked.

(22) *Ɔkɔ́dɔ   a   báa   dɔ́mba   nnyaŋá yamɛ na   gɛyɛ́nɛ́,*
      woman   she   P1   pass   house   my   with   morning

          ɛ   éda   a   yúŋenye   moɔnɔ́   bɛhé.
          she   go   she   nurse   baby   her
      A woman passed my house this morning, nursing her baby as she
      went.

Again, in (22), the time is set by the tense marker on the first verb and
the second verb is a relative use of the present form to show simultaneity.

2.2. Anteriority. In this section, various ways in which speakers of
Nugunu may indicate that one event is anterior in time to another are
considered. These constructions differ from the simultaneous constructions
of §2.1 in that both clauses are marked for perfective aspects.

Anteriority marked by subordination. One way of indicating that an
event occurred anterior to another is to express the first event by a
perfective form of any of the past tenses in a subordinate clause introduced by *aŋa*, a conjunction which introduces circumstantial clauses and
may be translated as 'when' or 'since' depending on whether the circumstance is temporal or causal. The succeeding action is then expressed
in the main clause by a perfective verb form.

Although theoretically the verb in the main clause can be marked either as the same tense as the first action or as a more recent past tense, in most instances we find it is represented by the narrative past or by the infinitive instead of by an absolute tense. This is because such sentences are most often found in narrative discourses, either personal accounts or folk tales. If one of these narrative forms is used, the hearer will interpret the action as occurring at the time established in the setting at the beginning of the discourse. We see again from this construction that both the narrative past and the infinitive used in narrative discourse are perfective forms. An example of each follows in (23) and (24).

(23) *Iyó   ŋgɛ ɛ́ ɛ́dá mɛ́sɛ́ go bigúlí   bɛ́námányɛ.*
     yesterday I   P2 go mass   at hour   eight

     Aŋa   mɛ́sɛ́ má á   ná   húmé,
     when   mass it P2 DEP let^out

     m bɛ́ɛ ɛ́dá naá   nyonyí, go go ɔ́ndɔ boyɛ́ga.
     I NP go   to   market for INF buy   pineapple
     Yesterday I went to mass at eight o'clock. When mass let out, I
     went to market to buy a pineapple.

(24) *Aŋa nó mbaá mo síŋgílídé tíŋí   kúnúu   go hɔnɛdɔ.*
     when it P3 him catch   tightly Tortoise INF laugh
     When it caught him tightly, Tortoise laughed.

Absolute relative tenses. Nugunu has constructions similar to the pluperfect and future perfect in European languages which allow the speaker to specifically locate a situation as previous in time to a point of reference other than the present. In discussing these constructions we find it helpful to adopt the formulae of Comrie (1985:125–126), repeated here in (25), where E refers to the event in question, R to the reference point, and S to the present or moment of speaking.

(25) Absolute relative formulae

     Pluperfect   = E before R before S
     Future Perfect = E before R after S

Nugunu basically uses one device to establish the relationship between R and S whether R is future or past. This device is the addition of another section to the verb phrase using the auxiliary ŋá (§1.4). Given Nugunu's rich tense system, it is possible to establish R at any of the three degrees of remoteness of past or future. The anteriority relationship E before R, on the other hand, is shown by the periphrastic perfective construction in (7), using P1 followed by the perfective infinitive. It is not possible to use either of the other past tenses with this relative time reading, although P3 does occur to indicate absolute past perfective situations.

(26) *A   mba ŋá a   báa go dúe fɛa   séhé,*
      he P3   do he P1   INF sell avocados her

      gɛcamɛna géɛgɛ m mbaá bolá.
      time   which I P3^DEP arrive
      He had already sold her avocados when I arrived.

(27) *A   báa ŋá a   báa go gúe,*
      he P1   do she P1   INF die

      gɛcamɛna géɛgɛ m bá ná bolá.
      time   which I P1 DEP arrive
      He had already died when I arrived.

(28) *Nobólá nó ŋga ŋá nó báa go naáa,*
      rain   it F3   do it P1   INF fall

      gɛcamɛna géɛgɛ o   ŋgaá gúlúgé.
      time   which you F3^DEP return
      The rain will already have fallen when you return.

We observe from (26)–(28) that there is agreement between the tense marker in the *ŋá* section of the first clause, establishing R, and the tense marker in the second clause. These agreeing markers indicate absolute time, whereas the P1 marker which precedes the INF marker is used to indicate relative past and does not imply any degree of remoteness.

Comparison of pluperfect with unrealised intention. There are other constructions in Nugunu where P1 is used in other than its primary sense. For example, there is a construction quite similar in form to the pluperfect, but which, instead of showing anteriority in the past, expresses an intention in the past which was not fulfilled. This construction also uses P1 in the second section of the verb phrase. Any of the past tenses may be used with the auxiliary *ŋá* to set the time reference.

(29) *M báa ŋá m bɔ́ɔ ɔ́ndɔ nnámbɔ́,*
      I P1 do I P1   buy meat

    kané cɛ báa lé na muinyí.
    but I^NEG P1 BE with money
I was going to buy meat, but I didn't have any money.

(30) *M mba ŋá m báa légalɛga go bɛa ɔkɔ́dɔ múunyu,*
      I P3 do I P1 want INF have woman that

    kané bisée bá mbi inyée.
    but parents they P3 refuse
I would have liked to have married that woman, but her parents refused.

The crucial difference between this construction expressing unfulfilled intention and the pluperfect is the presence in the pluperfect of *go* (INF) after *báa* (P1) in the second section of the verb phrase. If this is left out, the event did not actually take place. Compare (31) and (32).

(31) *Dɛ mba ŋá dɛ báa mo bófolio.*
      we P3 do we P1 him forget
We would have forgotten him (but something reminded us.)

(32) *Dɛ mba ŋá dɛ báa go mo bófolio.*
      we P3 do we P1 INF him forget
We had already forgotten him (when something else happened.)

2.3. Posteriority. In Nugunu, it is also possible to specify events as occurring subsequent to a reference point other than the present, although this rarely occurs. Different constructions are used to specify future in reference to the past and future in reference to the future. Comrie (1985:128) represents such constructions as in (33).

(33) Relative future formulae

    Future in the past   = E after R before S
    Future in the future = E after R after S

Future in the past. Any of the three future tenses may be used to describe actions subsequent to a situation in the past, irrespective of whether or not the action has happened at the time of speech, as indicated in (34)–(36).

(34) *Mmáa   a   mba lé   a   bala ntémé,*
      Mother   she P3   BE   she clear field

      goaké   nobóla nó nú úle   naá   ofé   ya mars.
      because rain   it F2 come at   month of March
      Mother was clearing the field because the rains would come in March.

(35) *Ɔkɔ́dɔ a mba lé a námba oká,*
      woman she P3   BE she prepare cassava^leaves

      goaké   ohaŋa bɛhé a   guú úlé   go ukúle.
      because son   her   he F1 come   for visit
      The woman was cooking cassava leaves because her son would come (later that day) for a visit.

(36) *Ohaŋa   a   mba bédégáná muinyí,*
      young^man he P3   save   money

      goaké   buisí búmmue a   ŋga lúgé   okɔ́dɔ.
      because day   one   he F3 marry   wife
      The young man saved money because one day he might marry.

The same construction occurs with verbs of speaking, thinking, or knowing in the past as in (37). Notice that future tenses are relative with respect to R, the time established in the first clause, but are not necessarily future with respect to S. They do, however, retain their contrast in degrees of remoteness.

(37) *Kúnúu   a   mba lé   i   íyimene,*
      Tortoise he P3   BE   he   know

      goŋaá a gɛɛ́ ɛ́dá naá Makóa.
      that he F1 go to Makoa
      Tortoise knew that he would go to Makoa (later that day).

Future in the future. It is also possible to indicate immediate future in the future by combining a future tense marker with a periphrastic construction meaning 'to be on the point of doing something'. We may have, for instance, the absolute use of the imminent future construction, as in (38).

(38) *A ná   lέ ba go gúe.*
      he already BE of INF die
      He is about to die.

This may be extended by any of the three future tenses and the auxiliary *ŋá* to indicate that at a future time he will be about to die.

(39) *A gaá ŋá a ná   lέ ba go gúe.*
      he FI   do he already BE of INF die
      He will be about to die.

F2 and F3 can be used as well before *ŋá* to establish the reference point as subsequent to S, but it seems that the imminent future construction is the only way to indicate that the event is posterior to R. This restriction parallels the past perfect and future perfect constructions, where any of the tense markers can be used to set the point of reference; but only one construction is used to indicate anteriority (§2.2).

3. Summary

Some of the ways by which speakers of Nugunu locate events relative to each other in time have been examined. Present, past, and future tense markers are all used in relative ways once an absolute time frame has been established for a sentence. The aspectual distinction between perfective and imperfective has also been shown to be vital in distinguishing whether certain situations are anterior to or simultaneous with others.

References

Comrie, Bernard. 1976. Aspect. Cambridge: Cambridge University Press.
———. 1981. Language universals and linguistic typology. Chicago: University of Chicago Press.
———. 1985. Tense. Cambridge: Cambridge University Press.
Gerhardt, Phyllis. 1989. Les temps en nugunu. In Daniel Barreteau and Robert Hedinger (eds.), Descriptions de langues camerounaises. Paris: Agence de Coopération Culturelle et Technique et ORSTOM.

Orwig, Carol. 1989. Extensions verbales en nugunu. In Daniel Barreteau
    and Robert Hedinger (eds.), Descriptions de langues camerounaises.
    Paris: Agence de Coopération Culturelle et Technique et ORSTOM.
Robinson, Clinton. 1980. The internal structure of Gunu narrative text.
    Cahiers de Littérature Orale 8:99–123.
———. 1984. Phonologie du gunu, parter yambassa (langue bantoue du
    Cameroun). Paris: SELAF.

Section Two

Grassfields Bantu Languages

Conditionals in Mundani

Elizabeth Parker

Abstract

Mundani is a Western Grassfields Bantu language of the Momo subgroup. Conditional sentences in Mundani are divided into four types: simple or open conditionals, hypothetical conditionals, counterfactual conditionals, and concessive conditionals. Each of these four types is defined in semantic terms, and then their syntactic features are described, including morphological marking, verb forms, and possible combinations of tenses and aspects.

An attempt is made to fit this description of conditionals in Mundani into the typology drawn by Sukari Saloné in the article "Typology of conditionals and conditionals in Haya" (1979). Saloné suggests a typological link between the kind of tense-aspect system that predominates in a given language and the presence or absence of crucial tense distinctions in the categories of real and imaginary conditionals. These tense distinctions mesh with a third factor—whether open future conditionals pattern syntactically with conditionals that are semantically real or with those that are unreal.

Mundani may be said to exhibit the following characteristics:

- tense prominence
- tense distinctions in both real and imaginary conditionals
- open future conditionals that pattern syntactically with real conditionals.

In these respects, it seems to fit Saloné's typological scheme. There is some ambivalence, however, in the classification of open future conditionals. A historical connection may eventually be established between the marker of general future tense and the hypothetical marker, in which case future conditionals would be seen to pattern syntactically with conditionals that are semantically unreal, and Mundani would prove to be a counterexample to the suggested typology.

It is further noted that the language sample on which Saloné's observations are based is small and unrepresentative. More research is needed to discover whether the proposed typological links hold over a wide range of languages.

165

Résumé

Le mundani est une langue bantu des Grassfields de l'ouest, sous-groupe momo. Les phrases au conditionnel en mundani sont réparties en quatre types: les conditionnels simples ou ouverts, les conditionnels hypothétiques, les conditionnels contrefactifs et les conditionnels concessifs. Chacun de ces quatre types se définit d'abord du point de vue de la sémantique. Les caractéristiques d'ordre syntaxique sont présentées ensuite, y compris les morphèmes, les formes verbales et les différentes combinaisons d'aspects et de temps, qui sont spécifiques à chaque type.

Cette description des phrases au conditionnel s'insère dans le cadre d'une typologie formulée par Sukari Saloné dans son article intitulé 'Typology of conditionals and conditionals in Haya' (1979). Saloné propose un lien typologique entre le système des temps et des aspects dans une langue donnée, et la présence ou l'absence dans cette même langue de certaines oppositions temporelles dans les phrases au conditionnel réelles et imaginaires. Il faut tenir compte aussi de la structure syntaxique des phrases au conditionnel ouvertes au temps futur, en ce qu'elle situe ces phrases soit dans la catégorie des conditionnels réels, soit parmi les conditionnels imaginaires.

Le mundani manifeste les caractéristiques suivantes:

- prééminence du système des temps sur le système aspectuel
- oppositions temporelles pertinentes dans les phrases conditionnelles réelles et imaginaires
- phrases conditionnelles ouvertes au futur qui ressemblent du point de vue de leur syntaxe aux phrases conditionnelles réelles.

Sous ces trois rapports, le mundani semble cadrer avec la typologie de Saloné. Pourtant, le classement des phrases conditionnelles au futur reste quelque peu ambigu. S'il existe un lien diachronique entre la marque du futur général et la marque de l'aspect hypothéthique, il faudra regrouper les phrases conditionnelles au futur avec celles qui sont irréelles, et pas avec celles qui sont sémantiquement réelles. Le mundani irait alors à l'encontre de la typologie proposée.

On remarquera de plus que l'échantillon des langues qui forme la base des observations de Saloné est très réduit et peu représentatif. Il faudrait élargir le domaine des recherches pour savoir si les rapports typologiques proposés sont valables dans un nombre important des langues du monde.

This study of conditionals in Mundani[1] was prompted by Saloné (1979) on Haya, which suggests there may be a typological link between the kind of tense-aspect system that predominates in a given language and the syntactic distinctions that the language makes between reality and unreality in conditional sentences. Conditional sentences in Mundani are examined to discover whether they fit this proposed typological scheme.

1. Conditionals

Following Saloné, I divide conditionals into three semantic categories:

1. simple or open conditionals
2. hypothetical conditionals
3. counterfactual conditionals

To these I add a fourth category:

4. concessive conditionals

Saloné uses the term SIMPLE conditionals for the first type. I have chosen to call them OPEN conditionals in order to avoid confusion between this type of conditional sentence and simple (as opposed to complex) sentences, which consist of only one clause. Each of these four types is defined in semantic terms first. Their syntactic features are then described, including distinctive morphological marking and verb forms, and the various possible combinations of tenses and aspects.

Some preliminary generalizations can be made about conditional sentences. First, the consequence clause normally follows the antecedent clause, reflecting the temporal connection in the real world. Secondly, the condition-consequence relation may be signalled by either of the markers

---

[1]The Mundani language is spoken by an estimated population of 30,000 people in the Fontem Subdivision of Manyu Division, S.W. Province, Republic of Cameroon. Population figures are not available for the large numbers of Mundani-speaking people who have settled outside the home area, in the plantations and urban centers of N.W. and S.W. Provinces and elsewhere. Mundani is a Western Grassfields Bantu language of the Momo Subgroup.

I should like to thank the many Mundani people who furnished the texts used as a source of examples for this paper; also Mr. Kedju Emmanuel and Mr. Lekunze Richard for help in checking the data. My thanks go also to Prof. Bernard Comrie of the University of Southern California and to Dr. Carol Stanley and Dr. Stephen C. Anderson of the Summer Institute of Linguistics for their suggestions and encouragement in writing up the material.

ko or *m̀bə* introducing the consequence clause. These markers can both be translated 'if ... then' in English.

There is an alternative way of constructing a conditional sentence that is less commonly used. In this second type, the consequence clause precedes the antecedent clause instead of following it. The condition-consequence relation is marked by the particle *na* (COND) introducing the antecedent clause, which is closed by the subordinator *la*, (SUB) as seen in (1).[2]

(1)   *A-a lɔ́ʔɔ à lạ   akɨ̀ŋ,*
       2sS-F F1 2sS cook cooking^pot

      na à bakà   bɔ   afàʔ la.
      COND 2s NEG^PFV have work SUB
       You should cook a meal if you don't have any work to do.

Since this type of conditional sentence is rare and quite straightforward, it is not discussed further in this paper.

1.1. Open conditionals. Open conditionals "state that a proposition results if another proposition holds" (Saloné 1979:65). There is little doubt or uncertainty regarding the actualization of the event or action expressed by the verb in either clause, as in (2)–(5).

(2)   Open past

      Tà lè ghɨ̂ ale ǹ-gà   apfə̀   ane àli yu,
      3sS P3 do thus FACT-go LOC^compound on c7^day c7^DEF

      ko/m̀bə Manyì gha apfə̀   mɨ̂.
      COND   Manyi go^PFV LOC^compound also
       If he went home on that day, then Manyi went home also.

---

[2]Other abbreviations used in the examples are: c(#) noun class number; COMPL complement; CONT continuous; DEF definite; EMPH emphatic; INDEF indefinite; LOC locative; LOG logophoric; NEG negative; O object; PFV perfective; POSS possessive; PROG progressive; and S subject; a cedilla under a vowel signals nasalization.

Tones are marked as follows: ˋ low or extra-low tone (L), ˇ rising tone, ˆ falling tone, ´ high tone (H), and − mid-tone (M). High and mid tone are left unmarked except where it is desired to draw attention to them.

(3)   Open present—particular case[3]

À   me kɨ   e-ye   atò afɨʔ?   yaa,
2sS   SIM want   NFACT-see 3sO time   this

ko/m̀bə   tà   wu   a   lob.
COND   3sS   be   LOC   house
If you want to see him now, he is in the house.

(4)   Open present—general statement

Bɔ̀   me dzɨ   ekab   nyaŋ,
3pS   SIM eat money   much

ko/m̀bə   bɔ̀   me nɨ   bèzi   m̀-bi   bɔ̰   nengaa.
COND   3pS   SIM take wives FACT-give^birth children through
If they earn a lot of money, they take wives and have children by
them.

(5)   Open future

À   ghà   a   M̀bɔ̀ʔ   atetsɔʔ,
2sS   go^PFV   LOC   Bamumbu   tomorrow^morning

ko/m̀bə   ma-a e-tèʔa   akpèn.
COND   1sS-F NFACT-remain behind
If you go to Bamumbu tomorrow morning, I'll remain behind.

Several observations can be made about the formal properties of these
open conditionals.

First, the conditional marker *ko* or *m̀bə* is normally present, and the
choice between the two markers seems to depend on personal preference.
The marker is deleted only in order to make a very strong assertion. For
example, if *ko* or *m̀bə* is deleted from (5), the meaning can be ap-
proximated as 'if you go to Bamumbu tomorrow morning, I'll definitely
remain behind.' Put another way, the presence of the conditional marker
serves to soften the force of the speaker's assertion.

Secondly, Mundani allows the same range of tense distinctions in open
conditionals as in simple declarative sentences. Thus, the open past conditional could contain any of the available past tenses: general past (P),

---

[3]The nonfactive prefix *e-* attached to infinitival forms drops out in rapid speech.

today past (P1), yesterday past (P2), or before-yesterday past (P3), while the simple future conditional could contain any of the available future tenses: general future (F), today future (F1), tomorrow future (F2), or after-tomorrow future (F3).[4] Notice, however, that the tense marking is not necessarily the same in both clauses. This is the case in (2), (3), and (5) above, and the reasons for the differences are discussed below.

In a past tense sentence such as (2), the past tense is marked in the initial (antecedent) clause only. The verb in the following (consequence) clause is a perfective form unmarked for tense. Note in passing that this pattern of past-tense marking in open conditionals resembles the pattern found in narrative. The past tense is marked overtly only in the initial clause of the narrative, or at the beginning of a major new episode within it; the main event line is then carried forward by means of perfective verb forms which are unmarked for tense.

Moving to the present tense conditionals in (3) and (4), if these examples were recast as simple declarative sentences, present imperfective (IMP) verb forms would normally be used. An exception is the stative verb *ewu* 'to be', which would retain its perfective form to indicate a state regarded as complete in itself (Parker 1985a:44). The parallel declarative sentences would read as in (6) and (7).

(6) Present tense—particular case[5]

   a.   *A-à*   *ǹ-kɨ-∅*   *e-ye*   *atò*
       2sS-IMP FACT-want-IMP NFACT-see 3sO
       You want to see him.

   b.   *Tà wu*   *a*   *lob.*
       3sS be^PFV LOC house
       He is in the house.

---

[4]The tense system of Mundani is described in Parker 1985a and 1985b.

[5]Postverbal imperfective marking is frequently deleted following the verbs *ekɨ* 'want' and *eghɨ* 'do, make', even though phonologically the vowel sequence /ɨ/ + /a/ is permitted in the language. The reason for the deletion is not known.

(7) Present tense—general statement[6]

a. *Bɔ-ɔ̂*   *ǹ-dzì-a*   *ekab*   *nyaŋ.*
    3pS-IMP FACT-eat-IMP money much
    They earn a lot of money.

b. *Bɔ-ɔ̂*   *è-nì-a*   *bèzi* *m̀-bì-a*   *bɔ̀*   *nengaa.*
    3pS-IMP FACT-take-IMP wives FACT-give^birth-IMP children through
    They take wives and have children by them.

When these pairs of declarative sentences are linked in a condition-consequence relationship, the imperfective aspect is replaced by *me* marking simultaneity (SIM), followed by the main verb. *Me* links two situations that are simultaneous in the sense of overlapping, but which are not necessarily coextensive. It can operate anaphorically or cataphorically, and the grammatical subjects of the verbs need not be coreferent. *Me* only rarely occurs with a tense marker, and in the least marked context the time reference of the main verb is normally interpreted as present, as in (4) above.

It is noticeable that, in the data collected so far, there is only one case of the use of an imperfective present verb form in a conditional sentence. One possible explanation for this restriction in the use of the imperfective aspect may be that in Mundani it is obligatorily combined with factive marking (FACT), as in (6) and (7). Factive marking implies a high degree of certainty regarding the realization of the situation expressed by the verb concerned. It is, therefore, an unsuitable mood for conditionals, even open ones, where no doubt is overtly expressed concerning the possible realization of a given situation.[7]

In the open future conditional (see (5) above), a present perfective verb form has been used in the antecedent clause to encode future time reference. This encroachment of the present tense form on the domain of the future tense is restricted to conditional clauses and to some other subordinate clause types, for example, temporal adverbial clauses (which have much in common with conditionals). Such an extended use of the present tense may not occur in a main clause. Thus a future conditional may have a present tense in the antecedent clause and a future tense in the consequence clause, as in (5) above, or a future tense in both clauses,

---

[6]The homorganic nasal consonant marking the factive mood has a variant *è-* preceding another nasal consonant. This variant form often drops out in rapid speech.

[7]For a brief account of factive and nonfactive (NFACT) marking in Mundani, see Parker 1985a:1–9.

as in (8). A present tense in the consequence clause, however, whether
imperfective, as in (9a), or perfective, as in (9b), would be ungrammatical.

(8) Open future

> *À-á   sàʔa   e-ghǎ   a   Ṁbəʔ,*
> 2sS-F   F2   NFACT-go   LOC   Bamumbu

> *ko/ṁbə   ma-a   e-tèʔa   akpèn.*
> COND   1sS-F   NFACT-remain behind
> If you go to Bamumbu (tomorrow), I'll remain behind.

(9) Open future—ungrammatical forms

a. * *À-á   sàʔa   e-ghǎ   a   Ṁbəʔ,*
>   2sS-F   F2   NFACT-go   LOC   Bamumbu

> *ko/ṁbə   ma-à   ǹ-tèʔ-a   akpèn.*
> COND   1sS-IMP FACT-remain-IMP behind
> If you go to Bamumbu (tomorrow), I'll remain behind.

b. * *À-á   sàʔa e-ghǎ a Ṁbəʔ,   ko/ṁbə   ma teʔa   akpèn.*
> (Same as (9a))   COND   1sS remain^PFV behind
> If you go to Bamumbu (tomorrow), I'll remain behind.

Notice in the antecedent clause in (8) that the tonal pattern on the
subject pronoun and future tense marker is L-H (à-á). This pattern is
characteristic of several subordinate clause types, such as relative clauses
and complement clauses introduced by *ǹdɨ* 'how'. In a main clause the tone
pattern on subject pronoun and future-tense marker would be H-M (á-ā).
The two contrasting patterns are illustrated in (10) and (11).

(10) Main clause

> *Tá-ā   e-bene   aben   yu.*
> 3sS-F   NFACT-dance c7^dance c7^DEF
> He will dance the dance.

(11) Subordinate clause

> àben   yu   tà-á   e-bene   la
> c7^dance   c7^DEF [3sS-F   NFACT-dance   SUB]
> the dance that he will dance

The L-H pattern in the antecedent clause in (8) indicates that this clause is subordinated syntactically to the consequence clause, and not the reverse.

There are cases where two clauses could be interpreted semantically as having a condition-consequence relationship even though there is neither a characteristically subordinate tone pattern nor a conditional marker *ko* or *m̀bɔ*. In such cases, one might ask what phonological or syntactic features indicate whether these are two clauses linked in a conditional sentence or a sequence of two simple, independent, declarative sentences.

There are, in fact, two such markers. First, in conditional sentences, the clauses form a single unit in terms of sentence intonation. The falling intonation marking the termination of a sentence occurs at the end of the final (consequence) clause, but not at the end of the antecedent clause. This characteristic intonation consists of a slight downward shift in the pitch of the last two or three syllables of the sentence; thus, a downshifted high tone may be realized on the same phonetic level as a mid tone, a mid tone as a low, and so on.

Secondly, where a verb in the present perfective occurs in final position in the antecedent clause, it appears in its B form—that is, the form which occurs only with an immediately following context—and not in its A form, which would occur only before a pause (Parker 1985a:30–35). Thus in (12), the perfective form of *efa* 'to be/become big' is *fàa* (B form, L-H) and not *faŋ* (A form, H); in (13) the perfective of *ekiʔi* 'to come' is *kíʔi* (B form, H-H) and not *kíʔì* (A form, H-L).

(12)   *Tà fàa,*   *ko*   *à*   *tsaa*   *atò akatè*   *mî̠.*
       3sS become^big^PFV   COND 2sS send^HORT 3sO LOC^school also
       If he has become big, you should also send him to school.

(13)   *À   kíʔi,*   *à*   *lòòte*   *mètsɔ̀*   *batoʔ*   *bu.*
       2sS come^PFV 2sS cut^PFV mouths c2^calabashes c2^DEF
       If you come, you cut the mouths of the calabashes.

The use of these perfective B forms is therefore another indication that the two clauses concerned are linked together.

1.2. Hypothetical conditionals. In a hypothetical conditional (HYP), the antecedent clause "introduces a hypothetical or imaginary proposition (where that proposition is not assumed to be false)" (Saloné 1979:66). That is, the situation expressed by the verb in the antecedent clause is unrealized at the moment of utterance, and its eventual realization may even seem unlikely. It is, nevertheless, assumed that, if this antecedent proposition were to hold, then the consequence proposition would also hold. Examples are given in (14) and (15) below.[8]

(14)   *N-dzé-á   fǫ,   ko/m̀bə   ma-a e-lùùla.*
        1sS-see-HYP buffalo COND   1sS-F NFACT-run^away
        If I saw a buffalo, I would run away.

(15)   *Tà kíʔ-á   a   apfə̀   am,*
        3sS come-HYP LOC compound 1sPOSS

        ko/m̀bə àghi ako ma ŋa   atò   la   a   ǹtsè.
        COND   thing INDEF 1sS give LOC^3sO SUB   c7^s^it be^not
        If he came to my compound, I would not give him anything.

In these examples, as in open conditionals, the conditional marker *ko* or *m̀bə* is normally present, and the choice between them seems to depend on individual preference. Deletion of the conditional marker is rare, and tends to introduce the notion that the situation, although hypothetical, is very likely to be realized.

(16)   *A-a lí-á   ǹ-gà,   ∅   à   tsaʔte   atò abua am.*
        2sS-F F3-HYP FACT-go COND 2sS greet^HORT 3sO for 1sO
        If (when) you go, you should greet him for me.

The verb in the antecedent clause consists of the verb root, carrying its inherent tone (high in each of the three examples above) plus the high-tone suffix *-á*. The verb in the consequence clause will normally be in the future tense, as in (14). In (15), the verb *ǹtsè* 'be not' is an invariant form that cannot combine with a tense marker. In (16), the verb *tsaʔte* 'greet' in the consequence clause is a hortatory (HORT) form. The future tense is therefore marked instead in the antecedent clause, since hortatory and future markers do not occur together in the same clause. Note, in this

---

[8]The homorganic nasals *N* and *ǹ* are reduced forms of the first person singular subject pronoun *ma*.

example, that -*á* is suffixed to the auxiliary verb marking tense F3, and not to the main verb.

With regard to the marking of the verb in the antecedent clause, it is worth noting that the suffix -*á* is homophonous with the general future marker -*á*, and possibly also with the imperfective indicator -*a*, although I have been unable so far to posit an underlying tone for this marker.[9] The various verb forms in which -*a* appears are illustrated in (17), with high and mid tones marked. The imperfective form receives double marking in preverbal and postverbal positions; the general future has single marking in the preverbal slot; the hypothetical form receives a single postverbal marker.

(17) Imperfective: *tà-à ǹ-kɨʔâ*   'He is coming.'
                                                    'He comes (habitually).'

      General future: *tá-ā (ē-)kɨʔɨ*   'He will come.'

      Hypothetical   *tà kɨʔ-á*   'if he came'
      conditional: 'if he were to come'

The tonal phenomena in these verb forms are complex and not fully understood at present. As they come to be better understood, the relatedness (or nonrelatedness) of the four suffixes should become more apparent. In particular, it is not known why the general future marker carries a mid tone rather than a high tone in the type of construction illustrated above. The fact that in negative constructions this future marker is shifted to final position in the clause, where it carries a high tone (Parker 1985b:26–28) suggests that its underlying tone is high.

Another article by Parker (1985a:41–42) discusses a possible relationship between the imperfective and general future markers, suggesting that the latter may have been formerly an imperfective marker which has shifted its function to become, synchronically, a marker of general future. The question then arises as to whether this same marker has been further extended diachronically to assume a special function in conditional sentences. This kind of process is attested in other languages. For example, in Haya, the marker of tense F1 "has achieved a status in simple conditionals beyond its usage as an indicator of future. That is, it is the indicator of 'conditionality' in these sentences" (Saloné 1979:71). In Mundani, the suffix -*á* is clearly not a general marker of conditionality, since it does not occur in open conditional sentences. Neither does it necessarily imply that the proposi-

---

[9]In the neighboring language Ngyemboɔn, the corresponding imperfective marker -*à* is thought to have an underlying low tone (Anderson 1983:88).

tion made in the antecedent clause is unlikely to be realized. In (18) and (19), for example, the verb in the initial clause (or clauses) consists of the verb root plus -á, but does not express an impossible situation: it is reasonably certain that the maize will begin to flower, and that the calabash will be nicely decorated.

(18) Te   bùʔ-á   te   me kòʔte,   à   me ghǎ ǹ-dìnk-â.
     c10^3pS begin-HYP until SIM flower 2sS SIM go FACT-look-IMP
     If (when) they (the maize plants) start to flower, you go and look at them.

(19) À ghɨ̀-à   à   me ye, è   tsíʔ-á   ŋmàʔà   ŋmàʔa,
     2sS do-HYP 2sS SIM see c1^s^it become-HYP decorated decorated
     |_____ HAB[10]_____|

     à   me màke   nê ...
     2sS SIM wonder COMPL^that
     If (whenever) you see it (the calabash) and it is nicely decorated, you wonder that ...

This 'reasonably certain' interpretation of (18) and (19) is supported by the fact that these sentences can be translated into English using 'when' rather than 'if'. In fact, in these examples, we seem to be dealing with clauses describing the temporal circumstances of the action or event expressed by the main clause, rather than with a condition-consequence relation. The dividing line between the two kinds of relation is not clear cut, however. Different speakers disagree as to whether the conditional marker ko or m̀bə could actually be inserted into sentences such as (18) and (19) or into example (16). This ambivalence seems to arise from the fact that the situation expressed by the verb in the initial clause is, on the one hand, hypothetical in the sense that it has not been realized at the moment of utterance; on the other hand, its realization is considered by the speaker to be virtually certain. In contrast, certain language assistants have no hesitation in including a marker of conditionality in sentences (14) and (15), where it is considered unlikely that the situation expressed by the verb in the initial clause will ever be realized.

On examining the verb forms in the initial clauses of all these examples, whether conditional or nonconditional, we find components of meaning which we can call the perfective component and the hypothetical com-

---

[10]This construction is commonly used to express the notion of habituality (HAB). It may be diagrammed as s + eghɨ̌ 'do' + s + v.

ponent. In (14), for instance, the verb form *dze-a* implies that the buffalo will already have been seen before I run away from it (perfective), but that it has not actually been seen at the time of speaking (its being seen is still hypothetical). In (18), the maize will already have begun to flower when you go to look at it (perfective), but it is not necessarily flowering at the time of speaking, since the speaker is merely setting up a hypothetical situation and telling the hearer what is normally done when that situation arises.

Given these common semantic components, we may call this verb form the hypothetical perfective and the suffix -*á* the hypothetical marker. The question of whether this marker is derived from the marker of imperfective aspect and/or the general future marker remains open, but a relationship between the three markers seems plausible from a semantic point of view. This matter will be raised again in §2.1.

1.3. Counterfactual conditionals. A counterfactual conditional is one in which "the antecedent asserts a proposition which is assumed to be false" (Saloné 1979:66) or at least highly unlikely. In (20) and (21), the antecedent proposition in each case is clearly untrue: I am not you (20), she had not cooked food (21a), and he had not stolen the money (21b). In each of these three examples, the consequence clause is introduced by *ko* or *m̀bɔ*. The conditional marker is normally obligatory in a counterfactual sentence. One language associate allowed its omission from (20), but said that this would result in a very strong negation in the consequence clause ('I would never ever tell him under any circumstances!').

(20) Counterfactual—present tense

> *N-gu   àwɔ̀,   ko/m̀bɔ   n̄-ka   su   atò.*
> 1sS-be^PFV 2sEMPH COND   1sS-NEG tell 2sO
> If I were you, I would not tell him.

(21) Counterfactual—past tense

a. *Tà ghɨ ale n̄-dą   èghɨdzɨ, ko/m̀bɔ mâ   ghɨ̂ n̄-dzɨ.*
   3sS PI thus FACT-cook food   COND   1sS PI   FACT-eat
   If she had cooked food, I would have eaten.

b. *Tà ghɨ ale   ǹ-tsɔ   ekab   wu,*
    3sS P1 thus FACT-steal c3ˆmoney c3ˆDEF

    ko/m̀bə tà bakà   su   abua bɔkefen.
    COND   3sS NEGˆPFV tellˆPFV to policemen
    If he had stolen the money, he would not have told the police.

Text material has also yielded one instance (22) of a counterfactual conditional sentence where neither *ko* nor *m̀bə* is present.

(22) *È ka wu   zìa   ka   ye   bə̰ə̰ Ǹgbìnyə̰ la,*
     it NEG beˆPFV 3sEMPH EMPH LOG catch Leopard SUB

    ∅   à zi   avi   akìŋ   ane, yè pfə.
    COND 2sS putˆinˆPFV LOGˆo LOCˆcookingˆpot thus LOG die
    If it were not I myself who caught Leopard, (then) when you put me into the cooking-pot in this way, I should die.

Since the notions of future time and counterfactuality are seen as incompatible in Mundani, future counterfactuals are not possible. Speakers of Mundani can, however, use both present and past tenses with counter-factual meaning. Examples (20) and (22) are in the present tense; (21a) and (21b) have a past tense form in their antecedent clauses. The form used consists of the P1 auxiliary *ghɨ̂*, followed by the consecutive form of the main verb, carrying factive marking. In Mundani, this verb form func-tions not only as tense P1 (past today), but also as a past anterior (A had done X before Y occurred). The same past tense form appears in the consequence clause in (21a). The consequence clause in (21b) is negated and has a present perfective verb form. The reason for this may be that a simple perfective negative form is preferred to the rather complex form of the negative past anterior (or P1). Alternatively, it may be that the perfec-tive is functioning here as a perfect tense, expressing a situation that has occurred in the recent past and has implications in the present (Parker 1985a:44).

In past tense counterfactuals, the position of the adverbial *ale* 'thus' in the linear order of the antecedent clause is crucial. If *ale* is shifted to final position in the clause, the sense becomes factual—an assertion that the given situation actually occurred—and the consequence clause, in turn, can only be interpreted as a statement of fact. In other words, the initial clause becomes adverbial, describing the circumstances of the past situation ex-pressed by the main clause. The conditional marker *ko* or *m̀bə* cannot occur. These changes are illustrated in (23), which is a restructuring of (21a).

(23) *Tà ghî̀ n̄-dạ*   *èghɨdzɨ ale,   mâ ghî̀ n̄-dzɨ.*
      3sS P1 FACT-cook   food   thus 1sS P1 FACT-eat
      As she had cooked food (earlier today), I ate it (earlier today).

1.4. Concessive conditionals. In a concessive (CONC) conditional, the antecedent clause indicates a condition that would seem to be opposed to the statement made in the consequence clause. Thus, the sentence as a whole expresses a situation that is surprising, altogether contrary to normal expectations.

In a present or future conditional sentence, the concessive notion is grammaticized by the auxiliary verb *màà* occurring immediately before the main verb in the antecedent clause. The main verb occurs in its consecutive form and is marked for factive mood.[11] *Màà* can be translated into English as 'even (if)'. As in counterfactual conditionals, the marker of the condition-consequence relationship is *ko* or *m̀bɔ*, and deletion of these markers is normally unacceptable.

(24) Concessive—present tense

      Bɔ-ɔ̀   màà   n̄-gù-a   n̄-kpà?t-à   wu   a   kàbɔ̀ŋ,
      3pS-IMP CONC FACT-CONT-IMP   FACT-plan-IMP only   c1^o   evil

      ko/m̀bɔ ntɨ̰̀   am   aà   m̄-bɔ̀.
      COND   heart 1sPOSS IMP   FACT-be^good
      Even if they are planning only evil, I am happy.

(25) Concessive—future tense

   a. *Ba-a màà n̄-gà   a   ǹtɔ?,*
       1sS-F CONC FACT-go LOC palace

       ko/m̀bɔ ba kà   ye   a   Fɔ̀   zìambɔŋ a.
       COND   1pS NEG see c1^o Fon   3sEMPH   F
       Even if we go to the Palace, we shall not see the Fon himself.

---

[11]Consecutive verb forms are described in Parker 1985a:1–9.

b. *A-a màà ǹ-gà   a   M̀bə̀ʔ,*
    2sS-F CONC FACT-go LOC Bamumbu

    ko/m̀bə ma-a e-tè ʔa   akpèn.
    COND   1sS-F NFACT-remain behind
Even if you go to Bamumbu, I'll remain behind.

The marker *màà* is not used to express a concessive notion in past tense sentences. In such cases, a condition-consequence sentence is not used at all. Instead, the concessive notion is expressed by means of two coordinated clauses in a contrastive relationship, linked by *ka* 'but'. This type of construction normally has two readings. In (26), for example, reading (i) leaves open the possibility that the child was not sent, while reading (ii) implies that he was.

(26) Concessive—past tense

    Tà-à tʉ   wə̰   wu   tesi,   ka Manyì ka ye atò.
    3sS-P2 send c1^child c1^DEF yesterday but Manyi NEG see 3sO

    (i) Even if he sent the child yesterday, Manyi did not see him.
    (ii) He sent the child yesterday, but Manyi did not see him./
        Although he sent the child yesterday, Manyi did not see him.

Note, finally, that the use of *màà* to mark concessive is confined to conditional sentences. In nonconditional sentences the same function is performed by the auxiliary verb *ebate*, which appears before the main verb in the subordinate clause and may be translated into English in various ways, for example, 'even though/although/despite the fact that'. The verb *ebate* may be used with the full range of tenses—past, present, and future. Example (27) is in the past tense.

(27) *M̀bìŋ li m-batè   me lu ale, tà kɨʔɨ wu kɨʔɨ.*
    rain P3 FACT-AUX^CONC SIM fall thus 3sS come only come
Even though it was raining, he still came.

A nonconditional concessive may also be expressed using two coordinated clauses linked by *ka*, as illustrated in (26).

2. Typology of conditionals

2.1. Reality and unreality in conditional sentences. Saloné (1979:66f) suggests that languages vary in the way they segment the reality continuum and that this variation is reflected in different strategies for forming conditional sentences. For example, open future conditionals are semantically unreal, and in this respect they are similar to hypothetical and counterfactual conditionals. Some languages, such as Yoruba, exhibit a closer syntactic relationship between open future conditionals and hypothetical or counterfactual types than they do between open future conditionals and those types of conditional—open past or present—that are semantically real. In other words, the semantic unreality of the open future conditional is encoded in its syntactic structure. Other languages, however, including some Bantu languages, such as Haya and Tikar (Stanley, personal communication), display little syntactic affinity between open future conditionals and hypotheticals or counterfactuals. Instead, they group open future conditionals with open past and present conditionals that are semantically real. That is, Haya, on the one hand, and Yoruba, on the other, make the real-unreal division at different points along the reality continuum. This difference is diagrammed in (28).

(28)   REAL   UNREAL

   Haya   open conditionals (past,   hypotheticals
             present, and future)   counterfactuals

   Yoruba   open conditionals (past   open future conditionals
             and present)   hypotheticals
                                        counterfactuals

In Mundani, a comparison of open future conditionals with hypothetical and counterfactual types reveals little similarity in terms of syntactic structure, except for the presence of the conditional marker *ko* or *m̀bə*, and of a future tense form in the consequence clause of open futures and hypotheticals. The main syntactic features of the three types are summarized in (29).

(29) Open future: *ko/m̀bə* optional. Future tense marked in both
                         clauses or present tense in the antecedent clause
                         and future tense in the consequence clause.

     Hypothetical: *ko/m̀bə* normally present. Perfective hypothetical
                         verb form in the antecedent clause; future tense
                         or absence of tense marking in the consequence
                         clause.

     Counterfactual: *ko/m̀bə* normally present. Present tense in both
                         clauses or past tense in both clauses.

It would appear, therefore, that Mundani resembles Haya in placing open future conditionals on the real side of the real-unreal divide. In §1.2, however, we referred to the possibility of a historical connection between the general future marker -*á* and the hypothetical marker -*á*. If this connection can be established in future research, open future conditionals and hypothetical conditionals can be said to share an important syntactic feature. Thus Mundani would fall together with Yoruba as a language that places open future conditionals on the unreal side of the diagram in (28).

2.2. Tense distinctions in imaginary conditionals. Saloné (1979:74) uses the term IMAGINARY to refer to "that subset of unreal conditionals which indicates divergence from this world." In semantic terms, imaginary conditionals include those which express imaginary or hypothetical situations and those which express a situation that could have occurred in the real world but did not actually occur.

Saloné comments that it is a characteristic of imaginary conditionals to have restricted tense possibilities, since tense distinctions are generally unnecessary for the correct interpretation of these sentences. This observation is borne out in Mundani, as seen in the examples of hypothetical and counterfactual conditionals in §§1.2 and 1.3. It is possible, however, to make a distinction in Mundani between past and nonpast in counterfactual conditionals (20–22), a distinction which many languages lack.

From a comparison of four languages, including Haya and Yoruba, Saloné makes the interesting observation that those languages in which open future conditionals pattern syntactically with real conditionals are also those which can make a past vs. nonpast distinction in imaginary conditionals. On the other hand, those languages which place open future conditionals on the unreal side of the real-unreal divide lack tense distinctions in imaginary conditionals. Haya would illustrate the former type of language, and also Tikar (Stanley, personal communication); Yoruba would belong to the latter type. These characteristics are diagrammed in (30).

(30)   Open future conditionals   Imaginary conditionals

    Haya   real   past/nonpast distinction
    Yoruba   unreal   no tense distinction

The sample of languages on which Saloné bases this observation is very small and unrepresentative. It comprises English (an Indo-European language), Haya and Chagga (Bantu languages of Tanzania), and Yoruba (a Kwa language of Nigeria). Comrie points out (personal communication) that there are counterexamples to this kind of patterning. In Russian, for example, open future conditionals resemble other open conditionals in terms of their syntax, but there is no tense opposition in imaginary conditionals. Further research must establish whether the correlation suggested by Saloné would hold cross-linguistically, even in statistical terms.

How does Mundani fit the suggested grouping? If we discount a possible connection between the general future and hypothetical markers and assume that open future conditionals pattern with conditionals that are semantically real (at least synchronically), then Mundani belongs to the same subgroup as Haya and lends support to Saloné's thesis. If, however, the hypothetical marker is closely related to the general future marker, open future conditionals pattern with semantically unreal conditionals. This observation, taken together with the existence of a tense opposition in imaginary conditionals, means that Mundani would be a counterexample to the correlation diagrammed in (30).

2.3. Tense prominence and aspect prominence. Saloné (1979:78) points out that the way a language distinguishes between reality and unreality is related to tense. Languages which group open future conditionals with other open conditionals are observing a future tense distinction within the category of open conditional sentences; those languages that include open future conditionals with unreal conditionals are ignoring that tense distinction. The languages that ignore this future tense distinction are also those which lack a past vs. nonpast distinction in imaginary conditionals. That is, the coincidence of the features charted in (30) is not accidental, since both have to do with tense.

Saloné then develops the correlation a step further, suggesting that the languages which ignore the above-mentioned tense distinctions in their formation of conditional sentences are languages which are ASPECT-PROMINENT, that is, where aspect and mood may be marked without any overt reference to tense. The languages where these tense distinctions are observed in conditional sentences are TENSE-PROMINENT languages, in which mood and aspect can be referred to only in the presence of a particular tense marker. Haya is an example of a tense-prominent language, while Yoruba is an aspect-prominent language. Once again, it should be noted that the language sample used to arrive at this correlation is very small.

In attempting to characterize Mundani as a tense- or aspect-prominent language, we can start from the preliminary review of the Mundani system of mood, aspect, and tense in Parker 1985a. The basic aspectual distinction is between perfectivity and imperfectivity. Perfective and imperfective verb forms are illustrated in (31). There is no neutral form that can be said to be neither imperfective nor perfective. Perfective aspect is unmarked; imperfective aspect is marked by both preverbal and postverbal -a.

(31)   Perfective: tà bén   'he has danced'
       Imperfective: tà-à m̀-bèn-á   'he dances, he is dancing'

Imperfective aspect, accompanied obligatorily by the nasal consonant marking factive mood, may occur without any overt reference to tense. It may also be accompanied by the auxiliary verb *wua* marking continuous aspect or by the progressive marker *na*, still without reference to tense.[12]

(32) Imperfective—continuous

   Tà-à   wua   m̀-bèn-a.
   3sS-IMP   CONT   FACT-dance-IMP
   He is in the process of dancing.

(33) Imperfective—progressive

   (a) *Bòt   ko   na-à   ǹ-gì-∅   è   nu   awɔb*
       people PART   PROG-IMP FACT-do-IMP they drink 3pO
       |_____HAB_____|

       tê   m̀-be.
       until   FACT-beˆdrunk
       Some people are always drinking until they become drunk.

   (b) *bèzi   bu   nà-a   ǹ-tsèk-a   apfɔ̀   am la*
       women   DEF   [PROG-IMP FACT-stay-IMP LOCˆcompound my SUB]
       the women staying (temporarily) in my compound

---

[12]As mentioned in §1.1, *me* (simultaneity) likewise normally occurs without tense marking (see (3) and (4)).

From these facts, it might appear that Mundani is an aspect-prominent language. On closer investigation, however, it is seen that the tenseless forms described above cannot be combined with past or future time adverbials, and will almost invariably be interpreted as present tense.[13] In fact, perfective and imperfective verb forms without overt tense marking function as present tense forms in the language, identifiable by contrast with the overt marking of past and future tense forms (Parker 1985b:1–2).

One can speculate that the perfective vs. imperfective distinction was, historically, the fundamental distinction in the language, and that a complex tense system is in the process of being superimposed on this basic aspectual opposition. There are many indications that the tense system is still evolving. One example is the way in which certain auxiliary verbs are losing their verbal character to become frozen forms marking tense, or the changing functions of the perfective forms *ghî* and *lô?*, which are becoming markers of tense—P1 and past anterior, respectively.[14]

At the present state of its development, the tense system seems to have achieved preeminence over the aspectual system. This is borne out by the fact that, in certain tenses, important aspectual distinctions are not made at all. For instance, as mentioned in §1.2, the imperfective indicator appears to have shifted its function in clauses with future time reference to become, synchronically, a marker of general future tense, while the various degrees of remoteness in future time are encoded by auxiliary verbs. Since the imperfective marker has received this extended function as a future marker, one cannot make a distinction between perfectivity and imperfectivity in future tenses nor between continuous and noncontinuous aspect, since the continuous aspect may appear only in the presence of imperfective marking.

Such features of the Mundani tense-aspect system suggest that the language should be classified, synchronically at least, as a tense-prominent system.

3. Conclusion

This overview of conditionals in Mundani, and of the type of tense-aspect system that predominates in the language, enables us to see

---

[13]Two exceptions to this rule are (1) the use of tenseless perfective forms in narrative (where the past tense setting is marked overtly only at the beginning of the narrative or of an episode within the narrative), and (2) the future time reference assigned to some tenseless verb forms in future conditional sentences §1.1.

[14]See Parker 1985b for a detailed discussion of some of these features.

whether or not Mundani fits into the typological scheme suggested by Saloné. If, at the present state of the language, we accept that the hypothetical and general future markers are not closely connected (even if a historical connection can eventually be established between the two), then we can assert that Mundani open-future conditionals pattern with other open conditionals—that is, with conditionals that are semantically real—and that a future vs. nonfuture tense distinction is made within this category of real conditionals. Furthermore, a past vs. nonpast tense distinction is made in counterfactual conditionals. In the light of these two significant tense distinctions in conditional sentences and the overall tense-prominence of the language, Mundani would seem to belong to the same subset of languages as Haya in the typology drawn by Saloné. The ambivalence surrounding open future conditionals should be noted, however. If they are interpreted as belonging on the unreal side of the real-unreal divide, then Mundani is a counterexample to the suggested typology.

It remains to be seen whether the proposed typological link between tense-aspect systems and conditional sentences can be established in a wide range of the world's languages, or whether it tends to be limited areally to sub-Saharan Africa or to a particular subgroup of languages, namely, Niger-Congo, to which Haya, Chagga, Yoruba, Tikar, and Mundani all belong.

References

Anderson, Stephen C. 1979. Verb structure. In Larry M. Hyman (ed.), Aghem grammatical structure, 73–136. Southern California Occasional Papers in Linguistics 7. Los Angeles: University of Southern California.

———. 1983. Tone and morpheme rules in Bamileke-Ngyembɔɔn. Ph.D. dissertation. Los Angeles: University of Southern California.

Beekman, John, John Callow, and Michael Kopesec. 1981. The semantic structure of written communication. Dallas: Summer Institute of Linguistics.

Comrie, Bernard. 1985. Tense. Cambridge: Cambridge University Press.

Marchese, Lynell. 1976. La subordination en godié. Abidjan: Institut de Linguistique Appliquée/Société Internationale de Linguistique.

Parker, Elizabeth. 1985a. Mood, tense, and aspect in Mundani. ms.

———. 1985b. Keeping time in Mundani: a study of relative time reference. Paper presented at the 16th West African Linguistics Society Congress, March 25–30, 1985. Yaoundé, Cameroon.

Saloné, Sukari. 1979. Typology of conditionals and conditionals in Haya. Studies in African Linguistics 10(1):65–80.

Schachter, Jacqueline C. 1971. Presupposition and counterfactual conditional sentences. Ph.D. dissertation. Los Angeles: University of California at Los Angeles.

Schaub, Willi. 1985. Babungo. London: Croom Helm.

Watters, John Robert. 1981. A phonology and morphology of Ejagham, with notes on dialect variation. Ph.D. dissertation. Los Angeles: University of California at Los Angeles.

Complex Sentences and Subordination in Mundani

Elizabeth Parker

Abstract

Mundani is a Grassfields Bantu language of the Momo subgroup, spoken in the S. W. Province of Cameroon.

This study defines the complex sentence as any sentence of more than one clause, whether those clauses are conjoined or subordinated one to another. In Mundani, the complex sentence (so defined) can take a variety of forms: a series of consecutivized clauses; a series of independent clauses that are juxtaposed without any overt indication of the relationship between them; a cluster of two or more clauses whose semantic relations are formalized by various markers. Apart from the markers of contrastive and conditional relations, there are four markers in Mundani that can be considered "basic". These markers, plus various compounds of them, permit a whole range of semantic relations to be formalized.

In addition to the marking of semantic relations, grammatical subordination may be signalled in certain clauses by means of the particle *lá* in final position, and/or a L-H tone pattern on the subject pronominal complex in the imperfective aspect or in future tenses. The coincidence of these markers of grammatical subordination with semantic dependency is almost (but not quite) complete. A discrepancy exists in two clause types that are semantically dependent but not subordinated grammatically, and a possible explanation for this discrepancy is proposed.

Résumé

Le mundani est parlé dans la province du Sud-Ouest du Cameroun. Il appartient au groupe bantu des Grassfields, sous-groupe momo.

Dans cette étude, la phrase complexe sera définie comme une phrase composée de deux ou de plusieurs propositions, sans tenir compte des relations de coordination ou de subordination qui existent entre celles-ci. En mundani, la phrase complexe ainsi définie se manifeste sous plusieurs formes. Elle peut se composer d'une série de propositions consécutives, ou d'une série de propositions indépendantes juxtaposées, sans marque explicite des relations qui les unissent. La phrase complexe peut également se composer d'une séquence de deux ou de plusieurs propositions dont les rapports sémantiques sont signalés par des morphèmes. En plus des marqueurs des relations contrastives et conditionnelles, il existe quatre marqueurs en mundani que l'on peut considérer commes formes de base. Ces formes et leurs composés permettent d'exprimer toute une gamme de relations sémantiques.

En plus des relations sémantiques, la subordination grammaticale est signalée dans certaines phrases au moyen de la particule *lá* en finale et du schème tonal B-H accompagnant un sujet pronominal complexe à l'imparfait et au futur. Ces marques de subordination grammaticale correspondent de façon presque exacte à la dépendance sémantique. Une divergence est relevée pour deux types de propositions, dépendantes du point de vue sémantique, mais indépendantes du point de vue grammatical. Un essai d'explication de cette divergence entre la dépendance sémantique et grammaticale sera proposé.

The following study of the complex sentence in Mundani is based on observations made during the period 1986–1989. The data were collected from written texts and from oral sources, and were checked and elaborated by James Jih Ndam with Sampson Akem Ketu.

The topics are grouped according to semantic rather than formal factors. Relative clauses are not included, as these are described in Parker 1985b. Conditional clauses are mentioned in §§5 and 7, but a more comprehensive description is found in the preceding paper in this volume.

For the purposes of this study, the complex sentence is defined as any sentence of more than one clause, whether those clauses are conjoined or subordinated one to another. For each type of complex sentence, certain formal features are noted, namely, the order of the clauses and the markers showing the relationship between them. Semantic features—the kinds of information encoded—are dealt with briefly. Section 8 of this study examines the occurrence of particular tone patterns on the subject pronominal complex in different clause types. It is seen that the tone pattern selected depends on the clause type, and that one of the two sets of patterns almost always coincides with the presence of the subordinator *la*.

1. Chronological ordering of events

1.1. Consecutive constructions. Consecutive constructions consist of a series of two or more verbs that share a common subject and a common tense-aspect specification. The subject and tense are expressed overtly only before the first verb in the series. Imperfective (IMPV) aspect is marked by the suffix -*á* attached to each verb in the sequence; perfective (PFV) aspect is unmarked and can be assumed throughout the sequence when imperfective marking is absent. Each verb after the first in the series carries a prefix signalling 'same subject'. This prefix does not indicate the person-number category of the subject nor the tense-aspect specification of the verb. It can take one of the following two forms, depending on whether the verb to which it is attached is factive (FACT) or nonfactive (NFACT).

Factive Ǹ-. This prefix is a syllabic nasal consonant which carries low tone and is homorganic with the initial consonant of the verb root to which it is attached. It has a low tone variant /è-/ preceding a voiceless fricative or nasal consonant (but frequently deleted before a nasal).[1]

(1) *Tà   lè   kiʔi   ǹ-tsèkê   ǹ-dzi   èghidzi.*
    3sS P3   come   FACT-sit   FACT-eat   food
    He came, sat down and ate.

Nonfactive ē-. This prefix is a mid vowel with a mid tone and it is often elided with a preceding vowel.

(2) *Ta-a   e-kiʔi   e-tseke   e-dzi   èghidzi.*
    3sS-F NFACT-come   NFACT-sit   NFACT-eat   food
    He will come, sit down and eat.

Parker 1985a:2–7 sets out further details of verb forms used in consecutive constructions, and of the interaction of the factive-nonfactive distinction with tense and aspect. Various kinds of semantic information encoded in the consecutive construction are also outlined (Parker 1985a:8–9). Note that one of the consecutive's main functions is to express the coordination of two or more events. The verbs that express the events are usually (but not invariably) arranged in the chronological order in which the events actually occur in the real world. This normal ordering is seen in (1) and (2). Occasionally, however, a verb in the series falls outside the main

---

[1]Abbreviations used in the examples—not mentioned elsewhere—are: c(#) noun class number; CONT continuous; DEF definitizer; EMPH emphatic; F1 today future; F2 tomorrow future; F3 after tomorrow future; IMP imperative; INCEPT inceptive; INT interrogative; LOC locative; NEG negative; O object; PO possessive; PROG progressive; REF reflexive; S subject; SIM simultaneity; a cedilla under a vowel signals nasalization.

Tones are marked as follows: ` low or extra-low tone (L), ˇ rising tone, ^ falling tone, ´ high tone (H), and – mid-tone (M). High and mid tone are left unmarked except where it is desired to draw attention to them.

chronological sequence. This is the case with *eye* in (3), which expresses
the purpose of the preceding verb *ǹgà*: it was Lucas' intention to see him,
but it is not certain whether he actually did so.

(3) *Lukàs   dzɔ̀   ǹ-gà   àbȩ   e-ye   atò,*
     Lucas   PFV^go^out FACT-go outside NFACT-see   3sO

     ǹ-dɔ̀ʔ   Ø-nɨ   ambè   vi   ǹ-gà.
     FACT-then FACT-take cl^bag cl^3sPO FACT-go[2]
     Lucas went outside to see him, then took his bag and went.

The time sequence may be made more explicit by including *elɔ̀ʔɔ* or *ebɔ*
in the series of consecutive verbs. *Elɔ̀ʔɔ* exists as an independent verb
meaning 'move, finish'; *ebɔ* is an auxiliary verb with the sense 'then (do
something)'. When inserted into a consecutive construction, either verb
may be translated as 'then' or 'afterwards'.

(4) *Tà   dzɨ   ǹ-dɔ̀ʔ   Ø-nu*
     3sS PFV^eat   FACT-then FACT-drink

     m̀-bɔ̂   ǹ-dɔʔɔsi   me   e-ghǎ.
     FACT-then FACT-get^up   INCEPT   NFACT-go
     He ate, then drank, and afterwards got up to go.

1.2. Juxtaposition of clauses. Where actions or events in a series do
not share a common agent, they may be expressed as a series of separate,
juxtaposed clauses, each with its own subject and verb. The clauses are
normally arranged in the same order as the order of the events in time.
There is a sequence of three such clauses in (5). The clauses are bound
together by a single sentence intonation (with lowered pitch on the final
two or three syllables), and so they are separated orthographically only by
commas.

---

[2]The noun class of specific nouns is marked in the examples only where there is a
concord marker which agrees with it in the immediate context, in which case both the
noun and its corresponding agreement marker have their noun class indicated.

(5) Tà tsì   èkpę   nyą̀ bu,
     3sS PFV^remove c8^bones meat c8^DEF

     tà màʔtè   a silob, abə kɔʔ   ǹ-gbi.
     3sS PFV^throw LOC floor dog PFV^get^up FACT-grab
     He removed the meat bones, he threw them on the floor, Dog got
     up and grabbed them.

1.3. The chronological marker _ka_ 'before'. In addition to consecutive
constructions and simple juxtaposition of clauses, a chronological sequence
of events may be expressed by linking two clauses by the marker _ka_
'before', as in (6). _Ka_ may occur with the full range of tenses—past,
present, or future.

(6) Ma-a ghǎ adzì   ka   tsě ghǎ akatè.
     1sS-F go LOC^stream before pass go   LOC^school
     I'll go to the stream before going on to school.

2. Complement clauses

Complement clauses expressing the content of a verb of speaking, thinking, feeling, or hearing may be introduced by one of two separate com-
plementizers—_nê_ '(say) that' or _ǹdɨ_ 'how'. These two forms are illustrated
in (7) and (8). In (7), the verb _su_ 'say' is in parentheses to show that it
may be optionally deleted before the complementizer (COMP) _nê_.

(7) Tà (su) nê,   à   ka   ǹ-gà.
     3sS (say) COMP^that 2sS NEG FACT-go
     He says that you should not go.

(8) Màlià nà-à   ǹ-kpàʔt-à   ǹdɨ,
     Mary PROG-IMPV FACT-plan-IMPV COMP^how

     yè-á   lɔʔɔ lą akìŋ   la.
     LOG^SUB-F F1   cook cooking^pot SUB
     Mary is planning how she will cook a meal.

In (8), a complement clause introduced by _ǹdɨ_ is closed by the subordinator
(SUB) _la_ and uses the characteristically subordinate tone pattern on the
subject pronominal complex—in this case _yè-á_ (L-H) instead of the H-M
pattern that would appear in a main clause (§8). The logophoric (LOG)

pronoun *ye* appears in subject position in the complement clause, instead of
the normal third-person-singular pronoun *ta*. In complement clauses introduced by either *ǹdɨ* or *nê*, the use of logophoric pronouns is obligatory to
indicate coreference with a third-person-singular subject in the main clause.
Logophoric forms and their functions are described in Parker 1986:151–56.

Unlike *nê*, *ǹdɨ* does not permit the deletion of a preceding verb of
speaking. A complement clause introduced by *ǹdɨ* always has to do with
the manner in which something is done, so it is not surprising that *ǹdɨ* also
functions as a marker of certain adverbial clauses of manner (§6).

3. Comparison

A common way to express a comparative notion in the language involves
the use of the consecutive form of the verb *ētsě* 'pass, surpass'.

(9) *Tà kô   ǹ-tsè   am.*
     3sS PFV^know   FACT-surpass 1sO
     He knows more than I do. (lit. He knows and surpasses me.)

A comparison may also be implied by an adverbial clause of manner
introduced by *m̀bɨʔɨ* 'as' or the more emphatic form *wu m̀bɨʔɨ* 'just as'.

(10) *Ghɨa   m̀bɨʔɨ tà-á   è-sù-a   awê   la.*
     IMP^do as   3sS^SUB-IMPV NFACT-tell-IMPV 2sO   SUB
     Do as he is telling you!

(11) *Tà-à   ǹ-gɨ-à   mènɔ̀   mi*
     3sS-IMPV FACT-do-IMPV c6a^matters c6a^3sPO

     wu   m̀bɨʔɨ tàt   vi   lè wua ǹ-gɨ-à   la.
     just as   c1^father c1^3sPO P3 CONT FACT-do-IMPV SUB
     He is behaving just as his father used to do.

As seen in (10) and (11), an adverbial clause of manner introduced by *m̀bɨʔɨ*
is closed by the subordinator *la*. It adopts the characteristically subordinate
tone pattern on its subject pronoun—*tà-á* (L-H), in (10), instead of *tà-à* (L-L),
which would be the form used in a corresponding main clause (§8).

Close semantic links between the notions of comparison, circumstance,
manner, and purpose are reflected in Mundani by the possibility of using
the same marker *m̀bɨʔɨ* for each of them, although various other formal
features distinguish the different clause types. Compare sentence (10)

above with (16), (17), and (23) below. See also Beekman et al. (1981:99–100) for comments on these semantic relationships.

4. Contrast

Two coordinate clauses in a contrastive relationship are linked by the marker *ka* 'but'. This marker is homophonous with the negative marker in future tenses, as in (12), and with the emphatic marker used in certain relative clauses, as in line 4 of (13).

(12) *Mâ nɨ   ekab   wu   te   ǹ-dɔ̂ʔ,*
      1sS PFV^take c3^money c3^DEF until FACT-finish

        ka   à   ka   su   wòt.
        but 2sS NEG tell person
        I have already taken the money, but you should not tell anyone.

Where the relationship of contrast exists between a conditional (COND) sentence and an immediately preceding sentence (i.e., a minimum of at least three clauses), *ka* is replaced by the marker *m̀bə*, 'but (if)'. In (13), the preceding sentence happens also to be conditional, but this is not a prerequisite for the use of *mbɔ̀* as a marker of the contrastive relationship. Note that *m̀bə* is homophonous with one of the two possible markers of the conditional construction itself, but it occurs in initial position in the antecedent clause, whereas the conditional marker is placed between the antecedent and consequence clauses (compare (13) with (14a)).

(13) *Àfâʔ   yaa   bɔ   fàʔà   la   wu   àghɨ-a*
      c7^work c7^DEM 3pS work SUB be c7^thing-c7^morning

        wɔbę̀   e   tanke la,   ko   a-à   ǹ-gà   leme.
        c1^human^being c1S plan SUB COND c7S-IMPV FACT-go disappear

        M̀bə a   wu àghɨ-a   Mbɔɔmà ka   tà tanke la,
        but c7S be c7^thing-c7^morning God   EMPH 3sS plan SUB

        ko   betsiʔa bɨ ka   liimè.
        COND can 2pS NEG destroy
        If this work that they have been doing is something that a human being has planned, then it will disappear. But if it is something that God has planned, you will not be able to destroy it.

5. Circumstance

A subordinate clause giving the circumstances or setting of the event expressed in the main clause may be one of the following:
(a) The antecedent clause of a conditional sentence (if . . .)
(b) A temporal adverbial clause (when . . .)
(c) An adverbial clause of circumstance introduced by *m̀bɨʔɨ* (as, since . . .)

Examples of each clause type are given in (14–16).

(14) Antecedent clause of a conditional sentence
     a. With *ko* or *m̀bə*

     Bɔ́   me dzɨ èkab   nyaŋ,
     3pS^SUB[3] SIM eat money   much

     ko/m̀bə bɔ me nɨ   bèzi m̀-bi   bɔ̰   nengaa.
     COND   3pS SIM take wives FACT-give^birth children through
     If they earn a lot of money, they take wives and have children by
     them.

     b. With *na . . . la*

     A-a   lɔ́ʔɔ   à   lą   akɨŋ,
     2sS-F FI^HORT 2sS cook cooking^pot

     na   à   bakà   bɔ   afàʔ la.
     COND 2sS PFV^NEG have work SUB
     You should cook a meal if you don't have any work to do.

Conditional sentences are described in Parker 1989. In (14a), the conditional relationship is marked optionally by *ko* or *m̀bə* placed at the beginning of the consequence clause. The choice between the two markers depends on the personal preference of the speaker. The order of the clauses is antecedent-consequence, and the antecedent clause adopts subordinate tone patterns on the subject pronominal complex (§8).
     A different type of conditional structure is illustrated in (14b). The order of clauses is reversed (consequence-antecedent). The antecedent clause is

---

[3]In the antecedent clause of a conditional sentence, it has been observed that in the perfective a low tone replaces the normal high on the second- and third-person-plural-subject pronouns *bɨ* and *bɔ*.

introduced obligatorily by the conditional marker *na*. It is closed by the subordinator *la* and carries subordinate tone patterns on its subject pronominal complex. This second type of conditional sentence is less common than the first.

In (15), a temporal clause precedes a main clause. It is unmarked except for a subordinate tone pattern on the subject pronominal complex—in this case *à-á* (L-H) instead of the pattern *á-ā* (H-M) characteristic of a main clause. An alternative way of expressing the temporal notion in (15) would be to use the nominal *àfîʔ* 'time' followed by a relative clause *Afîʔa [à-á kîʔ la]* 'At the time when you will come'. This type of structure could precede or follow the main clause.

(15) *À-á   kîʔ,   à   me   lòòte mètsɔ̀   batoʔ   bu.*
      2sS-F^SUB come 2sS INCEPT cut   mouths c2^calabashes c2^DEF
      When you come, you should begin to cut the mouths of the calabashes.

In (16), an adverbial clause of circumstance introduced by *m̀bîʔ* is closed by the subordinator *la*. In the imperfective or future, it would carry a subordinate tone pattern on the subject pronominal complex.

(16) *M̀bîʔ   tà   ghî n̂-dạ   èghɨdzɨ ale   la, mâ ghî n̂-dzɨ.*
      since   3sS P1   FACT-cook   food   thus SUB 1sS P1   FACT-eat
      Since she had cooked food (earlier today), I ate it (earlier today).

The relationship between the clause types illustrated in (14)–(16) is very close. In particular, the distinction between conditional and temporal types is neutralized where there is no conditional marker present.

6. Manner

Adverbial clauses of manner always follow the main clause to which they are subordinated. They may be introduced by one of two markers—*m̀bîʔ* 'as' or *ǹdɨ* 'how'—or by a compound marker in which *m̀bîʔ* or *ǹdɨ* is one component. In every case the adverbial clause of manner is closed by the subordinator *la* and employs subordinate tone patterns on the subject pronominal complex. Examples are given in (17)–(20). Note that these sentences are also comparisons (§3). The marker *ǹdɨ* and its compound forms always have to do with the MANNER in which a given action or event occurs. The emphatic form *wu m̀bîʔ* 'just as' is illustrated above in

(11). The emphatic form of *ǹdɨ* is *wu ndɨ* 'just how'. The form *ǹgù-ndɨ* always implies uncertainty.

(17)   *Ghɨa   m̀bɨʔɨ   tà   su   la.*
        IMP^do as   3sS   PFV^say   SUB
        Do as he says!

(18)   *Ta-a   li   e-mě   e-kɨʔɨ,*
        3sS-F   F3   NFACT-again   NFACT-come

        m̀bɨʔɨ-ndɨ   àkate   atò   a   su   la.
        as-how   c7^letter 3sPO   c7^s PFV^say SUB
        He will come back as his letter says.

(19)   *Dzɔ̌n   nà-à   ǹ-gɨ-à   mènɔ̀   mi*
        John   PROG-IMPV   FACT-do-IMPV   c6a^matters c6a^3sREF

        ǹdɨ   betsiʔa   wòt   ka   fèèle   atò la.
        how   can   person   NEG   blame   3sO SUB
        John is behaving in a way that no one can blame him.

(20)   *Tà   me lene   wą̀   wu*
        3sS   SIM beat   c1^child c1^DEF

        ǹgù-ndɨ   bɔ̀-ɔ́   ǹ-dèn-a   atò mɨ̂   la   â?
        be-how   3pS^SUB-IMPV FACT-beat-IMPV   3sO also   SUB   INT
        Does he beat the child in the same way that he is also being beaten?

7. Cause and effect

The antecedent-consequence relationship in conditional sentences, described briefly in §5, is one kind of cause-effect relation. Other cause-effect relations are illustrated in this section.

7.1. Means-purpose. Two initial generalizations can be made about purpose sentences. First, the order of clauses is always means-purpose. Second, the purpose clause is not marked by the subordinator *la*, and the subject pronoun does not carry a subordinate tone pattern. In other words, there is no indication in a means-purpose sentence that either clause is subordinated to the other.

There are three strategies for conveying the notion of purpose. The first is that two clauses can be simply juxtaposed, with no overt marker of the relationship between them. The purpose clause must follow the means clause and is normally in the hortatory (HORT) mood, as in (21).

(21) *Tà tɔ   atò, tà kiʔi   ŋa èghɨ   bu.*
      3sS PFV^call 3sO 3sS HORT^come give c8^things c8^DEF
      He called him to come and give the things.

The second strategy for indicating purpose is to use the speech introducer *nê* '(say) that' with its extended function as a marker of a means-purpose relation. In this case, it is translated as 'so that, in order that'. The presence of *nê* implies that the purpose is already fulfilled at the moment of speech or is certain to be fulfilled. This type of purpose sentence is illustrated in (22).

(22) *Tà wu-a   n̂-kɨ-a   awê,*
      3sS CONT-IMPV   FACT-search-IMPV 2sO

      nê,   à   kiʔi   n̂-gà adzì.
      so^that 2sS HORT^come FACT-go LOC^stream
      He was looking for you so that you should come and go to the stream.

Finally, the means-purpose relation may be marked by *m̀bɨʔɨ* 'so that, in order that'. In this case, the purpose is uncertain: it may or may not be fulfilled. *M̀bɨʔɨ* may also be used to express a negative purpose 'so that not, lest', without the further addition of a negative marker. The mood or tense specification of the verb in the purpose clause shows whether the sense is positive or negative. Future tense indicates a positive interpretation, as in (23a); the hortatory mood indicates a negative one, as in (23b).

(23) Explicit purpose marker *m̀bɨʔɨ*

      a. *Tɔ   atò m̀bɨʔɨ tá-ā kiʔi e-dzɨ   èghɨdzɨ bi.*
          IMP^call 3sO so^that 3sS-F come NFACT-eat c8^food c8^3sPO
          Call him so that he can come and eat his food!

      b. *Su   atò m̀bɨʔɨ tà kpen.*
          IMP^tell 3sO lest   3sS HORT^fall
          Tell him so that he will not fall!

7.2. Reason-result. The reason-result relation is commonly signalled by one of four markers—*ǹgunê, m̀bɨ̀ʔɨ̀nê, na,* or *m̀bɨ̀ʔɨ̀na*—any of which can be translated 'because, since, for'. With these markers, the result clause always precedes the reason clause. Examples are given in (24)–(27).

Examples (24) and (25) illustrate reason clauses introduced by one of two compound forms where *nê* is the main constituent: *ǹgu-nê* and *m̀bɨ̀ʔɨ̀-nê*. These clauses display no marks of subordination.

(24) *Pità   me ghǎ   abe̩   ale,*
       Peter SIM go   outside thus

       ǹgu-nê   atɨ̩   tà-á   tseke la   ǹtsě.
       since   chair [3sS^SUB-F sit   SUB] be^not
       Peter went outside since there was no chair for him to sit on.

(25) *Tɔ   Lukàs tà kɨ̀ʔɨ̀,   m̀bɨ̀ʔɨ̀-nê tà bakà   wu asi,*
       IMP^call Lucas 3sS HORT^come because 3sS PFV^NEG be present

       bà ka ko   ǹ-tsɔ̀ʔtè   ànəa   ngaa.
       1pS NEG know FACT-settle matter DEM
       Call for Luke to come, since if he is not present, we shall not be able to settle that matter!

A reason clause introduced by *na* or the compound form *m̀bɨ̀ʔɨ̀-na* is closed by *la*, and the subject pronominal complex carries subordinate tone marking. For example, *à-á* (L-H) occurs in (26) instead of the nonsubordinate *á-ā* (H-M). There is no observable semantic difference, however, between the subordinate and nonsubordinate constructions.

(26) *Me   ko   awê, na   à-á   kpene abeme ebɨ la.*
       INCEPT take^care 2sO   because 2sS^SUB-F fall   inside hole SUB
       Take care because you may fall into a hole!

(27) *Ka   ǹ-gà   angele tò, m̀bɨ̀ʔɨ̀-na tà wu   lɨ̩   la.*
       NEG FACT-go beside 3sPO because 3sS PFV^be wizard SUB
       Don't go near him because he is a wizard!

In the reason-result relation, the order of clauses is reversed when the relationship is marked by *ale* 'so', or by the emphatic form *è wu ale*, which is a complete clause in its own right meaning 'since it is so'. Examples of these are given in (28) and (29).

(28) *Vi   Pità   è   su   atò nê,   tà   gha   ǹ-dze*
       wife Peter c1S PFV^tell 3sO   COMP^that 3sS HORT^go FACT-see

        a   Fɔ̀, ale tà   sà?   atetsɔ?   ǹ-gà.
        c1^o chief so   3sS PFV^wake^up LOC^morning FACT-go
        Peter's wife told him he should go and see the chief, so the next
        morning he went.

(29) *Tàt   wê   nà-à   ǹ-gɔ̀ɔ̀n-à,*
       c1^father c1^2sPO   PROG-IMPV FACT-be^sick-IMPV

        è   wu ale, à nɨ   atò   ǹ-gà   a   wasipità.
        it be so 2sS HORT^take 3sO   FACT-go LOC hospital
        Your father is sick, so you should take him to the hospital.

Notice, finally, that in sentences (24)–(29) the semantic relationship between the two clauses could be interpreted as grounds-conclusion rather than as reason-result.

7.3. Grounds-conclusion. There are two main additional ways in which a grounds-conclusion relation may be expressed. First, the relation may be signalled by the compound marker *ǹdɨwu* 'since', introducing the grounds clause. With this marker, the order of clauses is not fixed—both grounds-conclusion and conclusion-grounds orders are acceptable. The grounds clause is always closed by *la* and, in the imperfective and future, carries a subordinate tone pattern on the subject pronoun. Examples (30) and (31) illustrate the grounds clause in initial and final positions, respectively.

(30) *Ǹdɨwu à   fà?à   àfà?   ayê   te   ǹ-dɔ?   la,*
       since   2sS PFV^work c7^work c7^2sPO until FACT-finish SUB

        à tsi?   me   tɔ   èkatè   bê.
        2sS HORT^instead INCEPT read c8^books c8^2sPO
        Since you have already completed your work, you should begin to
        read your books.

(31) *A-a lɔ?ɔ à   lą   akɨŋ,*
       2sS-F F1   2sS HORT^cook cooking^pot

        ǹdɨwu à   bakà   bɔ   afà? la.
        since   2sS PFV^NEG have work SUB
        You should cook a meal, since you don't have any work to do.

Finally, the grounds-conclusion relation may be marked by one of three
compound forms derived from *ǹkàà* 'because of'. These forms, which are
ǹkàà-nê, *ǹkàà-na*, and *ǹkàà-ndɨ*, introduce the grounds clause and may be
translated 'since'. The order of clauses with these markers is always conclusion-grounds, as in (32)–(34). A grounds clause introduced by *ǹkàà-nê*
has no marks of subordination. A grounds clause introduced by *ǹkàà-na* or
ǹkàà-ndɨ is closed by *la* and carries a subordinate tone pattern on the
subject pronominal complex. The verb *ǹgùa* 'being' normally precedes
ǹkàà-ndɨ.

(32) *Bà le tsi èlen-e*   *àli laane nê   wu Abùʔ,*
      1pS P3 put c5^name-c5^morning   day today say^that be Abuʔ

      ǹkàà-nê bɔ̀ le wua ǹ-dzɔ̀-a   ǹ-gà-∅
      because 3pS P3 CONT FACT-go^out-IMPV FACT-go-IMPV

      ǹ-kɨ-a   èbùʔ ane àli-a   ngaa.
      FACT-seek-IMPV slaves on c7^day-c7^morning DEM
      We called the name of this day Abuʔ because they would go out
      looking for slaves on that day.

(33) *Bɨ ka ǹ-gà èwen afɨʔ   yaa,*
      2pS NEG FACT-go market c7^LOC^time c7^DEM

      ǹkàà-nà m̀bɨ̀ŋ nà-à   ǹ-kɨ̌   e-lu   la.
      since rain PROG-IMPV FACT-want NFACT-rain SUB
      You should not go to market now, since rain is threatening to fall.

(34) *Ma me laʔa nê,*
      1sS SIM say COMP^that

      wą   am ka fàʔ àfàʔ yu ale,
      c1^child c1^1sPO NEG work c7^work c7^DEF thus

      ǹ-gù-a   ǹkàà-ndɨ tà-á   ǹ-gɔ̀ɔ̀n-a   la.
      FACT-be-IMPV since 3sS^SUB-IMPV FACT-be^sick-IMPV SUB
      I said that my child should not do the work since he is sick.

8. Tone patterns on the subject pronominal complex

8.1. Independent clauses. An independent clause is one which can stand alone in semantic terms and to which other clauses are linked in a dependent relationship. The forms of the subject pronominal complex in independent clauses are set out in (35).

Column A gives the tense-aspect specification of the clause in which given pronoun forms occur. These specifications are: perfective aspect (PFV) and imperfective aspect (IMPV), which are both unmarked for tense but normally interpreted as present; past before yesterday (P3); past yesterday/general past (P2/P, a single form with two functions); past today (P1); and future tenses (F). (For an outline of the tense-aspect system of Mundani, see Parker 1985a.)

In column B, the numbers 1, 2, and 3 represent first, second, and third persons, respectively. In column C are given the singular pronoun forms, and in column D the plural forms, with the tones written separately beside each form.

Notes on chart (35):

(a) Pronoun forms in positive and negative sentences are identical except where otherwise indicated.

(b) The basic pronoun form may be combined with a preverbal tense or aspect marker. Where this occurs, the marker has been separated from the pronoun proper by a hyphen. The preverbal imperfective marker is the suffix -à; the marker of tense P2/P is also -à. The marker of future tense in positive clauses is -ā, but in the negative this tense marker is displaced to clause-final position and carries a high tone. In third person plural pronoun forms, the vowel of the tense or aspect marker assimilates to the preceding root vowel /ɔ/; e.g., bɔ́-à → bɔ́-ɔ̀.

(c) Subject pronouns in the imperfective and tense P2/P are identical. The distinction between the two constructions is maintained in the verb forms.

(d) Tense P1 (past today) employs the same set of subject pronouns as the perfective. This is because P1 is signalled by an auxiliary verb—elɔ́ʔɔ, eghɨ̂, or eli—which in the perfective occurs as lɔ́ʔ, ghɨ̂, or li. The following main verb is in its consecutive form, e.g., mâ lɔ́ʔ m̀bēn 'I danced (earlier today).'

(e) A replacive low tone pattern overrides the pronoun tones in tense P3 and the future negative.

(35) Tone patterns on the subject pronominal complex in independent
    clauses

A TNS/ASP	B PERSON	C SG			D PL		
PFV	1	*mâ*		HL	*báà*		HL
		ḿ	(NEG)	H	*bá*	(NEG)	H
	2	*à*		L	*bɨ́*		H
	3	*tà*		L	*bɔ́*		H
IMPV	1	*má-à*		H-L	*bá-à*		H-L
	2	*à-à*		L-L	*bɨ́-à*		H-L
	3	*tà-à*		L-L	*bɔ́-ɔ̀*		H-L
P3	1	*ǹ*		L	*bàà*		LL
	2	*à*		L	*bɨ̀*		L
	3	*tà*		L	*bɔ̀*		L
P2/P	1	*má-à*		H-L	*bá-à*		H-L
	2	*à-à*		L-L	*bɨ́-à*		H-L
	3	*tà-à*		L-L	*bɔ́-ɔ̀*		H-L
P1	1	*mâ*		HL	*báà*		HL
	2	*à*		L	*bɨ́*		H
	3	*tà*		L	*bɔ́*		H
F	1	*má-ā*		H-M	*bá-ā*		H-M
		ǹ . . . á	(NEG)	L . . . H	*bà . . . á*	(NEG)	L . . . H
	2	*á-ā*		H-M	*bɨ́-ā*		H-M
		à . . . á	(NEG)	L . . . H	*bɨ̀ . . . á*	(NEG)	L . . . H
	3	*tá-ā*		H-M	*bɔ́-ɔ̄*		H-M
		tà . . . á	(NEG)	L . . . H	*bɔ̀ . . . á*	(NEG)	L . . . H

8.2. Dependent clauses. A dependent clause is defined as one which
cannot stand alone in semantic terms, that is, it makes sense only in
relation to an independent clause which it expands or modifies in some
way.

Most of the pronoun forms listed in (35) remain unchanged in dependent clauses. In certain dependent clause types, however, the subject
pronominal complex in the imperfective and future tenses carries a L-H
tone pattern throughout, as seen in (36).

(36) Tone patterns on the subject pronominal complex in some dependent clause types

A TNS/ASP	B PERSON	C SG		D PL	
IMPV/F	1	*mà-á*	L-H	*bà-á*	L-H
	2	*à-á*	L-H	*bì-á*	L-H
	3	*tà-á*	L-H	*bɔ̀-ɔ́*	L-H

Note that tense P2/P pronoun forms, which are homophonous with imperfective forms in independent clauses, do not carry a L-H pattern in dependent clauses, where they may thus be readily differentiated from the imperfective pronoun forms. On the other hand, the overlay L-H pattern neutralizes the distinctions between imperfective and future pronominal forms.

The L-H tone pattern on the subject pronominal complex is restricted not only to imperfective and future constructions but also to those imperfective and future constructions in a limited set of dependent clause types. In (37), column A lists the clause types where the independent tone patterns occur and column B lists clause types where the L-H pattern is found.[4]

Note that the L-H tone pattern coincides with the presence of the clause-final subordinator *la* in all but the last three clause types listed in column B of (37). The subordinator *la* is absent, however, from all the clause types listed in column A. This distribution indicates that the L-H pattern in imperfective and future clauses may be regarded, with *la*, as a feature of subordination.

Adverbial clauses of time and circumstance, antecedent clauses in conditional sentences, and interrogative clauses are not marked by the subordinator *la*, but their subject pronominal complexes do exhibit the L-H pattern in the imperfective and future forms. If, as we have suggested, the L-H pattern is a feature of grammatical subordination, it would appear that these three clause types are regarded as subordinated, at least to a degree, to some neighboring clause (which in the case of an interrogative would presumably be the response to the question being asked).

---

[4]Some minor tonal differences between independent clauses and relative clauses have been noticed in tense P3, the before-yesterday past tense. These tonal differences affect the main verb. They are described in an appendix to Parker 1985b. Further research is needed to discover if such tonal changes occur on the main verb of other dependent clause types.

(37) Tone patterns on the subject pronominal complex in different
clause types

A (tone varies) independent	B L-H dependent
All true independent clauses	
Clauses introduced by *nê*	Clauses introduced by *ǹdɨ*
	Clauses introduced by *na*
Clauses introduced by any marker that is a compound of *nê—ŋgu-nê, m̀bɨʔɨ-nê*, or *ǹkàà-nê*	Clauses introduced by any marker that is a compound of *ǹdɨ* or *na—ǹdɨ-wu, ŋgù-ndɨ, wu-ndɨ, ǹkàà-ndɨ, m̀bɨʔɨ-ndɨ, m̀bɨʔɨ-na*, or *ǹkàà-na*
	Relative clauses
Purpose clauses introduced by *m̀bɨʔɨ* or *nê*	Adverbial clauses introduced by *m̀bɨʔɨ*
	Adverbial clauses of time or circumstance (other than those introduced by *m̀bɨʔɨ*)
Consequence clauses in conditional sentences	Antecedent clauses in conditional sentences
	Interrogative clauses

The absence of *la* and the L-H tone pattern causes various clause types
to fall into the same category as independent clauses (column A).

In the case of the consequence clause in a conditional sentence, this
categorization is not surprising. The marker *ko* or *m̀bə*, although appearing
immediately before the consequence clause, does not seem to be an
essential part of it. Speakers pause not only before this marker but also
(although less emphatically) after it, and the marker is, in any case,
optional. For these reasons, we have labelled *ko* and *m̀bə* not as consequence markers, but rather as markers of the conditional relationship
(COND) existing between the antecedent and consequence clauses. The
consequence clause, then, can stand on its own. The antecedent clause, on
the other hand, cannot normally stand alone, and it is this clause that has
the subordinate L-H tones on its subject pronominal complex in the
imperfective and future.

A complement clause introduced by *nê* falls into the independent category. Unlike the complementizer *ǹdɨ*, *nê* is separated from the following complement clause by a noticeable pause (by a comma in written texts). This fact suggests that the marker is not actually considered a part of the complement clause at all and that, in semantic terms, the latter can function as an independent clause in its own right. In other words, *nê* links two independent clauses in a compound relationship and can be called a compound marker.

The other clause types in column A of (37) seem to be classified as independent chiefly by virtue of their connections with *nê*. Some are introduced by a compound marker that has *nê* as one of its components; others are purpose clauses introduced by either *nê* or *m̀bɨʔɨ*. Most of these clause types are semantically dependent, but the influence of the compound marker *nê* seems to account for the fact that this seeming semantic dependency is not reflected in the grammatical structure.

The use of the subordinate tone pattern in different clause types is seen in (38)–(46). The clauses concerned are closed by *la* in examples (38)–(43); in (44)–(46) *la* is absent.

(38) Clause introduced by *ǹdɨ*

> *Tà bakà   ko   ǹdɨ   tà-á   ghɨ̌ la.*
> 3sS PFV^NEG know COMP^how 3sS^SUB-F do SUB
> She doesn't know what (lit. how) she will do.

(39) Clause introduced by a compound of *ǹdɨ*

> *Wạ   wu   ka fàʔ   àfàʔ   yu   ale,*
> c1^child c1^DEF NEG HORT^work c7^work c7^DEF thus
>
> *ǹ-gù-a   ǹkàà-ndɨ tà-á   ǹ-gɔ̀ɔ̀n-a   la.*
> FACT-be-IMPV since   3sS^SUB-IMPV FACT-be^sick-IMPV SUB
> The child should not do the work, since he is sick.

(40) Clause introduced by *na*

> *Me ko   awê, na   à-á   kpene abeme ebɨ la.*
> SIM take^care 2sO because 2sS^SUB-F fall   inside hole SUB
> Take care because you may fall into a hole!

(41) Clause introduced by compound of *na*

> *Ka ǹ-ga   angele tò,   m̀bɨ̀ʔɨ-na tà -á   ǹ-gɨ̀-a*
> NEG FACT-go beside 3sPO because 3sS^SUB-IMPV   FACT-do-IMPV
>
> *a   kàbɔ̀ŋ la.*
> c1^o   evil   SUB
> Don't go near him because he does bad things!

(42) Relative clause

> *Bɔ   nɨ   atɨ̧   ǹ-gà   adzìʔ   a*
> 3sS   PFV^take chair FACT-go c7^LOC^place c7^morning
>
> *bɔ̀-ɔ́   e-lɔ́ʔɔ   e-ghă   e-lìa   la.*
> [3sS^SUB-F NFACT-F1 NFACT-go NFACT-end SUB]
> They took a chair to the place where they would end (the race).

(43) Adverbial clause introduced by *m̀bɨ̀ʔɨ*

> *Ghɨa   wu   m̀bɨ̀ʔɨ tà-á   Ø-sù-a   awê la.*
> IMP^do only   as   3sS^SUB-IMPV IMPV-tell-IMPV 2sO   SUB
> Do exactly as he is telling you!

(44) Adverbial clause of time or circumstance

> *À-á   e-lɔ́ʔɔ   e-kɨ̀ʔɨ,*
> 2sS^SUB-F NFACT-F1 NFACT-come
>
> *à   ŋa   èghɨ   bu   abua tò.*
> 2sS HORT^give c8^things c8^DEF to   3sPO
> When you come (later today), you should give the things to him.

(45) Antecedent clause in a conditional sentence

> *Tà-á   e-sàʔa   e-ghă   ewen,*
> 3sS^SUB-F NFACT-F NFACT-go market
>
> *ko   tá-ā e-yṵṵ   èghɨ   bi.*
> COND 3sS-F NFACT-buy c8^things c8^3sREF
> If she goes to market (tomorrow), she will buy her things.

(46) Interrogative clause

> *Bàa   mbɔŋ   bà-á   ghǐ na   â?*
> 1p   EMPH   1pŝSUB-F do how   INT
> And we, what shall we do?

9. Conclusion

In Mundani, the complex sentence can take a variety of forms—a series of consecutive marked verbs, a series of independent clauses that are juxtaposed without any overt indication of the relationship between them, or a cluster of two or more clauses whose semantic relations are formalized by various markers. Apart from the markers of contrastive and conditional relations, there are four markers that can be considered basic—*nê*, *ǹdɨ*, *na*, and *m̀bɨʔɨ*. Various compounds of these basic markers permit a whole range of semantic relations to be formalized.

In addition to marking semantic relations, grammatical dependency or subordination may be signalled in certain clauses by means of the particle *la* in final position, a L-H tone pattern on the subject pronominal complex in the imperfective aspect or in future tenses, or by the occurrence of both *la* and a L-H tone pattern. The coincidence of these markers of grammatical subordination with semantic dependency is almost, but not quite, complete. An area of discrepancy exists in circumstance or reason clauses introduced by a compound form of *nê* and in purpose clauses introduced by *m̀bɨʔɨ*. These clauses are dependent in semantic terms, but they are not subordinated grammatically. One possible explanation of this discrepancy is the influence of *nê*, which usually marks the relationship between two clauses that are both semantically and grammatically independent of each other.

References

Beekman, John, John Callow, and Michael Kopesec. 1981. The semantic structure of written communication. Dallas: Summer Institute of Linguistics.

Marchese, Lynell. 1976. La subordination en godié. Abidjan: Institut de Linguistique Appliquée/Société Internationale de Linguistique.

Parker, Elizabeth. 1985a. Mood, tense, and aspect in Mundani. ms.

———. 1985b. Relative clauses in Mundani. ms.

———. 1986. Mundani pronouns. In Ursula Wiesemann (ed.), Pronominal systems, 131–65. Continuum Schriftenreihe Zur Linguistik 5. Tübingen: Gunter Narr Verlag.

———. 1991. Conditionals in Mundani. In this volume.

Section Three

Chadic Languages

Tense and Aspect in Podoko Narrative and Procedural Discourse

Elizabeth Jarvis

Abstract

The Podoko verbal system has two binary distinctions: perfective vs. imperfective, and presence or absence of a focus position immediately following the verb. This gives four basic verb forms, all of which may be marked for tense by means of a past or future particle. The focus forms may also be marked with tonal downstep meaning 'nonpast'. The event line of narrative and procedural discourse uses the perfective, usually without focus, with no tense marking. Background material uses the focus perfective for events that took place prior to that point on the event line. The focus imperfective is used for repeated events, for events and states that are concurrent with the main events, and for explanations of a general nature. Reported speech generally uses focus forms in main clauses with the perfective for past events and the imperfective for present and future.

Résumé

Le système verbal en podoko connaît une double distinction binaire: la distinction perfectif/imperfectif et, celle de la présence ou absence d'une position de focalisation postposée au verbe. Ceci donne, donc, lieu à quatre formes verbales de base. Toutes ces formes sont susceptibles de prendre une particule de temps passé ou futur et, les formes avec focalisation peuvent être marquées aussi par un abaissement tonal signifiant non-passé. La succession d'événements dans une narration ou dans un récit technique est présentée dans le perfectif, normalement sans focalisation, le temps n'étant pas marqué. Le perfectif avec focalisation s'emploie pour les événements antérieurs au moment dont il est question dans le récit. L'imperfectif s'emploie pour les actions répétées, pour les actions et les états qui se passent en même temps que les événements principaux, et pour

les explications générales. Dans le discours rapporté on trouve le plus
souvent dans les propositions principales les formes avec focalisation: perfectif pour le passé, imperfectif pour le présent et le futur.

This paper briefly describes the Podoko[1] system of tense and aspect and
explores the use of various verb forms in narrative and procedural discourse.
The description of the system is presented in §1 including a discussion of
focus. The consecutive clause type is explained because of its significance for
discourse structure. In looking at narrative and procedural discourse, we
examine first how information on the event line is encoded (§2), then how
background information is presented (§3); finally, some observations are made
concerning verb forms used in reported speech within narrative (§4). A
Podoko text with translation is given in the appendix.

1. Tense and aspect in Podoko

1.1. Aspect. Podoko has a basic distinction between perfective and imperfective aspect.[2] The perfective form of a verb consists of the verb stem
with or without extensions, i.e., object marker, directional, and others. The
imperfective form of a verb varies according to whether the verb is
transitive or intransitive, but in neither case are extensions allowed (except
for indirect object marking where appropriate). If a form is transitive
imperfective, the stem is marked by palatalization (a word-level prosody,
indicated in the transcription by a superscript y at the beginning of the
word). If it is intransitive imperfective, the verb stem takes an -i suffix,
giving a form which is identical to that of the verbal noun.

The transitive imperfective prosody is glossed in the examples by IMPF
with a ligature (^) to show that the prosody applies to the entire word.
The intransitive imperfective suffix is glossed by IIMPF with a hyphen

---

[1]Podoko is a Chadic language of the central (Biu-Mandara) branch. It is spoken in
the district of Mora in north Cameroon by some twenty or thirty thousand people. The
research for this paper was done with the permission of the Ministry of Higher
Education, Computer Services, and Scientific Research of the Republic of Cameroon.
I wish to thank Ndoula Lagona and Maroua Jonas for their cooperation in providing
the texts and other data quoted in this paper; my colleague Jeanette Swackhamer for
her work on tone in Podoko; and Bernard Comrie for his guidance in writing this
paper.

[2]For a fuller description of this, see Jarvis 1989, §4.3.

because it can actually be separated from the root.[3] Thus the verb *gəl-* 'grow (up), bring up' has the intransitive perfective form *gala* 'grow', the transitive imperfective form *ʸgala* 'bring up', and the intransitive imperfective form *gəli* 'grow'. (A final *ə* is added to some forms to preserve syllable structure.)

Not all verbs show the perfective/imperfective aspectual distinction. Some verbs, such as *ngwá* 'want', *va* 'give', *nda* 'there is', *mba* 'know how', and *dzə́gwa* 'can' have a single form. These resemble perfectives rather than imperfectives, but their usage is often imperfective. The meaning of a stative verb such as 'know how' is necessarily perfective, whereas the verb 'give' may be used either as perfective or imperfective, even though there is only one form.

1.2. Focus. The basic perfective/imperfective aspectual distinction exists in both indicative and imperative moods. In the indicative, however, there is a further distinction of focus/nonfocus which affects both the verb form itself and the rest of the clause.[4] In a clause of the nonfocus type, the verb is unchanged; but the subject is marked, either with a high tone (H) on the first syllable if it is a noun (although some verbal extensions cancel this) or a pronoun with an irregular prefix *m-*. If the clause has a focus position, the verb is generally preceded by *a*. Sometimes this *a* is dropped, and, in certain cases, it is obligatorily absent, for example, after the conjunction *ʸtata* 'when'. An unfocused subject remains unmarked in a focus construction, and it no longer directly follows the verb. The basic word order VSO becomes: *a* V FOC S O, where the focus position comes between the verb and the subject.

These two binary distinctions give rise to four possibilities in the indicative mood, as in (1).

Examples of nonfocus perfectives are presented in (2) and (3), focus perfectives in (4) and (5), a nonfocus imperfective in (6), and a focus imperfective in (7). Note that the transitive verb form meaning 'bring up'

---

[3]The following abbreviations are used in the body of the paper: ANPH anaphoric; COLL collective; CON consecutive; DUM dummy focus; EMPH emphasis; EXT extension; FOC focus/focaliser/focus position; FUT future; H high tone; ID ideophone; IIMPF intransitive imperfective; IMPF imperfective; IMPV imperative; NEG negative; NFOC nonfocus; NPST nonpast; O object; PRF perfective; PST past; Q interrogative; REF reflexive/reciprocal; S subject; SUB subordinator; TOP topic; V verb; VN verbal noun; Ø zero morpheme; ! tonal downstep; ? unknown gloss; 1 first person; 1i first person inclusive; 1x first person exclusive; 2 second person; 3 third person; s singular; p plural.

[4]In Jarvis 1989, §§4.3, 6.1.2, and 6.3.1, the nonfocus perfective is referred to as 'aoriste'.

is used in (6) and (7) because intransitive imperfectives do not pattern with the other forms. They will be explained below.

(1) Indicative mood constructions

	− focus			+ focus		
perfective	v(EXT)	$\left\{\begin{array}{l}\text{s:noun }^{\text{H}}\\ \text{s:}m\text{-pronoun}\end{array}\right\}$	O	a v(EXT)	FOC	S O
imperfective (transitive)	^{y}v	$\left\{\begin{array}{l}\text{s:}^{\text{H}}+\text{noun}\\ \text{s:}m+\text{pronoun}\end{array}\right\}$	O	a ^{y}v	FOC	S O

(2)   *Gələ   údzəra.*
       PRF^grow NFOC^child
       The child grew up.

(3)   *Gələ   mayá.*
       PRF^grow NFOC^1s
       I grew up.

(4)   *A gə́lə   á dzangə   udzəra.*
       FOC PRF^grow on mountain child
       It was on the mountain that the child grew up.

(5)   *A gə́lə   á dzangə   yá.*
       FOC PRF^grow on mountain 1s
       It was on the mountain that I grew up.

(6)   *^{y}Manə ^{y}gələ   mayə́   udzəra, . . .*
       SUB   IMPF^grow NFOC^1s child
       The fact that I am bringing up the child, . . .

(7)   *A ^{y}gələ   udzərə yá.*
       FOC IMPF^grow child   1s
       It was the child that I was bringing up./I was bringing up the child.

In illustrations (4) and (5) of focus perfective, the focus position is filled by the locative expression 'on the mountain'. It is not uncommon, however, for the focus position to be filled by a reduplication of the verb stem, with no apparent emphasis on the meaning of the verb, as in (8).

(8)   *A gə́lə   gələ   udzəra.*
       FOC PRF^grow grow child
       The child grew up./The child has grown up.

The nonfocus imperfective is found only in subordinate clauses. Every main clause with an imperfective transitive verb has a focus position, and if no particular constituent is semantically in focus, the object is put in focus by default. Hence, the two readings for (7) are possible.

The imperfective constructions in (1) use only transitive forms. Intransitive imperfective forms are not found in nonfocus main clauses; they are found with preverbal *a*, but the focus position is optional, as in (9) and (10). In (9), there is a locative expression in focus position; in (10), the focus position is empty because the subject pronoun is not emphatic.

(9)   *A gəl-i   á dzangə udzəra.*
       FOC grow-IIMPF on mountain child
       It is on the mountain that the child was growing up.

(10)   *A gəl-i   ka.*
       FOC grow-IIMPF 2s
       You were growing up.

1.3. Tense. Tense may be marked by preverbal particles *sa* (past) or *da* (future). These particles are related to the verbs *s-* 'come' and *d-* 'go', respectively. The particle *sa* is used in discourse to indicate the past with reference to the time line. In clauses with focus, it replaces preverbal *a*. The particle *da* indicates absolute future time. In clauses with focus, it is placed between *a* and the verb stem.

(11)   *Sa gəl-i   udzəra.*
       PST grow-IIMPF child
       The child was growing up.

(12)   *A da ʸgələ   udzərə yá.*
       FOC FUT IMPF^grow child   1s
       I am going to bring up the child.

Sometimes it is difficult to distinguish the future-tense particle from the verb 'go' used as an auxiliary, as in (13).

(13)   *A   da   ᵞɓawǝ   udzǝrǝ   yá.*
FOC FUT   IMPF^call child   1s
I will call the child./I am going to call the child.

These tense markers may be used with the direct speech introducer *ngǝ́*
'say', even though it is not a standard verb.

(14)   *A dába "Hiyǝ mayǝ́" dá ngǝ́ ganǝ   lawá,*
because corn   my   FUT say squirrel TOP
Because Squirrel will say, 'It's my corn,'   (Appendix 15)[5]

In focus clauses only, tense may also be marked by clause-initial
downstep (!), which lowers all following low tones until a high tone occurs
to reset the register of subsequent tones. This downstep feature marks
nonpast time. In the imperfective, this is interpreted as present time, as in
(15). In the perfective, the downstep has a modal reading, as in (16).

(15)   *!A   ᵞgǝlǝ   udzǝrǝ yá.*
NPST^FOC IMPF^rear child   1s
I am bringing up the child.

(16)   *!A   gǝlǝ   gǝlǝ yá.*
NPST^FOC PRF^grow grow 1s
May I grow up.

1.4. Consecutive clauses. One special clause type needs to be presented
before we proceed to the description of the use of the tense/aspect forms in
discourse. This clause has the word order SVO, instead of the basic VSO. In
addition, the subject is marked with prenominal *ngǝ*, indicating consecutive
(CON) action (Jarvis 1989, §6.1.3). In the case of a pronoun subject, a special
pronoun is used and *ngǝ* is only optionally present with certain forms.[6] These
constructions are referred to as CONSECUTIVE CONSTRUCTIONS because they
are used primarily for actions that follow from previous actions (17), or in
purpose clauses (18). Also common in these constructions is the dummy
focus marker *ngá*, which is postposed to the verb—whether transitive or
intransitive—when no object follows.

---

[5]This sentence and others so marked, are found in context in the Appendix to this
paper.
[6]Subject pronouns are listed in (48), in the appendix to this paper.

(17) *Kəsa   nga   ʸudzə   ʸvərdəngə məná,*
     PRF^take NFOC^3s small   axe   3s

       kənə   dáda,   kənə   ʸkələ   dəgwásla.
       CON^3s bush   CON^3s IMPF^cut wood
       She took her little axe, went to the bush, and cut wood.

(18) *Kəzlalu   ndí   a   həlkwa,*
     PRF^close NFOC^one   with   basket

       a ɗaba ngə nabə́ga aká̰ dəkwa ngá.
       CAUSE   CON rain   NEG PRF^enter DUM
       One closes it (the granary) with a basket so that the rain may not
       get in.

2. Event line

When we look at both the genres of discourse that are built on an event
line (narrative and procedural), we see that the event line—the sequence
of events that form the backbone of the text—is clearly delineated in
Podoko discourse by using the perfective. The perfective is usually nonfocus and has no tense marking. A short illustration of this, from a
procedural text, is presented in (19).[7]

(19) *T-i   ʸpə́hi lakí, tədasə   ndí   yawə́ aká̰ hiyá.*
     cook-VN   beer TOP   PRF^pour^under NFOC^one water to   corn

       Ngəzla   nga   wa   də makə́ka kwətə́ra.
       PRF^break NFOC^3s mouth   in week   one

       ʸFətəlá   ndi   tá patsa. Mbələlə nga.
       PRF^spread NFOC^one for sun   PRF^dry NFOC^3s
       To brew beer, one pours water under grains of guinea corn. They
       germinate for a week. One spreads them out in the sun. They dry.

Even events in subordinate clauses are expressed with a nonfocus perfective, as long as they are in chronological order on the time line.

---

[7]The palatalization of the verb *ʸfətəlá* 'spread out' is lexical and not from the
imperfective marker.

Example (20) is taken from the text presented in the appendix to this paper (60–63).

(20) *Pələla   ndí   udzəra, ᵞndzədə́la ndá.*
     PRF^undo NFOC^one   child   PRF^seat NFOC^one

          ᵞManə tapavə́   ndí   lakí, də hala   gana.
          SUB   PRF^taste^REF NFOC^one TOP in ground squirrel

          Bandá mbávu gánə   lakí,
          soon^as PRF^rise NFOC^squirrel TOP
She untied the baby and sat it down. When they got hold of each other, Squirrel (was thrown) to the ground. As soon as Squirrel got up, . . .

After an ideophone, the consecutive clause is often used with a perfective verb, as in (21).

(21) *Gwək gwəgwək gwək ngə́ ndi gasa   gána.*
     ID   ID   ID   CON one PRF^catch squirrel
     One caught Squirrel.   (Appendix 158)

Focus perfectives are less commonly found on the event line, but they do occur. The focus position is usually filled by the reduplicated verb stem.

(22) *A   mbáhasə   mbáhə ndi ᵞsəgá.*
     FOC PRF^take^under take   one leg

     A   ᵞbətsa   ᵞbətsə ndi a   haya.
     FOC PRF^knock knock one with earth
One grabbed his legs. One knocked him over on the ground.
                                (Appendix 160, 161)

This same verb form is also used in presenting background (nonevent line) information (§3). In (22), however, it is clearly presenting event-line material, but it is not obvious what significance it has as opposed to a nonfocus perfective alternative.

Not every event on the time line is encoded by a perfective verb. The consecutive clause is often used with an imperfective verb to round off a paragraph. For example,

Now another day, he (Hornbill) returned (nonfocus perfective). He said to Pigeon, "Please lend me your beak to go on a journey," he said. "I won't give it to you," Pigeon said to him. "Please, I beg you," he said. "Alright," said Pigeon now. He gave (nonfocus perfective) him the beak. Then he (Hornbill) went off (*ngə* SV imperfective).

This may be analysed as the end of a paragraph because the story continues in a different location and the next sentence begins with TAIL-HEAD linkage (Longacre 1976:204), a device used for opening a section: 'When he had gone'.

This use of the imperfective in a consecutive clause is a common feature of narrative but is found less often in procedural texts. There, it is used not only to close paragraphs, but to indicate that something preceded it. It may even be used, on occasion, at the beginning of a paragraph, indicating that the paragraph follows on from the preceding one: 'Another time, the old woman went to get firewood now'. This is the opening of a new paragraph and the clause is of the consecutive imperfective type.

The consecutive clause type with imperfective verb may also be used for repeated action, as in (23). The particle *ngə* (consecutive) is not present in this example, but the word order clearly marks the construction as consecutive.

(23) *Tapa   nga   lakí,   a   tsaralu   tsára.*
     PRF^taste NFOC^3s   TOP   FOC PRF^good^3s good

     Kənə   ʸmətadə nga,   kənə   ʸmətadə   nga.
     CON^3s IMPF^lick DUM CON^3s IMPF^lick DUM
     He tasted it, it pleased him. So he licked and licked.

The same sort of repetition can be expressed using an intransitve imperfective verb, as in (24) and (25). Most final vowels become *a* prepause. Hence, the intransitive imperfective markers in (24) change from their normal *i* to *a*. The imperfective verb may be preceded by *bá* (focus), as in (25).

(24) *Ba   ʸmaná tapa   nga   lakí,   a   tsaralu   tsára.*
     when SUB   PRF^taste NFOC^3s   TOP   FOC PRF^good^3s good

     ʸNdakə bá mətad-a,   bá   mətad-a.
     then   FOC lick-IIMPF FOC lick-IIMPF
     When he tasted it, it pleased him. So then he licked and licked.

(25) *Ba mbáh-i   nda, ba mbáh-i   nda. Raha   ndí   bəhwa.*
FOC take-IIMPF one FOC take-IIMPF one PRF^fill NFOC^one sack
One kept taking (more and more grain). One filled several sacks.

One other form which occurs occasionally on the event line is a verbal
noun followed by an indirect object marked by the preposition *aká*. There
are two examples of this in the text in the appendix, but its significance is
not yet clear.

(26) *Mbáh-i aká ᵞtanəngá dá gága.*
take-VN to thing to termite^hill
He took the things into the termite hill.   (Appendix 64)

(27) *Zámbər-i aká nasi   bá ᵞtata a   slála   kə́nga.*
summon-VN to women FOC all   with district ANPH
She summoned all the women in that district.   (Appendix 109)

3. Background information

We turn now to material that is off the event line, excluding reported
speech which is discussed in §4. Let us look first at the use of the focus
perfective. It may be used for time setting, in which case tense is not
marked. The focus position is filled by the reduplicated verb stem or, more
rarely, by the verbal noun with the preposition *a* 'with'. In (28), the focus
marker *a* has dropped out (see §1.2).

(28) *Sədá   sə   nanə dá kayə dá Zətə mazláməná laki,*
PRF^come^out come 1x in house of God now   TOP

nganano daha   da sə   dzángə Slalaváda.
CON^1x go^down to under mountain Slalavada
When we had come out of church now, we went down to Mt.
Slalavada.

Very often, the verb used in time setting is a repetition of the verb of
the immediately preceding clause (TAIL-HEAD linkage), as in (29).

(29) *Kərɗa   ndí   mandzala,   hwaɗa   ndí*
     PRF^grind NFOC^one sprouted^grain PRF^mix NFOC^one

      dɔ́ mata tiyá. A   hwadá   hwaɗɔ́ ndi lakí, matadá
      in big pot FOC PRF^mix mix   one TOP PRF^split

      ndi   matá dəgwásla.
      NFOC^one   big   wood
      One grinds the sprouted grain, one mixes it (with water) in a big
      pot. When one has mixed it, one breaks up a lot of firewood.

In (30), the focus position is filled by the reduplicated verb stem, and in
(31), by 'with' and the verbal noun. This latter construction sometimes
seems to have the sense 'just when'.

(30) *Ndi   ʸwarə   nawɔ́ saha   navira ndá sla.*
     CON^one IMPF^lead goat   descend   with   COLL cow

      Saha   bá !a s-i   ndi sá ndərə zlá lakí,
      PRF^descend FOC with come-VN one to peanut again TOP
      One brought down the goats and cows. When one had come down
      to the peanut field again,

(31) *A   talakwa   bá !a tal-i   dá sə   slírə lakí,*
     FOC PRF^touch^in FOC with touch-VN to under tooth TOP
     Just when she had picked her teeth,   (Appendix 28)

An event which occurred prior to the point in time at which it is
mentioned in the story, or which occurred before the story began, is
marked by *sa* (past) and the focus position is filled with *a* and a verbal
noun.

(32) *A   nda ndə ʸngɔ́də nɔ́sa   sa davarə   !a d-i   dá nəwala.*
     FOC there^is certain woman PST PRF^leave with go-VN to man
     There was a woman who had gone to (another) husband.
                                    (Appendix 1)

(33) *Sa slərtəkwa !a   slərt-i   sləɓə gwə́mə dá slirə məná.*
      PST PRF^stick   with stick-VN meat   also   into tooth 3s

      ʸNdakə kəlada   nga   ʸkəlád͡a kə́nga.
      then   PRF^break NFOC^3s grass   ANPH

Some meat had got stuck between her teeth. So she broke off the
grass.   (Appendix 25, 26)

Example (32) gives information about what the woman had done before
the story began. Example (33) mentions the meat's getting stuck between
the woman's teeth, an event which must have happened at some earlier
time in the story. Past tense relative clauses often use the nonfocus rather
than the focus perfective. Compare (33), where we have focus perfective
in a relative clause, with (34).

(34) *A ndzi ʸtanəngá hənə hənə də́ dəfa sa ʸsəlu   dúla.*
      FOC be   thing   lie lie in 3s PST PRF^drink beer
      The thing that had drunk the beer was lying in (the field).

The imperfective, on the other hand, is used mainly for describing states
and events that are concurrent with the events on the time line, as in (35).

(35) *Mawə vǝ́ngwə ʸmanə́ hawə́ maká wa? ngə́ nda.*
      which mouth this   mouth 2s   Q   say one

      !A   ʸtalawə   vala nda.
      NPST^FOC IMPF^touch 3s one

"What sort of beak do you think you've got?" they said. They kept
touching it.

The touching is not a new event subsequent to the words of mockery.
Presumably the two were going on at the same time. Therefore the
imperfective is used.

Habitual actions that form the background to the story are also expressed by the imperfective.

(36) *A   nda ndə waládïya məná lakí, a   ʸɓawə   naləmani*
     FOC there^is servant 3s   TOP FOC IMPF^call herds

      ká   məná dá ndərā, ...
      ANPH 3s   to peanut
      He had a servant, and he used to lead his herds to the peanut
      field, ...

The story goes on to tell how the servant was stopped from grazing the
herds in the field and destroying the peanuts.

An aside, or explanation, may also use the imperfective. Part of an
account of how to make beer goes like this:

> One heats (nonfocus perfective) on the fire the liquid that has
> been squeezed out. It boils and boils (focus imperfective). One
> calls (focus imperfective) that 'brewing'.

The final clause is an aside from the main account, explaining a particular term that is used in making beer.

There is another use of the imperfective which is common, particularly
in procedural discourse, but its function is far from clear. In (37), an action
is stated first in the focus imperfective and then in the nonfocus perfective.

(37) *!a   ʸslə   təmazálə nda. Slálá   ndi   təmazála,*
     NPST^FOC IMPF^cut stalk   one PRF^cut NFOC^one stalk

      !a   ʸpalə   kayə nda. Pəlálá   ndi   kaya,
      NPST^FOC IMPF^thatch house one PRF^thatch NFOC^one house
      ... one cuts stalks. One cuts the stalks, one thatches the roof. One
      thatches the roof, ...

As each of the two actions in (37) (cutting and thatching) happened only
once, presumably only one verb of each pair can be on the event line.
Normally we expect nonfocus perfectives on the event line, so some other
explanation must be found for the preceding focused imperfectives. A
similar phenomenon has been observed in narrative, but there it is much
rarer. In (38), an imperfective verb is repeated in a consecutive clause and
followed by the same verb in perfective aspect.

(38) *Ngə ndi ᵞuzə*   *nga, ngə ndi ᵞuzə*   *nga, uzu*
      CON one IMPF^eat   DUM CON one IMPF^eat   DUM PRF^eat

     ndí   ɓəlva.
     NFOC^one berry
     One kept eating and eating; one ate some berries.

4. Reported speech

Finally, we look at reported speech as found in narrative. Some conversational exchanges are long enough and their context is such that they function as embedded narratives, so that they follow the pattern already observed. However, some exchanges are quite brief and of a different nature. In the text in the appendix, the longest single passage of reported speech is only seven clauses 80–86. In it the daughter explains to her mother how her baby was stolen. It contains no nonfocus perfectives. The only main clause nonfocus perfective in reported speech in this text is 88, which has a past tense marker and reports that the mother is reminding her daughter of what she had said to her before the baby was stolen: 'I told you, . . .' Generally, the focus perfective is used in reported speech for events that happened previous to the conversation, and the focus imperfective for events present and future in relation to the conversation. Thus we find the focus perfective used in 'Squirrel has stolen my daughter's child' (96), and focus imperfective in 'I'm dragging you off to the chief's' (34).

The focus imperfective is found either with the nonpast depressor tone (present tense) or with *da* (future).[8]

(39) *!A   ᵞtawə   tawɔ́ ka mudɔ́ nəsɔ́   na?*
      NPST^FOC IMPF^cry what 2s old   woman Q
      What are you crying for, old woman?

(40) *A   da də   yá da dátəka.*
      FOC FUT go^IIMPF 1s to house^your
      I will go to your house.

---

[8]The verb *də* (go) in (40) is irregular and lacks the normal intransitive imperfective suffix *-i* .

Nonpast focus perfectives are found with a variety of modal uses—request (41),[9] obligative (42), optative (43), or deliberative (44).

(41) *!A   vi   lá   ka vángwə maká ... wa?*
NPST^FOC PRF^give^1s NEG 2s mouth 2s   Q
Won't you give me your beak?

(42) *Sáyə !a   tidá   duli ka kwa.*
must NPST^FOC PRF^cook^1s beer 2s EMPH
You must brew me some beer.

(43) *!A   da təhaká   ganə   la.*
NPST^FOC FUT PRF^hit^2s squirrel NEG
May Squirrel not hit you./You must not let Squirrel hit you.

(44) *!A   ɓakavadə́ kənə nanə ya?*
NPST^FOC PRF^do   how 1p   Q
What are we to do?

Both perfective and imperfective imperatives are found but it is difficult to see the significance of the aspectual distinction. In the following example, the first imperative is perfective and the second imperfective; but they seem to have the same force.

(45) *Akwə́ !da   ʸdzaha   ʸdzáhə má   mawə mawə́ mə́nda ...*
IMPV NPST^go PRF^gather gather even which which person

    Akwə́ !da   ʸusalə́   ʸmanə́ nə́sə a   udzərə də́
    IMPV NPST^go IMPF^seek this   woman with child in

    gwagwa bá   ʸtata.
    back   FOC all
Go and gather everyone ... Go and look for every woman who has a baby on her back.

The use of tense and aspect in subordinate clauses in reported speech has not been thoroughly studied, but it is worth remarking that nonfocus verb forms, both perfective and imperfective, are common, as in (46) and (47).

---

[9]In the particular type of clause found in (41), the negative marker follows the verb instead of being clause final.

(46) *ʸManə ʸmbə́lidə́   ka   lakí, . . .*
      SUB   PRF^throw^1s NFOC^2s TOP
      The fact that you threw me, . . .

(47) *Na ʸmaná ʸtawə   mayá   ʸtaw-á.*
      it SUB   IMPF^cry NFOC^1s cry-VN
      That's why I'm crying.

5. Conclusion

Discourse, including embedded discourse which is built on a sequence of events, uses the perfective aspect for verbs on the event line. There are, however, some special cases where the imperfective is used, for example, in the consecutive clause. The nonfocus perfective is much more common than the focus perfective, but the latter is frequent enough that it should not be overlooked. Neither is marked for tense when referring to actions on the event line.

In background material, the focus perfective is used for events that took place prior to that point on the event line. If they are the immediately preceding event, there is no tense marker, but if they happened at some earlier point in the story or procedure, or even before the story began, they carry past tense. The imperfective is used for repeated events, for events and states that are concurrent with the main events, and for explanations of a general nature.

Reported speech most often uses focus forms in main clauses, especially if the conversational exchanges are brief—the perfective for the past and the imperfective for present or future. Nonfocus forms, both perfective and imperfective, are found in subordinate clauses.

References

Comrie, Bernard. 1976. Aspect. Cambridge: Cambridge University Press.

Jarvis, Elizabeth. 1989. Esquisse grammaticale de la langue podoko. In Daniel Barreteau and Robert Hedinger (eds.), Descriptions de langues camerounaises, 39–127. Paris: Agence de Coopération Culturelle et Technique et ORSTOM.

Longacre, Robert E. 1976. An anatomy of speech notions. Lisse: The Peter de Ridder Press.

Appendix

The following text provides an example of Podoko narrative. To aid the reader in interpreting the text, Podoko subject pronouns are listed in (48) in their basic, nonfocus, and consecutive-clause forms. The consecutive-clause forms are also used as subject pronouns of the verb *ngə́* 'say'.

(48) Subject pronouns

	basic	nonfocus	consecutive
1s	*yə́*	*mayə́*	*ngayə́*
2s	*ka*	*ka*	*(ngə) ka*
3s	*∅*	*nga*	*(ngə) kənə*
1i	*mə*	*mamə́*	*ngamə/ngamamə*
1x	*nanə*	*manánə*	*ngananə*
2p	*kwə*	*kwə*	*(ngə) kwə*
3p	*ta*	*mətá*	*ngita*

The Woman and Her Baby

1. *A   nda ndə ʸngə́də nə́sa   sa   davarə   !a   d-i   dá nəwala.* 2.*Mazláməná*
   FOC there^is certain woman PST PRF^leave with go-VN to man   now

ngə́ kənə taka nə́walənga, 3. *"Nəwalala, a   da ʸdzə́rə   ndá balə   yá*
say 3s   to   man^3s   man^1s FOC go IMPF^see COLL father^1s 1s

nínga," ngə́ kənə. 4. *"Aya," ngə́ nəwalənga.* 5.*Takwa   ngá   dafə́ dá*
today   say 3s   okay   say man^3s   PRF^cook^in NFOC^3s fufu into

kwəwə́   údzərə. 6. *ʸDálə́ dala sləɓa.* 7.*ʸNdakə kənə ʸkəsə   nga.* 8. *Mazláməná*
calabash child   good sauce meat   then   CON^3s IMPF^take DUM   now

dədá nga   da dá   bata. 9. *ʸTəta dədá   də da dá   bata   mazláməná*
PRF^go NFOC^3s to house father^3s   when PRF^go go to house father^3s now

lakí, 10. *ʸndakə talədá   máta   gwə́mə dalá sləɓa.* 11. *Ngə́ kənə taka*
TOP   then PRF^cook^3s NFOC^mother^3s also   sauce meat   says 3s   to

də́wə mana, 12. *"Dəwə mayá, ngá ka dədá lawá,* 13. *má !da   nəká   ba*
girl 3s   girl 1s   here 2s go TOP   even NPST^FUT PRF^see FOC

a   nək-í   ka ᵞkəláɗa á ᵞtəvə lakí, 14. *!da   ᵞkələ   la.* 15. *A ɗába 'Hiyə*
with see-vn 2s grass on path TOP   NPST^FUT IMPF^break NEG   because corn

mayə' dá ngə́ ganə   lawá, 16. *a   dá dzə́gwa ka gwádi gánə́   la.* 17. *!A*
1s   FUT say squirrel TOP   FOC FUT can 2s word squirrel NEG   NPST^FOC

da təhaká   ganə   la. 18. *Bí   !da   mbáhakadásə ᵞtakwasə́ maká bá*
FUT PRF^hit^2s squirrel NEG   perhaps NPST^FUT PRF^take^2s   thing   2s FOC

a   ndzə́di la,'' ngə́ mata   taka də́wə mənə. 19. *"Aya,'' ngə́ də́wa kə́nga.*
with force NEG say mother^3s to girl 3s   okay   say 3s ANPH

20. *ᵞNdakə kərɗaləkwa ndí   pəhwa.* 21. *Kənə da,*   22. *kənə   da,*
    then   PRF^grind^3s NFOC^one flour   CON^3s go^IIMPF   CON^3s go^IIMPF

23. *kənə da.* 24. *ᵞNdak kənə lakí, !a   ndzi ᵞkəláɗa.* 25. *Sa slərtəkwa*
    CON^3s go^IIMPF   ID   CON^3s TOP NPST^FOC be   grass   PST PRF^insert

!a slərt-i sləβə gwə́mə dá slirə məná. 26. *ᵞNdakə kəlada   nga   ᵞkəláɗa*
with stick-vn meat also   into tooth 3s   then   PRF^break NFOC^3s grass

kə́nga. 27. *Bandá kəlada   nga   ᵞkəláɗa,* 28. *a talakwa bá !a   tal-i*
ANPH   soon^as PRF^break NFOC^3s grass   FOC PRF^touch FOC with touch-vn

dá sə   slírə lakí, 29. *"Tá tawə́ hiyə mayə na?'' ngə́ gana.* 30. *"Hiyə maká*
to under tooth TOP   for what corn 1s   Q   say squirrel   corn 2s

ᵞkəláɗa na na?'' ngə́ nəsə́   kə́nga. 31. *"A, hiyə mayá.''* 32. *"ᵞTalawə   wayə́ la*
grass Q Q   say woman ANPH   yes corn 1s   IMPF^touch 1s NEG

gánə   bala,'' ngə́ ndi takiná. 33. *"Hiyə mayə wayə   lakí, 'ᵞTalawə   wayə́*
squirrel father^1s say one 3s   corn 1s   1s TOP IMPF^touch 1s

la' ngə́ ka taka wáya? 34. *!A   ᵞzalə   da dá   sləwandála yə́ waká,'' ngə́*
NEG say 2s to 1s   NPST^FOC IMPF^drag to house chief   1s 2s   say

gana. 35. *"!A   ᵞzalə   waká yə́ da dá   sləwandála,'' ngə́ gana.*
squirrel   NPST^FOC IMPF^drag 2s 1s to house chief   say squirrel

36. *"ᵞTalawə   wayə́ dəgíyə́ la,'' bá ngə́ nəsə́   kə́nga.* 37. *"!A   ᵞzalə*
    IMPF^touch 1s indeed NEG FOC say woman ANPH   NPST^FOC IMPF^drag

ᵞzálə́ yá waká da dá   sləwandála,'' ngə́ gana. 38. *ᵞNdaka tə́tapar tapar*
drag 1s 2s to house chief   say squirrel   then ID(grab) ID

sləgóla. 39. *ᵞNgwə́ts ganə   a   haya.* 40. *Tə́tapar tapar sləgóla.* 41. *ᵞNgwə́ts*
wrestle   ID   squirrel with earth   ID(grab) ID   wrestle   ID

gana   a   haya. 42.*Tátapar tapar akə́ makə́ra. 43. *Ngwáv ngə́ ndi   va*
squirrel with earth   ID(grab) ID   to three   ID   CON one PRF^give

*nga a   hayə bá   ndzə́dī mazlámə́ná. 44. *Ndaka "Dzə́mə má," ngə́ gana.*
DUM with earth FOC force now   then think 1i   say squirrel

45. *"Waka lakí, *mana nda ká   a   mə́tsə́dá narə táya sə́   maká kwalamá,*
    2s   TOP   SUB is NFOC^2s with bracelet and bead under 2s   ?

46. *dasə ká dá slíyu   ngá wa?" ngə́ kə́na. 47. "Palə́la   pala, bá kalá*
    when 2s FUT PRF^beat^1s DUM Q   say 3s   PRF^undo undo if NEG

!mbə́lakadə́ mayá," ngə́ gana taka nə́sə kə́nga. 48. Palə́la   nə́sə
PRF^throw^2s NFOC^1s say squirrel to woman ANPH   PRF^undo NFOC^woman

*kə́nga tayá, 49. palə́la   nga   mə́tsə́dá, 50. a   tə́ma   bá   *futi   sə*
ANPH bead   PRF^undo NFOC^3s bracelet   FOC remain FOC g-string under

nə́sə   kə́nga mazlámə́ná narə údzə́rə də́ gwagwa. 51. Ngə́ kə́nə takiná lakí,
woman ANPH   now   and child in back   say 3s   to^3s TOP

*"Wayə wayə wa. 52. *Manə *mbə́lidə́   ka lakí, 53. a   zla ndá   *futi*
alas alas alas SUB PRF^throw^1s NFOC^2s TOP   ? still COLL g-string

*sə   maká narə údzə́rə də́ gwagwa maká kwalamá, *tə́taká wa?" ngə́ kə́na.*
under 2s   and child in back   2s   ?   what   Q   say 3s

54. *Palə́la   nə́sə   kə́nga *futa, pala   ndí   də́ hala.*
    PRF^undo NFOC^woman ANPH   g-string PRF^put^down NFOC^one in ground

55. *Tapavə́   mə́tá   zlá6a, 56. də hala gana   zlá6a. 57. "*Manə*
    PRF^taste^REF NFOC^they again   in ground squirrel again   SUB

*nda ka   a   udzə́rə də́ gwagwa, 58. ina *manə́ kalá !slaku   mayə́*
is NFOC^2s with child in back   3s   SUB   NEG PRF^beat^2s NFOC^1s

na na?" ngə́ gana. 59. "Ká !pə́lə́la nga udzə́ra," ngə́ nə́sə   kə́nga.
Q Q   say squirrel   IMPV PRF^undo ? child   say woman ANPH

60 *Palə́la   ndí   udzə́ra, *ndzə́də́la ndá. 61. *Manə tapavə́*
   PRF^undo NFOC^one child   PRF^seat NFOC^one   SUB   PRF^taste^REF

ndí   lakí, 62. də hala gana.   63. Bandá mbávu gánə   lakí,
NFOC^one TOP   in ground squirrel   soon^as PRF^rise NFOC^squirrel TOP

64. *mbáh-i akə́ *tanə́ngá dá gága. 65. *Kə́sə́lu   ngá   udzə́rə zlá6a.*
    take-VN to thing   to termite^hill   PRF^take^up NFOC^3s child also

66. *Fətsa   nga   dá gága.*   67. *ʸNdakə ngə nəsə́   ka   taw-i*
PRF^flee   NFOC^3s to termite^hill   then   CON woman ANPH cry-IIMPF

mazláməná. 68. *Taw-i   nəsə́   kə́nga.* 69. *Nda gəra táw-i   nə́sə   kə́nga la.*
now   cry-IIMPF woman ANPH   is   equal cry-VN woman ANPH NEG

70. *"Ya nda yə́ la   mbala.*   71. *Ya kəsavarə   údzərə mayə́ gana," ngə́*
    ? is 1s NEG mother^1s   ? PRF^take^away child 1s   squirrel say

kənə. 72. *"Ya nda yə́ la."* 73. *Kənə   su   bá taw-i da dá   bata.*
3s   ? is 1s NEG   CON^3s come^up FOC cry-VN to house father^3s

74. *A   taka da dá   nəwalənga mazláməná la.* 75. *ʸNdaka, a   su*
    FOC try to house man^3s   now   NEG   like   FOC PRF^come^up

sə́   ma, 76. *"ʸTətaká wa?"* ngə́ *mata.* 77. *"A   nda udzərə mayə́ la.*
come TOP   what   Q   say mother^3s   FOC is child 1s   NEG

78. *A   ʸkəsiyu   ʸkə́sə gana."* 79. *"A   ɓakavadə́ kənə ka na?"* 80. *"A*
    FOC PRF^take^1s take squirrel   FOC PRF^do   how 2s Q   FOC

kəlada   ʸkəláɗa yə́ tá ʸtsakwazlə slirə   lakí, 81. *'Hiyə mayə́' ngə́ gana.*
PRF^break grass   1s for IMPF^clean tooth TOP   corn 1s   say squirrel

82. *ʸNdakə nganana slagála lakí,* 83. *'Pələla   pələ udzərə ʸtsə́ɗa,' ngə́*
    then   CON^1x wrestle TOP   PRF^undo undo child first   say

kənə taka wáyə lakí, 84. *ngayə́ pələla   udzərə narə táharə́ mayə́ bá ʸtata*
3s   to 1s TOP   CON^1s PRF^undo child and jewelry 1s   FOC all

lakí, 85. *mbatsí a   ʸɓaki dábariyá lakí,* 86. *ngá a   mbáhavarə mbáhə dá*
TOP   yet FOC do^1s trick TOP   here FOC PRF^take take   to

gága   məná," ngə́ *nəsə́   kə́nga taka máta.* 87. *"Tawə də́wə mayə́ na?*
termite^hill 3s   say woman ANPH to mother^3s   what girl 1s   Q

88. *Sa walakadá mayə́   gwáɗa,* 89. *ʸKəláɗa lawá, hiyə gánə   lawá, da*
    PST PRF^say^2s NFOC^1s word   grass TOP corn squirrel TOP FUT

ʸtalə   la,' sá ngə́ ngayə́ taka wáka. 90. *Mazláməná nga   ka   ʸkələ*
IMPF^touch NEG PST say 1s   to 2s   now   CON 2s IMPF^break

nga má, a ɗába tawə́ na? 91. *Ba zlu   zlə́   na.* 92. *Də́   mə dá sa*
DUM TOP because what Q   FOC PRF^finish finish ?   go^IIMPF 1i to at

mudə́ nəsə́   na, 93. *ngamə ndávasə akə́ gwáɗī sá məná,"* ngə́ nda. 94. *ʸNdakə*
old woman ?   CON^1i PRF^ask to word at 3s   say one   then

ngə ndi dá sa mudɔ́ nəsá.   95. *"A ɓakaha   tawɔ́ na?"* *ngɔ́ mudɔ́ nəsá.*
CON one to at old woman   FOC PRF^happen what Q   say old   woman

96. *"A kəsavarə údzərə dɔ́wə mayɔ́ ganə   lawá,* 97. *na ʸmanɔ́ ʸtsa manánə*
FOC PRF^take child girl 1s   squirrel TOP   it SUB   come NFOC^1x

sá sa maká lawá, 98. *ʹ!A   ɓakavadɔ́ kənə nanə ya?'* *ngɔ́ nganana,"* *ngɔ́ ndi*
to at 2s   TOP   NPST^FOC PRF^do how 1x   Q   say 1x   say one

taka múdə nəsá. 99. *"A ʸbɔ́lə   ʸmaká la,"* *ngɔ́ mudɔ́ nəsá.* 100. *"Akwɔ́*
to old woman   FOC difficult that NEG say old   woman   IMPV

ʸsulidá   ʸsulə ʸsləsli wayɔ́ na," *ngɔ́ mudɔ́ nəsá.* 101. *ʸNdakə sulalədá ndi*
PRF^fry^1s fry   egg   1s ?   say old   woman   then   PRF^fry^3s NFOC^one

ʸsləsla. 102. *Kənə ʸupadɔ́ nga,* 103. *kənə ʸupadɔ́ nga lakí,* 104. *"Amá !a*
egg   CON^3s IMPF^eat DUM   CON^3s eat   DUM TOP   but NPST^FOC

tsar-i   ʸsləsli makwɔ́ ina," *ngɔ́ mudɔ́ nəsɔ́ takitá.* 105. *"A lawá, akwɔ́*
good-IIMPF egg   2s   it   say old   woman 3p   ? ?   IMPV

!da   ʸdzaha   ʸdzáhə má mawə mawɔ́ mɔ́ndə gíva tá rəh-á. 106. *Akwɔ́*
NPST^go PRF^gather gather even which which person ?   for dance-VN IMPV

!da   ʸusalɔ́   ʸmanɔ́ nɔ́sə   a   udzərə dɔ́ gwagwa bá ʸtata," *ngɔ́ mudɔ́*
NPST^go IMPF^seek this woman with child in back FOC all   say old

nəsɔ́ taka nɔ́sə kɔ́nga. 107. *ʸNdakə "Aya,"* *ngɔ́ nəsɔ́ kɔ́nga.* 108. *Ba*
woman to woman ANPH   then   okay say woman ANPH   when

ʸmanɔ́ su   nɔ́sə   kɔ́nga lakí, 109. *zɔ́mbər-i   akɔ́ nasi   bá*
SUB   PRF^come^up NFOC^woman ANPH TOP   summon-VN to women FOC

ʸtata a   slála kɔ́nga, ndá mingwa, ndá ʸgwɔ́gwədʼa,   ndá gwɔ́mba bá
all with district ANPH COLL mosquito COLL mosquito^larva COLL frog FOC

ʸtata. 110. *ʸNdakə kəsada   nɔ́sə   kɔ́nga ʸtəmá.* 111. *Ngita   dá háwɔ́*
all   then   PRF^take^down NFOC^woman ANPH drum   CON^3p to mouth

gaga.   112. *Fəla   ndí   ʸtəmɔ́ dɔ́ hala.* 113. *Fada   ndá.*
termite^hill   PRF^put^down NFOC^one drum in ground   PRF^begin NFOC^one

114. *ʸNdakə ngə ndi ʸdəgɔ́   nga,* 115. *ndi   ʸdəgɔ́   nga,* 116. *ndi   ʸdəgɔ́*
then   CON one IMPF^hit DUM   CON^one IMPF^hit DUM   CON^one hit

ʸtəmá, 117. *ndi   ʸdəgɔ́   ʸtəmá.* 118. *"Dədá də waká ʸtangwə ʸtsɔ́dʼa,"* *ngɔ́*
drum   CON^one IMPF^hit drum   PRF^go go 2s   first   first   say

ndi taka míngwa.   119. *"ʸNdzəví ʸndzəvá, ʸngwa ʸngwa ʸngwa," ngə́ mingwə*
one to mosquito   ID   ID   ID   ID   ID   say mosquito

taka rə́h-a.   120. *"Dədá da," ngə́ ndi taka ʸgwə́gwəɗa.*   121. *"ʸZərəda muɓi,*
to dance-VN   PRF^go go say one to   mosquito^larva ID   ID

ʸzərəda muɓi, ʸzərəda muɓi," ngə́ ʸgwə́gwəɗa   taka rə́h-a.   122. *"Nda gəra*
ID   ID   ID   ID   say mosquito^larva to dance-VN   is   equal

mbá ka la,   123. *nda gəra   mbá   ka la," ngə́ ndi taka ʸgwə́gwəɗa.*
can 2s NEG   is equal of^can 2s NEG say one to   mosquito^larva

124. *"Dədá də waká," ngə́ ndi taka gwə́mba.* 125. *"Hədĩ həɗa kwakw, hədĩ həɗa*
       PRF^go go 2s   say one to   frog   ID   ID   ID   ID   ID

kwakw, hədĩ həɗa kwakw," ngə́ gwə́mba. 126. *"Ma   bá waká kəní a   mba mbə*
ID   ID   ID   ID   say frog   even FOC 2s   TOP FOC can can

ka," ngə́ nda.   127. *Ngə ʸngə́də nə́sə   dədá.*   128. *"Tambas mbas mbas, tambas*
you say one   CON certain woman PRF^go   ID   ID   ID   ID

mbas mbas mbas, tambas tambasas tambas," ngə́ kənə lakí, 129. *"Nda gəra*
ID   ID   ID   ID   ID   ID   say 3s   TOP   is   equal

mbá ka la," ngə́ ndi takiná. 130. *Ngə ndi ʸufadə́ ʸmbədəzə́ zlába.* 131. *Nda*
can 2s NEG say one 3s   CON one play   flute   also   is

gəra tsári ʸmáka ʸmbə́dəzə́ bá ʸwalá ʸwalá la. 132. *Ngə ndi ʸufadə́   nga,*
equal good that   flute   FOC really really NEG   CON one IMPF^play DUM

133. *ndi   ʸufadə́   nga.* 134. *ʸManə lakí akə́ ndələdá   gána.*
      CON^one IMPF^play DUM   this TOP ?   PRF^leap^out NFOC^squirrel

135. *"A ɓakaha   tawə́ háwə́ vəngwə káyə dálə wa?" ngə́ gana.* 136. *"A,*
      FOC PRF^happen what mouth mouth house 1s   Q   say squirrel   ?

!ʸpəzənə   vángwə la gána," ngə́ ndi takiná. 137. *" 'A ɓakaha   tawə́ ya?'*
NPST^rub^1x mouth NEG squirrel say one 3s   FOC PRF^happen what Q

ngə́ ngayá." 138. *"!A   rəh -i   nana."* 139. *"Ká   tala   ngá rəh-í*
say 1s   NPST^FOC dance-IIMPF 1x   IMPV PRF^touch ?   dance-VN

ká   gwə́ma," ngə́ kənə. 140. *Dədá   gánə   lakí,* 141. *"A   mba ka la,"*
ANPH too   say he   PRF^go NFOC^squirrel TOP   FOC can 2s NEG

ngə́ ndi takiná. 142. *"A dába tawə́ ya?" ngə́ kənə.* 143. *"Waka lakí a   nda*
say one to^3s   because what Q   say 3s   2s   TOP FOC is

mətsədɔ́ hávə maká la   lakí, 144. *ʸtətaká wa?"* ngɔ́ ndi takiná. 145. *Pawakwa*
bracelet body 2s   NEG TOP   what   Q   say one 3s   PRF^insert

ndí   mətsədá. 146. *Tala   ndí   rəh-á.* 147. *"A   tsəwə ká   ʸndáka*
NFOC^one bracelet   PRF^touch NFOC^one dance-VN   FOC good 2s   like^that

la," ngɔ́ ndi takiná. 148. *ʸNdakə ngwaɗavasə   nga   ndá tayá, ndá ʸfuti*
NEG say one 3s   then   PRF^tie^under NFOC^3s COLL bead COLL g-string

bá ʸtata. 149. *Kənə rəh-á.*   150. *"A mba ka la.* 151. *Hawə udzərə dɔ́*
FOC all   CON^3s dance-IIMPF   FOC can 2s NEG   where child in

gwagwa maká səka wanánə ya?" ngɔ́ ndi taka gána. 152. *ʸManə dəkwa*
back 2s   like 1x   Q   say one to squirrel SUB   PRF^enter

gánə   lakí, 153. *ngwaɗavəkwa ngá   udzəra.* 154. *ʸManə dədá*
NFOC^squirrel TOP   PRF^tie^in   NFOC^3s child   SUB   PRF^go

gánə   mazláməná lakí, 155. *"A ʸgwas ʸkwakwar ʸkwar ʸkwa ʸkwar,"*
NFOC^squirrel now   TOP   ID ID   ID   ID   ID   ID

ngɔ́ ganə   taka rɔ́h-i   mazláməná. 156. *"A mba mbə ka," ngɔ́ nda.*
say squirrel to dance-VN now   FOC can can 2s   say one

157. *Nasi   makɔ́rə lakí ndzawalu mətá   akɔ́ vɔ́ngwə gága.*   158. *Mazláməná*
women three   TOP   PRF^sit NFOC^3p to mouth termite^hill   now

lakí, gwɔk gwəgwɔk gwɔk ngɔ́ ndi gasa   gánə. 159. *"Ngayə fətsa   nga*
TOP ID   ID   ID   CON one PRF^catch squirrel   CON^1s PRF^flee DUM

dá gága,"   ngɔ́ ganə   lakí, 160. *kərtəng, a   mbáhasə   mbáhə ndi*
to termite^hill say squirrel TOP   ID   FOC PRF^take^under take one

ʸsəgá. 161. *A ʸbətsa   ʸbətsə ndi a   haya.* 162. *Tatəhi ngɔ́ ndi va nga.*
leg   FOC PRF^knock knock one with earth   ID   CON one give DUM

163. *Paləla   ndí   udzərə dɔ́ gwagwa məná narə táharɔ́ bá ʸtata.*
PRF^untie NFOC^one child in back   3s and jewelry FOC all

164. *ʸNdaka nda gərá   ngwábəlá ndi ganə   la.* 165. *ʸNdaka a   ngwá ʸməts-i*
then is equal hurt   one squirrel NEG   then FOC want die-IIMPF

gana. 166. *ʸNdaka.* 167. *A zlu   zlá.*
squirrel   like^that   FOC PRF^finish finish

Free English Translation

1. *There was a woman who had gone to (another) husband.* 2. *Now she said to her husband,* 3. *"My husband, I'm going to see my father's family today," she said.* 4. *"Okay," said her husband.* 5. *She cooked some food and put some of it in a child's calabash.* 6. *It was good meat sauce.* 7. *Then she took it.* 8. *Now she went to her father's.*

9. *When she arrived at her father's,* 10. *then her mother cooked some meat sauce for her too.* 11. *She said to her daughter,* 12. *"My daughter, now that you're leaving,* 13. *even if you see a grass on the path,* 14. *don't pick it!* 15. *Because Squirrel will say that it's his corn;* 16. *you won't be able to defend yourself against Squirrel.* 17. *Don't let Squirrel hit you.* 18. *Perhaps he will take your things by force," said the mother to her daughter.* 19. *"Okay," said the daughter.* 20. *Then the mother ground flour into (a calabash) for her.* 21. *She went,* 22. *she went,* 23. *she went.* 24. *Suddenly, there was a grass.* 25. *Some meat had got stuck between her teeth.* 26. *So she broke off the grass.* 27. *As soon as she had broken off the grass,* 28. *at the very moment she picked her teeth,* 29. *"Why did you touch my corn?" said Squirrel.* 30. *"Is the grass your corn?" said the woman.* 31. *"Yes, it's my corn."* 32. *"Don't touch me, father Squirrel," she said to him.* 33. *"It's my corn, and you tell me not to touch you?!* 34. *I'm dragging you to the chief's," said Squirrel.* 35. *"I'm dragging you to the chief's," said Squirrel.* 36. *"Don't touch me!" said the woman.* 37. *"I'm really dragging you to the chief's," said Squirrel.* 38. *Then he grabbed hold of her and they wrestled.* 39. *(She threw) Squirrel to the ground.* 40. *He grabbed hold of her and they wrestled.* 41. *(She threw) Squirrel to the ground.* 42. *He grabbed hold of her a third time.* 43. *She threw him to the ground with force now.* 44. *Then Squirrel said, "Let's think.* 45. *You, as long as you have your bracelets and beads,* 46. *when will you beat me?" he said.* 47. *"Take them off, if I can't throw you," said Squirrel to the woman.* 48. *The woman took off the beads.* 49. *She took off the bracelets.* 50. *There remained only the g-string on the woman now, and the baby on her back.* 51. *He said to her, "Alas!* 52. *You could throw me,* 53. *because you have still your g-string on and the baby on your back," he said.* 54. *The woman took off her g-string and put it on the ground.* 55. *They got hold of each other again.* 56. *Squirrel was on the ground again.* 57. *"Is it because you have a baby on your back* 58. *that I can't beat you?" said Squirrel.* 59. *"Let me undo the baby," said the woman.* 60. *She undid the baby and sat it down.* 61. *When they got hold of each other,* 62. *Squirrel (was thrown) to the ground.* 63. *As soon as Squirrel got up,* 64. *he gathered the things into the termite hill.* 65. *He picked up the baby too.* 66. *He escaped into the termite hill.* 67. *Then the woman cried now.* 68. *The woman cried.* 69. *The woman cried very much.* 70. *"Woe is me, mother.* 71. *Squirrel has taken my child," she said.* 72. *"Woe is me."* 73. *She came up weeping to her father's.* 74. *She didn't go to her husband's now.*

75. *Then, when she arrived,* 76. *"What's the matter?" said her mother.* 77. *"My child's gone.* 78. *Squirrel took him from me."* 79. *"How did you do that?"* 80. *"I broke off a grass to pick my teeth,* 81. *'It's my corn,' said Squirrel.* 82. *Then we wrestled.* 83. *'Untie the baby first,' he said to me,* 84. *so I undid the baby and all my jewelry,* 85. *but he tricked me.* 86. *See, he has carried off (everything) into his termite hill," said the woman to her mother.* 87. *"How, my daughter?* 88. *I told you,* 89. *'The grass is Squirrel's corn, don't touch it,' I said to you.* 90. *Now you have picked it, why?* 91. *It's done now.* 92. *Let's go to the woman* 93. *and ask her advice," she said.* 94. *So they went to the old woman.* 95. *"What's happened?" said the old woman.* 96. *"Squirrel has taken away my daughter's child,* 97. *that's why we've come to you;* 98. *we're asking what we should*

do," they said to the old woman. 99. "That's not difficult," said the old woman. 100. "Fry me an egg," said the old woman. 101. So they fried her an egg. 102. She ate, 103. she ate. 104. "But your egg is good," said the old woman to them. 105. "Listen, go and gather everybody to dance. 106. Go and look for every woman with a baby on her back," said the old woman to the woman. 107. Then the woman said, "Okay." 108. When the woman came up, 109. she summoned all the women in that district: mosquitoes, mosquito larvae, frogs, everyone. 110. Then the woman brought down a drum. 111. So they went to the opening of the termite hill. 112. She put the drum on the ground, 113. she began to play. 114. So then she played, 115. she played, 116. she played the drum, 117. she played the drum. 118. "You go first," they said to the mosquito. 119. The mosquito danced. 120. "Go," they said to the mosquito larva. 121. The mosquito larva danced. 122. "You're really good, 123. you're really good," they said to the mosquito larva. 124. "You go," they said to the frog. 125. The frog danced. 126. "You too, you can dance," they said. 127. Then a woman went 128. and danced. 129. "You can really dance," they said to her. 130. They played flutes too. 131. The flute-playing was very good. 132. They played 133. and played.

134. Now Squirrel jumped out. 135. "What's happened in front of my house?" said Squirrel. 136. "Don't talk to us, Squirrel," they said to him. 137. " 'What's happened?' I said." 138. "We're dancing." 139. "Let me dance too," he said. 140. Squirrel went. 141. "You can't do it," they said to him. 142. "Why?" he said. 143. "You, you haven't got bracelets, 144. what do you expect?" they said to him. 145. He put on the bracelets. 146. He tried to dance. 147. "You're no good like that," they said to him. 148. So he tied on the beads, g-string and everything else. 149. He danced. 150. "You can't do it. 151. Where's the baby on your back like us?" they said to Squirrel. 152. When Squirrel went inside, 153. he tied on the baby. 154. When Squirrel went now, 155. he danced. 156. "That's good," they said. 157. Three women, they sat right close to the opening of the termite hill. 158. Now they caught Squirrel. 159. "Let me escape to the termite hill," said Squirrel. 160. They quickly grabbed his feet. 161. They knocked him over on the ground. 162. They hit him. 163. They untied the baby on his back and all the jewelry. 164. They wore Squirrel out. 165. Squirrel almost died. 166. It was like that. 167. It's finished.

Tense and Aspect in Mofu-Gudur

Kenneth R. Hollingsworth

Abstract

This paper presents a new analysis of the tense and aspect system of Mofu-Gudur, a Chadic language spoken in Cameroon. The analysis is based on definitions proposed by Bernard Comrie (1976; 1985).

Mofu can be unmarked for tense and aspect or it can be marked for future (two ways), progressive/habitual, past, completive, or perfect. One also finds simultaneous expressions of completive action and progressive/habitual with and without future tense.

Résumé

Cet article est une nouvelle analyse du système aspecto-temporel du mofu-gudur (langue de la famille tchadique parlée au Cameroun), basée sur la définition des aspects et des temps telle que l'a proposée B. Comrie (1976; 1985).

En mofu-gudur, on relève un aspect/temps neutre (c'est-à-dire non marqué) par rapport à des aspects/temps marqués: le futur caractérisé par deux morphèmes différents; un progressif/habituel; un passé; un accompli et un parfait.

On observe également des expressions complexes de progressif/habituel et d'accompli; de progressif/habituel, d'accompli et de futur.

This paper presents the Mofu-Gudur tense and aspect system.[1] The analysis is similar to that proposed by Barreteau (1985) but differs in several ways. First, I interpret his progressive marker as a progressive/habitual. I also posit a perfect, and cite data which show the use of simultaneous completive and progressive/habitual markers in nonnegative statements. The analysis that completive and some subtype of imperfective can occur together could be a feature of most Chadic languages which has been overlooked until Wolff (1983:132) noted the compatibility of simultaneous expressions of completive action and the imperfective aspect in Lamang.

This paper focuses on tense-aspect in the indicative, in as much as mood has already been discussed elsewhere (Hollingsworth 1986).

I briefly describe the ordering of tense and aspect morphemes in the verb phrase (§1) and then illustrate the uses of the various tense-aspect constructions (§§2 and 3). In the concluding section (§4), I present the overall Mofu-Gudur tense-aspect system and discuss its unusual characteristics.

1. The Mofu verb phrase

The Mofu verb phrase consists of a subject pronoun (SUBJ)[2], progressive/habitual (P/H) marker, an optional tense (TNS) marker, an obligatory verb base (plus one or more suffixes), an optional object (O), and finally, an optional perfect (PERF) and/or completive (CMP) marker. These facts are presented formally in (1). Contrary to Lamang (Wolff 1983:137, 151), Daba (Lienhard and Wiesemann 1986:47–49), and Giziga in the negative (Jaouen 1974:16), Mofu-Gudur does not use grammatical tone to mark

---

[1]This article was written under Research Permit No. 05/87, authorized by the Ministry for Higher Education, Computer Services, and Scientific Research of the Republic of Cameroon and by the Ministry's subsidiaries, the Institute of Human Sciences and the Center for Anthropological Studies and Research. We thank these agencies for graciously permitting this research. I also wish to thank Mr. Jean-Baptiste Almara, my primary language associate for this paper, as well as Daniel Gamsouloum and Abdias Galla, who have been consulted during the writing of this paper. I am grateful to Bernard Comrie and Stephen C. Anderson for the insight and guidance they gave, and to Daniel Barreteau who provided help with the resume and read a draft of the paper.

Mofu-Gudur, also called Mofu-South, is a Chadic language spoken in northern Cameroon. According to Hoffmann, it belongs to the Biu-Mandara branch, Matakam group (1971:8). Dieu, Renaud, Barreteau, et al. have placed Mofu in the Central Branch, Mafa group, in a subgrouping with Giziga (1983:357).

[2]Except when the third person pronoun is deleted in the presence of the past tense marker ta.

either tense or aspect except for one rarely used form of irrealis conditional (Barreteau, personal communication).

(1) VP→SUBJ (P/H) (TNS) verb (O) (PERF) (CMP)

2. Mofu tense and aspect morphemes

Tense is a grammatical category used for locating events in time (Comrie 1985:vii). Like many Chadic languages, Mofu-Gudur can grammatically mark time by using past- or future-tense markers, or it can leave the time unmarked if the time frame is unimportant or if it is clear from the context. Present-time reference is assumed in the absence of tense or aspect markers or time adverbials. Present time is discussed further in the section on unmarked tense-aspect.

Aspect, on the other hand, does not concern itself with locating events in time, but is a way of "viewing the internal temporal constituency of a situation" (Comrie 1976:3). We can look at the structure of a situation in two different ways: perfectively or imperfectively. Comrie defines PERFECTIVE aspect as looking "at the situation from the outside, without necessarily distinguishing any of the internal structure of the situation, whereas the IMPERFECTIVE looks at the situation from the inside, and as such is crucially concerned with the internal structure of the situation" (1976:4).

In Mofu-Gudur, we find the unusual combination of completive used with subtypes of the imperfective. We also find various perfect constructions, which fit neither tense nor aspect definitions, but which refer "to a past situation which has present relevance" (Comrie 1976:12) and pattern like the completive aspect marker.

2.1. Unmarked tense and aspect. Verb phrases often occur without tense or aspect morphemes and can be said to be grammatically unmarked

for these qualities.[3] The unmarked tense-aspect construction is the one
most frequently used in conversation when the time setting is known or
when tense and aspect need no particular emphasis or when referring to
a situation that does not relate to a specific marked tense or aspect. For
instance, if I am about to leave I can say 'I am going to market' without
marking tense or aspect because this situation does not usually need tense
or aspect to be marked in Mofu.[4] If on the path walking to market,
however, I am asked where I am going, it is most natural to reply using a
progressive form since I am actually in the process of going somewhere.

Example (2) is translated as a progressive in English in an attempt to
show its nonpast, nonfuture sense, but it is not marked for progressive or
habitual. It could be used in answer to the question 'What is he doing?'

(2)   *A cá   zána.*
       he weave cloth
       He is weaving cloth.

Unmarked tense-aspect does not mean the situation could not acquire
other meanings in more marked contexts. While an unmarked verb phrase
has no tense or aspect of its own, time adverbials may be used to indicate
future, past, progressive, habitual, or iterative meanings. For example, an
additional adverbial phrase can be used to indicate a habitual sense
without any change to the marking of tense or aspect, as in (3).

(3)   *Mándaw   mándaw   a cá   zána.*
       tomorrow tomorrow he weaves cloth
       Every day he weaves cloth.

---

[3]Barreteau calls such forms AORIST (1985:45–46). Comrie has noted that aorist has
often been associated with past perfective constructions in traditional grammars of
some languages (1976:12). Hoffmann uses this term for a construction in Margi which
"usually indicates an action of the past" (1963:174). So there is some precedent in
Chadic languages for using the term in connection with the past tense, but the
unmarked Mofu verb phrase is not normally past tense.

Other Chadic linguists have used the term GRUNDASPEKT for this unmarked or
neutral tense-aspect (Jungraithmayr 1966; Wolff 1979). Lienhard and Wiesemann use
the term NEUTRAL for unmarked aspect (1986:47). Wolff, in a later work, prefers the
term ZERO ASPECT (1983:134). Since this construction in Mofu is unmarked for both
tense and aspect, I refer to it simply as UNMARKED to avoid possible confusion by
calling it aorist.

[4]I can also choose to reinforce nonpast by using *lá* (completive) without *ta* (past).

When a speaker switches to a monologue style, he may use a marked tense or aspect to set the time frame and then, once the context is set, whether to past or future, he may use constructions unmarked for tense or aspect to carry the storyline. An example of such an unmarked construction with a past perfective interpretation is shown in (4), taken from a narrative text.[5]

(4)   *Zlee zlé ná,   yá zə́mey slaw ŋgá dəvá   makwálakáya.*
      before TOP I   eat   meat of   panther dried
      Some time ago, I (once) ate dried panther meat.

Example (4) could be modified to indicate past habitual action by using further time adverbials, as in (5).

(5)   *Zlee zlé ná,   mándaw   mándaw*
      before TOP tomorrow   tomorrow

      yá zə́mey slaw ŋgá dəvá   makwálakáya.
      I   eat   meat of   panther dried
      A while back, I ate dried panther meat all the time.

Examples are also found with no marked tense or aspect, but which require future time reference because of time adverbs, as in (6).

(6)   *Gwágway mamba a   sawa.*
      festival   soon   it   come
      The festival will soon be here.

The unmarked tense-aspect construction is also used in narrative texts for events on the event line. Other marked tense or aspect constructions are used off the event line to summarize, project, or describe. Example (7) illustrates an unmarked series of events taken from the beginning of a folk story.

---

[5]The following abbreviations are used in the examples: CMP completive aspect; DIR directional suffix; FUT future; ID ideophone; NEG negative; PERF perfect; PL plural; P/H progressive/habitual; PST past tense; QUES question; REL relative; and TOP topic.

(7) *Mabár á   yéy   bəzéy ŋgá hay a   léy.*
     lioness she give^birth child her PL   in   field

    Ndaw péy, a   péy waw. Wúwar! Áwaw á wúwurtá   tábiyá.
    man ID he light fire ID   fire   it burn^them all

    Mabár a   sawa ná, tá   a   tuway, a   tuway.
    lioness she come TOP then she cry   she cry

The lioness gave birth to her cubs in a field. Someone set fire (to
the field), and whoop, the fire burned them all up. When the
lioness came, she cried and cried.

2.2. Marked progressive/habitual aspect *fá*. Comrie defines progressiveness as "the combination of continuousness with nonstativity" (1976:
12). He defines continuousness as "imperfectivity that is not occasioned by
habituality" (1976:33). Habituality, in turn, describes "a situation which is
characteristic of an extended period of time, so extended in fact that the
situation referred to is viewed not as an incidental property of the moment, but precisely, as a characteristic feature of a whole period" (Comrie
1976:27). The preverbal morpheme *fá* is a progressive/habitual (P/H) marker
because it can have both progressive and habitual readings, but it never
occurs with a stative verb. Consider example (8) as a response to the
question 'Where are Banay and Mana?'

(8) *Áta fá   pəkam   cúwe.*
     they P/H take^walk^PL together
     They are taking a walk together.

Example (8) is clearly progressive, but the same statement can also be
interpreted as habitual when not referencing what Banay and Mana are
doing at a specific moment, but making a general statement that 'They
take walks together', referencing a situation interpreted as "a characteristic
feature of a whole period."

    In order to say that *fá* is a progressive/habitual marker and not a general
imperfective marker, it should not mark statives. Barreteau (to appear)
shows that any Mofu verb can take the stative form. This stative form is
marked by a "nominalizing prefix *ma-* and a suffix *-káya* before which one
can insert a plural infix *-ta-*" [translation mine]. The progressive/habitual
marker, however, is ungrammatical with any verb in the stative form, as
shown by comparing (9) and (10).

(9)   *təɓáŋ   macəkrakáya*
       sheep   guard
       guarded sheep

(10)   **təɓáŋ fá   macəkrakáya*
       sheep   P/H guard
       guarded sheep

Another form of the stative in English is an equative sentence which uses the verb 'to be.' Mofu uses a verbless construction and the progressive/habitual marker for such sentences. The marker *fá* cannot be used with these verbless sentences, as shown by comparing (11) and (12).

(11)   *Áŋga mahurá.*
       he   big
       He is big.

(12)   **Áŋga fá   mahurá.*
       he   P/H big
       He is big.

It is also possible to consider other verbs such as 'know' and 'want' as stative verbs because once the state has begun it continues until something happens to change that state (Comrie 1976:49). Mofu speech does not allow *fá* to occur with such verbs.

Since *fá* does not occur with statives, we cannot say that it marks a general imperfective, but only the progressive and habitual subcategories of imperfective. In most of our examples we have glossed *fá* as either progressive or habitual since one can usually determine whether it is one or the other. Where the context is ambiguous, it seems that Mofu speakers first assume progressive meaning to be intended.

2.3. Marked completive aspect *lá*. The completive aspect marker *lá* is the only morpheme which can appear in the postverbal aspect position. This marker may or may not occur with the past tense morpheme *ta* (§2.5). This section looks at *lá* occurring on its own, as in (13).

(13)   *Ka gwáw ŋgá layáwa   lá   máy daw?*
       you can for take^me^DIR CMP also QUES
       Can you gather it up for me too?

With regard to perfective aspect, Comrie calls attention to the fact that perfective does not denote an action as simply being 'completed', in the sense of focusing on the termination of a situation, but rather as 'complete', by portraying a global view of a situation with a beginning and middle as well as a terminus (1976:18). Nevertheless, the perfective can have a 'completed' component.

Looking back at (13), the morpheme *lá* seems not so much perfective—looking at the whole situation—but completive—focusing on the termination of the action. So we use the term COMPLETIVE in place of PERFECTIVE for the aspect marked by *lá*. We further discuss the completive idea of *lá* below with a future meaning (§2.4), and occurring with past tense (§2.5).

2.4. Marked future tense *da*. The tense marker *da* indicates future tense which is glossed in English as 'going to', as in (14).

(14)   *A   da   kərey málágway.*
       she FUT grind corn
       She is going to grind corn.

Future time reference may also be indicated with the completive aspect marker *lá*. Though this is an aspect marker, Mofu speakers often translate it as 'will.' Example (15), illustrating a future meaning with *lá*, is not marked for tense, only completive aspect. That *lá* is usually read as indicating future tense probably results from the fact that marked past tense has a marker *ta* which must occur with *lá*, while the unmarked construction is tense neutral but generally implies present. If *lá* is neither past nor (unmarked) present, the only other tense to be implied is future.

(15)   *A   kərey málágway   lá.*
       she grind corn   CMP
       She will grind corn.

Native speaker reaction to the difference between (14) and (15) is one of 'close future' for the sentence with *da* (future) and 'sure future' for the sentence with *lá* (completive). One might wonder why the 'the-closer-the-surer' rule of future does not apply. Why would a native speaker have a close future vs. sure future rather than having close future imply sure future? The difference between the two meanings harks back to what are probably the basic meanings of the two morphemes. *Da* probably derives from the Mofu verb *daw* 'go'. *Lá*, being completive and not occurring with past tense, conveys the idea of completion in the future, hence 'sure future.' The completiveness leaves no doubt as to the action being finished.

In spite of the fact that these two meanings seem similar, they are both found in a variety of syntactic constructions. Both can occur in simple and complex declarative sentences. *Lá* is rarely found with a future reading in a topicalized construction, however, and is also avoided in questions where possible. Only *da* is found in negative obligation constructions (Hollingsworth 1986:96).

Comrie (1976:2 note) states that in cross-linguistic work one finds 'future' often behaving more like mood and not tense. Barreteau earlier described *da* as 'close future' (1978:24), but in his latest description (1985:52) has chosen to call it IRREALIS (VIRTUEL) to reflect modal quality. Sentence (14) could be interpreted as modal because it is the woman's intention to grind but she has not yet begun. The irrealis modal quality of *da* contrasts with the sense of realis conveyed by the completive future sense of *lá* in (15).

The difference between *da* and *lá*, however, does not seem to be irrealis/realis. When one looks at the complex use of tense-aspect markers, where *da* and *lá* are used with other tense or aspect morphemes, close future is always part of the reading of *da* and completive of *lá*. In addition, these morphemes appear to be the only source of the close future and completive readings.[6]

2.5. Marked past tense *ta*. Mofu-Gudur has only one marked past completive construction. It is indicated by the preverbal morpheme *ta* (PST) which always occurs with the postverbal morpheme *lá*. The underlying tone of *ta* is low but it may be realized as a phonetic high tone if the verb root has a preceding floating high tone which attaches itself to *ta*.

(16)   *Tasána ná, ya ta hɔtey méendɔɓké lá.*
        today   TOP 1s PST find   fresh^meat CMP
        As for today, I found fresh meat.

Some speakers pronounce *ta* (past) as *da* in the presence of first- and second-person subject pronouns. This *da* allomorph marks past tense and must be kept separate from *da* (future). Even those speakers who do not use *da* as past tense seem to have no trouble understanding those who do because of the obligatory presence of postverbal *lá* (completive) with past tense and its obligatory absence with (future). An example of past-tense *da* with *lá* (completive) is shown in (17).

---

[6]More examples of *da* and *lá* follow in §2.7.

(17)   *Ya da hɔtar ndaw   máyal a   wáy   ɗaw   lá.*
       1s PST find man   thief at house my   CMP
       I found a thief at my house.

2.6. Marked perfects *cáy, sém, sát.* The various perfect meanings, which
refer to past situations which have present relevance, are usually marked by
ta (past) occurring with either *cáy, sém,* or *sát.* These postverbal morphemes
are glossed as 'perfect' but they must occur with one or more preverbal
morphemes, usually with *ta,* (past), but occasionally also with the complex *fá
da* (progressive, past).

While *cáy, sém,* and *sát* mark perfect meaning, they also have further
semantic overtones. *Cáy,* the most simple or least marked perfect, indicates
that an action was terminated before another time of reference, as in (18).
Sém carries the additional meaning of a taking away or a disappearing that
is irreversible, as in (19). *Sát* also indicates this taking away or disappearing
but the action may be reversed, as in (20). *Sém* and *sát* are much less
frequently used than the more general *cáy.* In (18)–(20) these perfect
morphemes occur with *tá* (past).

(18)   *Mahurá, tá góley cáy.*
       big   PST grew PERF
       (He was) big; (he) had already grown up.

(19)   *Zlée zle ta va   sém.*
       before   PST seize   PERF^irreversible
       (At a time) before, (he) had seized it (and couldn't give it back).

(20)   *Baskwar ta nɔsey   sát.*
       bicycle   PST break   PERF^reversible
       The bike is broken (but repairable).

Perfect can also occur with completive aspect, the perfect morpheme
being used to emphasize a distancing from present time (or perhaps a
physical distancing from the present location). Example (21) illustrates *sém*
occurring with *lá* (completive), but *sát* and *cáy* may occur with *lá* as well.

(21)   *Ta handa   sém lá.*
       PST take^it PERF CMP
       (He) has already carried it all away.

Cáy, sém, and *sát* have a special use when they occur without *tá* (past), where they are used more like verbs, except that they cannot take verbal suffixes. *Cáy* appears alone or with *ná* (topic), and usually conveys a sense of 'having finished' or 'afterwards,' as in (22) and (23).

(22) *Ŋgá yah ná,   cáy.*
       for me TOP finish
       As for me, it is finished.

(23) *Ánja ka jáda ná nékɔ́dey gwáy bá   ná,*
       when you try^it TOP awhile only NEG TOP

       cáy   ná, ká vəldíwa.
       afterwards TOP you give^me^DIR
       When you try it, (try it) only for a little while, then afterwards, you give it (back) to me.

When used alone, *sém and sát* act like verbs in that they take a subject and convey a sense of 'having gone' or 'disappeared.'

(24) *Áŋga sém a   lúma.*
       he   go to market
       He has gone to the market.

(25) *Áyaŋ   fér gwes,   gwes, gwes, sát á   mánjára.*
       squirrel ID^sneak^out ID   ID   go to termite^hill
       Squirrel sneaks out and disappears into a termite hill.

Cáy can also occur as a perfect marker in close-future progressive constructions, as in (26).

(26) *Bay fá da zlehey   cáy ná,*
       chief P/H FUT give^a^speech CMP TOP
       When the chief was already about to begin giving a speech,

Past tense and perfect constructions are morphologically complex in that the tense morpheme must occur with a postverbal morpheme. In §2.5, I gave an example of past completive and perfect projected into hypothetical nonpast by use of time phrases and pragmatics. In §2.7, the remaining complex uses of tense and aspect markers will be examined.

2.7. Occurrence of tense with aspect markers. This section explores the occurrence together of various combinations of two or more tense-aspect morphemes in a single verb phrase. The possibilities which we have already discussed are listed in (27).

(27)   §2.5: *tá . . . lá*
        §2.6: *ta . . . cáy, ta . . . sém, ta . . . sát*
        ta . . . sém lá, ta . . . cáy lá, and *ta . . . sát lá*[7]

The possibilities yet to be explained are listed in (28).

(28)   *fá da, fá . . . lá,* and *fá da . . . lá.*

As mentioned above, *fá* and *da* can appear together to indicate a close future progressive situation, one which is about to occur. Example (29) is an illustration of the use of progressive and close future together. Do not confuse the verb 'take' of (29), which has an attached third-person object resulting in *lá*, with homophonous *lá* (completive). In (29), the future progressive indicates relative time since it is related to the past because of the time adverb.

(29)   *Ŋgaa kwana   ya sawa ná,*
        of   yesterday I   come TOP

        ndaw   máyal fá da lá   dalá   d̶aw.
        man   thief P/H FUT take money my
        Yesterday when I came, a thief was just about to steal my money.

The occurrence of *fá* with *lá* is rare, but I have found two examples in texts, both in quotations of direct speech. First, (30) shows an elicited *fá . . . lá* version of (29). Next, (31) represents one of the two examples of *fa . . . lá* uncovered in natural text.

---

[7]One might also expect *da* with *lá*, which would express a future completive idea, but this sense is already contained in *lá* when used alone. In actual language use, there are speakers who use *da* with *lá*, but *da* is always interpreted as past in this context (§2.5).

(30) *Ŋgáa kwána   ya sawa ná,*
     of   yesterday I come TOP

       ndaw máyal fá lá   dalá   daw lá.
       man thief   P/H take money my   CMP
       Yesterday when I came, a thief was taking all my money.

(31) *Bay mahura fá   hándáya lá.*
     chief big   P/H carry^me CMP
     The big chief (elephant) is taking me completely away.

The context of (31) is that a squirrel is being carried off by the elephant
to be killed. As they are going along the squirrel sees various animals and
wonders who will make the pretty markings on them because the elephant
is in the process of taking him completely away, to kill him. This phrase
marks both the progressiveness of the action—the elephant taking him
away—and the completiveness of the elephant's taking him away—his
death that is to come.

In addition to *fá* with *lá* which marks progressive action that will be
completed, and *fá* with *da* which marks progressive action about to begin,
we also find all three morphemes together. A close future progressive with
the perfect, *fá* with *da* and *sém*[8] is also possible. Many of these complex
examples in texts were also marked as negative. Example (32) shows how
the verb in our elicited example can be used to show a progressive
completive situation that has not yet happened.

(32) *Ŋgáa kwána   ya sawa ná,*
     for yesterday I come TOP

       ndaw máyal fá da lá   dalá   daw lá.
       man thief   P/H FUT take money my   CMP
       Yesterday when I came, a thief was about to begin taking all my
       money.

Illustration (33) is a positive example of *fá* with both *da* and *lá* that
comes from a procedural text.

---

[8]It might be possible to also use the other perfect markers *cáy* and *sát*, but I have
not yet found them with *fá da*.

(33) *Ndaw   ta   kədá   lá   ná,*
      man   PST kill^it CMP   TOP

    a   nə́key   dáa déy   ŋgá   masa   fá   da   kədey   lá.
    he see   in   eye   his   that   P/H FUT kill   CMP
    As for when the man took it (the playing piece), he saw that he
    would be taking it (or else the other man would take his piece.)

2.8. Marked iterative aspect. When subject and verb are repeated
several times, unmarked aspect allows for an iterative meaning. Examples
(34) and (35) illustrate iterative meaning with unmarked aspect and with
fá, respectively. Length on *fá* in (35) is caused by the particular verb root
employed and not by the reiteration of the verb.

(34) *Ŋgwas   á   kə́rey,   á   kə́rey.*
      woman   she grind   she grind
      The woman grinds and grinds.

(35) *Amá   áŋgá   ná,   fáa   wésey,   fáa   wésey.*
      but   3p   TOP   P/H   tremble P/H   tremble
      As for him, he was trembling and trembling.

3. Tense and aspect in relative clauses

    The relative clause in Mofu consists of a head and a restricting clause.
The restricting clause is marked by the relative clause marker *ma* (relative)
plus a verb phrase.

(36) *Kah,   ma   hətatiwa   təɓaŋ   daw hay   kede,*
      you   REL find^them   sheep   my   PL   there
      You, who found my sheep there for me,

    The only tense-aspects which have been found in relative clauses, other
than unmarked aspects, are *da* (future), *lá* (completive), and *cáy* (perfect).
When *ma* (relative) is used with postverbal morphemes in discourse, the
verb of the relative clause is always the same as the verb in the main
clause.
    Da (future) is used for relatives which refer to future time, as in (37).

(37) *Wárá   ma da guzlalahakwará déy kwar?*
      afterward who FUT write^for^you   eye your
      Afterwards, who will make markings (over) your eyes?

When used with *ma* (relative), *lá* (completive) always marks past completive and never future, as it does in main clauses.

(38) *Áta ma diyam lá a wáy tá   dəbá ná,*
      they REL go^PL CMP to house their then TOP
      They, having gone to their house,

When used with *ma* (relative), *cáy* (perfect) is always interpreted as a past perfect even without the past-tense marker which is necessary in main clauses.

(39) *Á má kə́ra   cáy,*
      3p REL grind^it PERF
      She, having already ground it,

No examples of either *fá* (progressive/habitual) or *ta* (past) with *lá* (completive) have been found in relative clauses.

(40) **ma fá kə́ra...*
      REL P/H grind^it

      *ma tá kə́ra   lá...
      REL PST grind^it CMP

      *ma tá kə́ra   cáy...
      REL PST grind^it PERF

4. Conclusion

Several charts are used to summarize the Mofu-Gudur tense-aspect system. The first chart (41) displays unmarked tense, past, and close future on one axis with unmarked and progressive/habitual aspect on the other axis.

The second chart (42) adds *lá* (completive) to the same variables.

The final chart (43) shows the same variables again, this time when they occur with either of the three perfect markers.

(41) Tense and progressive/habitual

	∅	ta (PST)	da (FUT)
∅	unmarked	*	close future
fá (P/N)	progressive habitual	*	progressive close future

(42) Tense and progressive/habitual, all with *lá* (completive)

	∅	ta (PST)	da (FUT)
∅	sure future	past	*
fá (P/H)	progressive completive	*	progressive close future completive

(43) Tense and progressive/habitual, all with *cáy, sém or sát* (perfect)

	∅	ta (PST)	da (FUT)
∅	(used as verbal ideophone)	past perfect	*
fá (P/H)	*	*	progressive close future perfect

References

Barreteau, Daniel. 1977. Le mofu-gudur, langue tchadique du nord-Cameroun. Africana Marburgensia 10(1):3–33.

————. 1978. La transcription d'un texte mofu-gudur, problèmes linguistiques. In H. Jungraithmayr and J.-P. Caprile (eds.), Cinq textes tchadiques (Cameroun et Tchad), 7–54. Berlin: Verlag von Dietrich Reimer.

————. 1985. Du mbara au mofu-gudur: approche comparée des systèmes verbaux. Langues tchadiques et langues non tchadiques en contact en Afrique Centrale, 37–60. Documents, Afrique 10, Contacts de langues et contacts de cultures 5. Paris: SELAF.

————. (to appear). La transitivité en mofu-gudur. Paris: SELAF.

Comrie, Bernard. 1976. Aspect. Cambridge: Cambridge University Press.

————. 1985. Tense. Cambridge: Cambridge University Press.

Dieu, Michel et Patrick Renaud. 1983. Situation linguistique en Afrique Centrale, Inventaire préliminaire: le Cameroun. Paris/Yaoundé: ACCT CERDOTOLA DGRST (Atlas linguistique de l'Afrique Centrale: Atlas linguistique du Cameroun). cartes.

Hoffman, Carl. 1963. A grammar of the Margi language. London: Oxford University Press.

————. 1971. Provisional checklist of Chadic languages. Chadic Newsletter, Special issue. (January, 1971). Marburg.

Hollingsworth, Kenneth R. 1983. Mofu-Gudur tense-aspect as it relates to discourse structure. ms.

————. 1986. Modal categories in Mofu-Gudur. Journal of West African Languages 16:91–98.

Jaouen, René. 1974. Le verbe en giziga. Paper presented at the 11th West African Linguistics Society Congress, 1–5 April, 1974. Yaoundé, Cameroon.

Jungraithmayr, H. 1966. Zum bau der aspecte im Westtschadohamitischen. Zeitshrift der Deutshen Morgenländischen Gesellschaft 116:227–34.

Lienhard, Ruth and Ursula Wiesemann. 1986. La modalité du verbe daba. Journal of African Languages and Linguistics 8:41–68.

Wolff, Ekkehard. 1979. Grammatical categories of verb stems and the marking of mood, aktionsart, and aspect in Chadic. Afroasiatic Linguistics 6(5):161–208.

————. 1983. A grammar of the Lamang language. Glückstadt: Verlag J.J. Augustin.

Summer Institute of Linguistics and
The University of Texas at Arlington
Publications in Linguistics
(* = in microfiche only)

1. **Comanche texts,** by Elliott Canonge. 1958. *
2. **Pocomchi texts,** by Marvin K. Mayers. 1958. *
3. **Mixteco texts,** by Anne Dyk. 1959. *
4. **A Synopsis of English syntax,** by Eugene A. Nida. 1960. *
5. **Mayan studies 1,** ed. by Benjamin F. Elson. 1961. *
6. **Sayula Popoluca texts, with grammatical outline,** by Larry Clark. 1961. *
7. **Studies in Ecuadorian Indian languages 1,** ed. by Benjamin F. Elson. 1962. *
8. **Totontepec Mixe phonotagmemics,** by John C. Crawford. 1963. *
9. **Studies in Peruvian Indian languages 1,** ed. by Mildred L. Larson. 1963. *
10. **Verb studies in five New Guinea languages,** ed. by Alan Pence. 1964.
11. **Some aspects of the lexical structure of a Mazatec historical text,** by George M. Cowan. 1965. *
12. **Chatino syntax,** by Kitty D. Pride. 1965. *
13. **Chol texts on the supernatural,** by Arabelle A. Whittaker and Viola Warkentin. 1965. *
14. **Phonemic systems of Colombian languages,** ed. by Viola G. Waterhouse. 1967. *
15. **Bolivian Indian tribes: classification, bibliography and map of present language distribution,** by Harold Key and Mary R. Key. 1967.
16.1. **Bolivian Indian grammar 1,** by Esther Matteson. 1967. *
16.2. **Bolivian Indian grammar 2,** by Esther Matteson. 1967. *
17. **Totonac: from clause to discourse,** by Aileen A. Reid, Robert E. Longacre, and Ella M. Button. 1968. *
18. **Tzotzil grammar,** by Marion M. Cowan. 1969.
19. **Aztec studies 1: phonological and grammatical studies in modern Nahuatl dialects,** ed. by Dow F. Robinson. 1969.
20. **The phonology of Capanahua and its grammatical basis,** by Eugene E. Loos. 1969.
21. **Philippine languages: discourse, paragraph and sentence structure,** by Robert E. Longacre. 1970.
22. **Aztec studies 2: Sierra Nahuat word structure,** by Dow F. Robinson. 1970.
23. **Tagmemic and matrix linguistics applied to selected African languages,** by Kenneth L. Pike. 1970.
24. **The grammar of Lamani,** by Ronald L. Trail. 1970.
25. **A linguistic sketch of Jicaltepec Mixtec,** by C. Henry Bradley. 1970.
26. **Major grammatical patterns of Western Bukidnon Manobo,** by Richard E. Elkins. 1970.
27. **Central Bontoc: sentence, paragraph and discourse,** by Lawrence A. Reid. 1970.
28. **Identification of participants in discourse: a study of aspects of form and meaning in Nomatsiguenga,** by Mary Ruth Wise. 1971.
29. **Tupi studies 1,** ed. by David Bendor-Samuel. 1971.
30. **L'énoncé Toura (Côte d'Ivoire),** by Thomas Bearth. 1971.

31. **Instrumental articulatory phonetics: an introduction to techniques and results,** by Kathryn C. Keller. 1971. *

32. **According to our ancestors: folk texts from Guatemala and Honduras,** ed. by Mary Shaw. 1971. *

33. **Two studies on the Lacandones of Mexico,** by Phillip Baer and William R. Merrifield. 1971.

34. **Toward a generative grammar of Blackfoot (with particular attention to selected stem formation processes),** by Donald G. Frantz. 1971. *

35. **Languages of the Guianas,** ed. by Joseph E. Grimes. 1972. *

36. **Tagmeme sequences in the English noun phrase,** by Peter H. Fries. 1970.

37. **Hierarchical structures in Guajajara,** by David Bendor-Samuel. 1972.

38. **Dialect intelligibility testing,** by Eugene H. Casad. 1974.

39. **Preliminary grammar of Auca,** by M. Catherine Peeke. 1973.

40.1. **Clause, sentence, and discourse patterns in selected languages of Nepal 1: general approach,** ed. by Austin Hale. 1973.

40.2. **Clause, sentence, and discourse patterns in selected languages of Nepal 2: Clause,** ed. by Austin Hale and David Watters. 1973.

40.3. **Clause, sentence, and discourse patterns in selected languages of Nepal 3: texts,** ed. by Austin Hale. 1973.

40.4. **Clause, sentence, and discourse patterns in selected languages of Nepal 4: Word lists,** ed. by Austin Hale. 1973.

41.1. **Patterns in clause, sentence, and discourse in selected languages of India and Nepal 1: Sentence and discourse,** ed. by Ronald L. Trail. 1973.

41.2. **Patterns in clause, sentence, and discourse in selected languages of India and Nepal 2: clause,** ed. by Ronald L. Trail. 1973.

41.3. **Patterns in clause, sentence, and discourse in selected languages of India and Nepal 3: texts,** ed. by Ronald L. Trail. 1973.

41.4. **Patterns in clause, sentence, and discourse in selected languages of India and Nepal 4: word lists,** ed. by Ronald L. Trail. 1973.

42. **A generative syntax of Peñoles Mixtec,** by John P. Daly. 1973.

43. **Daga grammar: from morpheme to discourse,** by Elizabeth Murane. 1974.

44. **A hierarchical sketch of Mixe as spoken in San José El Paraíso,** by Julia D. Van Haitsma and Willard Van Haitsma. 1976.

45. **Network grammars,** ed. by Joseph E. Grimes. 1975.

46. **A description of Hiligaynon syntax,** by Elmer Wolfenden. 1975.

47. **A grammar of Izi, an Igbo language,** by Paul E. Meier, Inge Meier, and John T. Bendor-Samuel. 1975.

48. **Semantic relationships of Gahuku verbs,** by Ellis W. Deibler. 1976.

49. **Sememic and grammatical structures in Gurung,** by Warren W. Glover. 1974.

50. **Clause structure: surface structure and deep structure roles,** by Shin Ja Joo Hwang. 1975.

51. **Papers on discourse,** ed. by Joseph E. Grimes. 1978.

52.1. **Discourse grammar: Studies in indigenous languages of Colombia, Panama, and Ecuador 1,** ed. by Robert E. Longacre and Frances Woods. 1976.

52.2. **Discourse grammar: Studies in indigenous languages of Colombia, Panama, and Ecuador 2**, ed. by Robert E. Longacre and Frances Woods. 1977.

52.3. **Discourse grammar: Studies in indigenous languages of Colombia, Panama, and Ecuador 3**, ed. by Robert E. Longacre and Frances Woods. 1977.

53. **Grammatical analysis**, by Kenneth L. Pike and Evelyn G. Pike. 1977.

54. **Studies in Otomanguean phonology**, ed. by William R. Merrifield. 1977.

55. **Two studies in Middle American comparative linguistics**, by David Oltrogge and Calvin R. Rensch. 1977.

56.1. **An overview of Uto-Aztecan grammar: Studies in Uto-Aztecan grammar 1**, by Ronald W. Langacker. 1977.

56.2. **Modern Aztec grammatical sketches: Studies in Uto-Aztecan grammar 2**, ed. by Ronald W. Langacker. 1979.

56.3. **Uto-Aztecan grammatical sketches: Studies in Uto-Aztecan grammar 3**, ed. by Ronald W. Langacker. 1982.

56.4. **Southern Uto-Aztecan grammatical sketches: Studies in Uto-Aztecan grammar 4**, ed. by Ronald W. Langacker. 1984.

57. **The deep structure of the sentence in Sara-Ngambay dialogues, including a description of phrase, clause, and paragraph**, by James Edward Thayer. 1978.

58.1. **Discourse studies in Mesoamerican languages 1: Discussion**, ed. by Linda K. Jones. 1979.

58.2. **Discourse studies in Mesoamerican languages 2: texts**, ed. by Linda K. Jones. 1979.

59. **The functions of reported speech in discourse**, by Mildred L. Larson. 1978.

60. **A grammatical description of the Engenni language**, by Elaine Thomas. 1978.

61. **Predicate and argument in Rengao grammar**, by Kenneth J. Gregerson. 1979.

62. **Nung grammar**, by Janice E. Saul and Nancy F. Wilson. 1980.

63. **Discourse grammar in Gaᵃdang**, by Michael R. Walrod. 1979.

64. **A framework for discourse analysis**, by Wilbur N. Pickering. 1980.

65. **A generative grammar of Afar**, by Loren F. Bliese. 1981.

66. **Phonology and morphology of Axininca Campa**, by David L. Payne. 1981.

67. **Pragmatic aspects of English text structure**, by Larry B. Jones. 1983.

68. **Syntactic change and syntactic reconstruction: a tagmemic approach**, by John R. Costello. 1983.

69. **Affix positions and cooccurrences: the PARADIGM program**, by Joseph E. Grimes. 1983.

70. **Babine & Carrier phonology: A historically oriented study**, by Gillian L. Story. 1984.

71. **Workbook for historical linguistics**, by Winfred P. Lehmann. 1984.

72. **Senoufo phonology, discourse to syllable (a prosodic approach)**, by Elizabeth Mills. 1984.

73. **Pragmatics in non-Western perspective**, ed. by George Huttar and Kenneth J. Gregerson. 1986.

74. **English phonetic transcription**, by Charles-James N. Bailey. 1985.

75. **Sentence initial devices**, ed. by Joseph E. Grimes. 1986.

76. **Hixkaryana and linguistic typology**, by Desmond C. Derbyshire. 1985.

77. **Discourse features of Korean narration**, by Shin Ja Joo Hwang. 1987.

78. **Tense/aspect and the development of auxiliaries in Kru languages,** by Lynelle Marchese. 1986.
79. **Modes in Dényá Discourse,** by Samson Negbo Abangma. 1987.
80. **Current trends and issues in Hispanic linguistics,** ed. by Lenard Studerus. 1987.
81. **Aspects of Western Subanon formal speech,** by William C. Hall. 1987.
82. **Dinka vowel system,** by Job Malou. 1988.
83. **Studies in the syntax of Mixtecan languages 1,** ed. by C. Henry Bradley and Barbara E. Hollenbach. 1988.
84. **Insights into Tagalog: reduplication, infixation, and stress from nonlinear phonology,** by Koleen M. French. 1988.
85. **The verbal piece in Ebira,** by John R. Adive. 1989.
86. **Comparative Kadai: Linguistic studies beyond Tai,** ed. by Jerold A. Edmondson and David B. Solnit. 1988.
87. **An etymological dictionary of the Chinantec languages: Studies in Chinantec languages 1,** by Calvin R. Rensch. 1989.
88. **Lealao Chinantec syntax: Studies in Chinantec languages 2,** by James E. Rupp. 1989.
89. **Comaltepec Chinantec syntax: Studies in Chinantec languages 3,** by Judi Lynn Anderson. 1989.
90. **Studies in the syntax of Mixtecan languages 2,** ed. by C. Henry Bradley and Barbara E. Hollenbach. 1990.
91. **Language maintenance in Melanesia: Sociolinguistics and social networks in New Caledonia,** by Stephen J. Schooling. 1990.
92. **Comanche dictionary and grammar,** ed. by Lila W. Robinson and James Armagost. 1990.
93. **Development and diversity: Language variation across time and space (A Festschrift for Charles-James N. Bailey),** ed. by Jerold A. Edmondson, Crawford Feagin, and Peter Mühlhäusler. 1990.
94. **Ika syntax: Studies in the languages of Colombia 1,** by Paul S. Frank. 1990.
95. **Syllables, tone, and verb paradigms: Studies in Chinantec languages 4,** ed. by William R. Merrifield and Calvin R. Rensch. 1990.
96. **Survey on a shoestring: a manual for small-scale language surveys,** by Frank Blair. 1990.
97. **Can literacy lead to development? A case study in literacy, adult education, and economic development in India,** by Uwe Gustafsson. 1991.
98. **The structure of Thai narrative,** by Somsonge Burusphat. 1991.
99. **Tense and Aspect in Eight Languages of Cameroon,** ed. by Stephen C. Anderson and Bernard Comrie. 1991.

For further information or a catalog of S.I.L. publications write to:

International Academic Bookstore
7500 W. Camp Wisdom Road
Dallas, TX 75236